THANKS!

How Practicing Gratitude
Can Make You Happier

Robert A. Emmons, Ph.D.

HOUGHTON MIFFLIN COMPANY
BOSTON · NEW YORK

First Houghton Mifflin paperback edition 2008
Copyright © 2007 by Robert A. Emmons
ALL RIGHTS RESERVED

For information about permission to reproduce selections from
this book, write to Permissions, Houghton Mifflin Company,
215 Park Avenue South, New York, New York 10003.

www.houghtonmifflinbooks.com.

Library of Congress Cataloging-in-Publication Data

Emmons, Robert A.
Thanks! : how the new science of gratitude can make
you happier / Robert Emmons.
p. cm.
Includes bibliographical references and index.
ISBN-13: 978-0-618-62019-7
ISBN-10: 0-618-62019-2
1. Gratitude. I. Title.
BF575.G68E46 2007
179'.9 — dc22   2006030297

ISBN: 978-0-547-08573-9 (pbk)

Printed in the United States of America

DOC 10 9 8 7 6 5 4 3

CREDITS   Figure 2.1 on page 23: Source: Lyubomirsky, Sheldon, & Schkade (2005).
Reprinted by permission. Figure 3.1 on page 72: Copyright © 2001 Institute of Heart-
Math. Reprinted by permission. Cartoon on page 100: Reprinted by permission from
http://www .CartoonStock.com. "Blessed Be the Name of the Lord" on page 117:
Copyright © ThankYou Music. Reprinted with permission.

ACKNOWLEDGMENTS

It's been said that the only certainties in life are death and taxes. Closely following in third place is the certainty of debt. As humans, we are in debt. Not financial debt, though that is reality for many of us as well, but an emotional and personal debt to all those who have helped us on our journeys. From cradle to grave, we are in debt to the countless individuals who make us what we are and on whom we depend. Debts of gratitude are different from other kinds of debts, however, in that they are pleasant. This form of gratitude is a glad indebtedness. I am gladly indebted to a large number of persons who have helped make this book possible.

Mike McCullough was my collaborator on the gratitude research project, and I owe him a special thanks. Mike has been a good friend and co-conspirator on various projects over the years, and without his expertise and encouragement little of the research in this book could have been conducted. A number of other students, colleagues, and mentors have made important contributions to the science of gratitude, including Barbara Fredrickson, Bob Roberts, Brother David Steindl-Rast, Charles Shelton, Chris Peterson, Dacher Keltner, Dan McAdams, David Myers, Jeffrey Froh, Jo-Ann Tsang, Jon Haidt, Marty Seligman, Patrick McNamara, Peter Stewart, Philip Watkins, Ray Paloutzian, Sol Schimmel, Stefanie Gray-Greiner, Stephen Post, and Todd Kashdan. Discussions, collaborations, and friendships with these individuals have deepened my understanding of the vital role that gratitude plays in human affairs.

Locally, I am indebted to Ted Abresch and Craig McDonald at the University of California–Davis Medical Center for allowing me to participate in their research and training grant on the quality of life in persons with neuromuscular disease. I thank all those who participated in this research and were generous with their time and self-disclosure. Lisa

Krause was invaluable in managing this aspect of the project. Over the past several years, I have benefited from the support of my department chair, Phil Shaver, and Deans Steven Sheffrin and Steven Roth in the College of Letters and Science. I thank Gabriel Unda of Campus Mediaworks for his photographic skills. Special thanks goes to Sarah Schnitker for keeping my lab alive and running while I took a sabbatical leave to complete this book.

Esmond Harmsworth, from the Zachary Shuster Harmsworth Literary Agency, was everything a novice writer could ask for in an agent, and much more. I am so grateful for his insight, wit, wisdom, and encouragement throughout this process. The book is so much better because of his attentiveness and support, and I am indebted to him. Thanks also go to Jane Rosenman, my editor at Houghton Mifflin, for her twin passions of clear, concise writing and the New York Yankees, over both of which we had many discussions and shared e-mails. I thank Beth Burleigh Fuller, manuscript editor at Houghton Mifflin, for her conscientiousness in guiding the manuscript through production. I've become convinced that copy editors are really the unsung heroes in the publishing business.

Much of the research reported in this book was supported through generous grants from the John Templeton Foundation. I am especially indebted to Executive Vice President Arthur Schwartz for his unflagging support and enthusiasm and his desire to translate basic research into forms that will have the greatest impact in society. I am also grateful for the support of Senior Vice-President Chuck Harper, President Jack Templeton, Senior Fellow Mary Ann Meyers, Joanna Hill, editor of the Templeton Foundation Press, and Sir John Templeton. I'll never forget the moment when Sir John stood up at a gratitude conference and posed the question to the audience, "How can we get six billion people around the world to practice thanksgiving?" May this book be a modest beginning toward this goal.

My wife, Yvonne, and our two boys, Adam and Garrett, have provided me with countless opportunities for gratitude. As the main sources of thanksgiving in my life, this book is dedicated to them.

CONTENTS

THANKS!

1

THE NEW SCIENCE
OF GRATITUDE

> I cannot tell you anything that, in a few minutes, will tell you
> how to be rich. But I can tell you how to feel rich, which is far
> better, let me tell you firsthand, than being rich. Be grateful . . .
> It's the only totally reliable get-rich-quick scheme.
>
> — BEN STEIN, actor, comedian, economist

IN 1999, the renowned writer Stephen King was the victim of a serious automobile accident. While King was walking on a country road not far from his summer home in rural Maine, the driver of a van, distracted by his rottweiler, veered off the road and struck King, throwing him over the van's windshield and into a ditch. He just missed falling against a rocky ledge. King was hospitalized with multiple fractures to his right leg and hip, a collapsed lung, broken ribs, and a scalp laceration. When later asked what he was thinking when told he could have died, his one-word answer: "Gratitude." An avowedly nonreligious individual in his personal life, he nonetheless on this occasion perceived the goodness of divine influence in the outcome. In discussing the issue of culpability for the accident, King said, "It's God's grace that he [the driver of the van] isn't responsible for my death."

This brief glimpse into the private life of the most successful horror novelist of all time reveals that gratitude can occur in the most unlikely of circumstances. Specializing as he does in writing about the darker, more fearful side of life, the "King" of terror is an unlikely poster person for gratitude. Normally we associate gratitude with the more elevated, exalted realms of life. For centuries, theologians, moral philosophers, and writers have identified gratitude as an indispensable manifestation of virtue and excellence of character. One contemporary philosopher recently remarked that "gratitude is the most pleasant of virtues and the most virtuous of pleasures."

Despite such acclaim, gratitude has never, until recently, been examined or studied by scientific psychologists. It is possible that psychology has ignored gratitude because it appears, on the surface, to be a very obvious emotion, lacking in interesting complications: we receive a gift — from friends, from family, from God — and then we feel pleasurably grateful. But while the emotion seemed simplistic even to me as I began my research, I soon discovered that gratitude is a deeper, more complex phenomenon that plays a critical role in human happiness. Gratitude is literally one of the few things that can measurably change peoples' lives.

It is perhaps inevitable that work rectifying such a glaring scientific omission would, like so many other breakthroughs, begin serendipitously. As a professor at the University of California, Davis, in the 1980s, I had become interested in what is now known as positive psychology, the study of human emotions that are healthy and pleasurable aspects of life (as opposed to the field's prior concentration on clinical and emotional problems). From the late 1980s to the late 1990s, the focus of my research was on happiness and goal strivings. Then, in 1998, I was invited to attend a small conference on what were deemed the "classical sources of human strength": wisdom, hope, love, spirituality, gratitude, humility. Each scientist was given the charge of presenting the known body of knowledge on his or her topic and developing a research agenda for the future. My first choice, humility, was taken; instead, I was assigned gratitude. I canvassed the theological, philosophical, and social science literatures, culling insights from these disciplines in an attempt to understand the essence of this universal strength. I soon came to believe that the capacity for gratitude is deeply woven into the fabric of the human species and possibly other species as well.

After the conference, I began a program of scientific research in collaboration with Michael McCullough, psychologist at the University of Miami, in which we made several important discoveries about gratitude. We discovered scientific proof that when people regularly engage in the systematic cultivation of gratitude, they experience a variety of measurable benefits: psychological, physical, and interpersonal. The evidence on gratitude contradicts the widely held view that all people have a "set-point" of happiness that cannot be reset by any known means: in some cases, people have reported that gratitude led to transformative life changes. And, even more important, the family, friends, partners, and others that surround them consistently report that people who practice gratitude seem measurably happier and are more pleasant to be around.

This book showcases the new science of gratitude. Woven into the narrative is a discussion of how the great religious leaders, philosophers, theologians, and writers have written about gratitude in different cultures and historical periods. To encourage the reader to begin the journey of gratitude practice, I include a discussion of practical techniques that will increase readers' gratitude and happiness. I intend this book to provoke intellectual interest as well as self-examination; I hope to provide you with information that might inspire you to make life-altering decisions.

What Gratitude Is

What exactly do we mean by *gratitude?* Most of us have an everyday sense of the concept. When I am grateful, I acknowledge that I have received a gift, I recognize the value of that gift, and I appreciate the intentions of the donor. The benefit, gift, or personal gain might be material or nonmaterial (emotional or spiritual).

From a scientific perspective, though, gratitude defies easy classification. Some years ago, the Web site for a popular radio talk show sold T-shirts emblazoned with the motto "Gratitude is an Attitude." It certainly is an attitude, but it is much more. Gratitude has also been depicted as an emotion, a mood, a moral virtue, a habit, a motive, a personality trait, a coping response, and even a way of life. The Oxford English Dictionary defines gratitude as "the quality or condition of being thankful; the appreciation of an inclination to return kindness." The word *gratitude* is derived from the Latin *gratia,* meaning "favor," and *gratus,* meaning "pleasing." All derivatives from this Latin root have to do with kindness, generousness, gifts, the beauty of giving and receiving, or getting something for nothing. Gratitude is pleasing. It feels good. Gratitude is also motivating. When we feel grateful, we are moved to share the goodness we have received with others.

Gratitude Is Recognizing and Acknowledging

In my own thinking about gratitude, I've found it very helpful to conceive of it in terms of two stages. First, gratitude is the *acknowledgment* of goodness in one's life. In gratitude we say yes to life. We affirm that all things taken together, life is good and has elements that make it worth living. The acknowledgment that we have received something gratifies us, either by its presence or by the effort the giver went into choosing it. Second, gratitude is *recognizing* that the source(s) of this goodness lie at least partially outside the self. The object of gratitude is other-directed; one can be grateful to other people, to God, to animals, but never to oneself. This is one significant way in which gratitude differs from other emotional dispositions. A person can be angry at himself, pleased with herself, proud of himself, or feel guilty about doing wrong, but it would be bizarre to say that a person felt grateful to herself. Even if you bought yourself a lavish dinner, as I am inclined to do when I order room service, it would be peculiar if I were to give thanks to myself. Thanks are directed outward to the giver of gifts.

From this angle, gratitude is more than a feeling. It requires a willingness to recognize (a) that one has been the beneficiary of someone's kindness, (b) that the benefactor has intentionally provided a benefit, often incurring some personal cost, and (c) that the benefit has value in the eyes of the beneficiary. Gratitude implies humility — a recognition that we could not be who we are or where we are in life without the contributions of others. Gratitude also implies a recognition that it is possible for other forces to act toward us with beneficial, selfless motives. In a world that was nothing but injustice and cruelty, there would indeed be no possibility of gratitude. Being grateful is an acknowledgment that there are good and enjoyable things in the world.

These two terms, *recognition* and *acknowledgment*, need some unpacking. First, they suggest that gratitude (or thankfulness) is an effortful state to create and maintain. It is not for the intellectually lethargic. Thanking belongs to the realm of thinking: the two words stem from common etymological roots. Prominent existential philosopher Martin Heidegger was fond of saying "*Denken ist Danken*" ("thinking is thanking"). The French language is especially rich in expressions having to do with thanking. The term *reconnaissance* is from the French *reconoissance,* meaning an inspection or exploration for the purpose of gathering information. It typically has a military connotation, but in the context of gratitude it refers to inspecting or exploring one's life for the purpose of seeing to whom thanks should be given. The French expression "*je suis reconnaissant*" is translated as a three-part construal: (1) "I recognize" (intellectually), (2) "I acknowledge" (willingly), and (3) "I appreciate" (emotionally). Only when all three come together is gratitude complete.

This brief etymological detour suggests already that gratitude is much more than mere politeness or a superficial feeling. Recognition is the quality that permits gratitude to be transformational. To *recognize* is to cognize, or think, differently about something from the way we have thought about it before. Think about an experience in your life when what was initially a curse wound up being a blessing in disguise. Maybe you were terminated from a job, a marital relationship dissolved, or a serious illness befell you. Gradually, you emerged from the resulting darkness with a new perception. Adversity was transformed into opportunity. Sorrow was transformed into gratefulness. You *re-cognized* the event. The re-cognizing might also involve matters much more mundane than downsizing, divorce, or disability. Driving to work on an ordinary day, we may for the first time notice a sunrise, a meadow bursting with spring blooms, or a formation of geese overhead, and find ourselves suddenly overcome with grateful awe.

Gratefulness is a knowing awareness that we are the recipients of goodness. In gratitude we remember the contributions that others have made for the sake of our well-being. On the recipient side, we acknowledge having received a benefit, and we realize that the giver acted intentionally in order to benefit us. On the giver side, we acknowledge that the receiver was in need of or worthy of the benefit, and we recognize that we are able to provide this benefit. We cannot be grateful without being thoughtful. We cannot shift our mental gears into neutral and maintain a grateful lifestyle. This is why gratitude requires contemplation and reflection.

The Heart and the Head

Lest we overintellectualize gratitude (an occupational hazard for an academic like myself), we must keep in mind that the affective, or feeling, component can be profound. Gratitude engages the heart as well as the mind. *The International Encyclopedia of Ethics* says that "gratitude is the heart's internal indicator when the tally of gifts outweighs exchanges." Nearly 200 years ago, the Scottish philosopher Thomas Brown defined gratitude as "the delightful emotion of love to him who has conferred a kindness on us, the very feeling of which is itself no small part of the benefit conferred."

I have come to believe that inside of us looms a powerful need to express gratitude for the goodness we have received. For some people, on some occasions, the feeling wells up inside until it spills over. Perhaps this is why we find that often we cry tears of gratitude. Gratitude calls out for expression until it can no longer be contained.

Elizabeth Bartlett is a professor of political science at a Midwestern university. At the age of 42, chronic tachycardia (an irregular heartbeat) necessitated a heart transplant. Four years earlier she suffered a cardiac arrest, and medication failed to improve her condition. In her book chronicling her journey, she describes this sense of overflowing gratitude:

> Yet I have found that it is not enough for me to be thankful. I have a desire to do something in return. To do thanks. To give thanks. Give things. Give thoughts. Give love. So gratitude becomes the gift, creating a cycle of giving and receiving, the endless waterfall. Filling up and spilling over. To give from the fullness of my being. This comes not from a feeling of obligation, like a child's obligatory thank-you notes to grandmas and aunts and uncles after receiving presents. Rather, it is a spontaneous charitableness, perhaps not even to the giver but to someone else, to whoever crosses one's path. It is the simple passing on of the gift.

Getting What We Don't Deserve

An additional, essential aspect of gratitude is the notion of *undeserved merit*. When I am grateful, I recognize that I have no claim on the gift or benefit I received; it was freely bestowed out of compassion, generosity, or love. One philosopher of ethics thus defines gratitude as "the willingness to recognize the unearned increments of value in one's experience." The theological term for this is *grace*. So we have another trio of terms that go together: *grace, gratis,* and *gratitude*. They flow into one another. Perceive grace and you will naturally feel grateful. Grace is unearned. It is a free gift. If you believe in grace, you believe that there is a pattern of beneficence in the world that exists quite independently of your own striving and even your own existence. Gratitude thus depends upon receiving what we do not expect to receive or have not earned, or receiving more than we deserve or earned. Grace is why the discussion of gratitude is so at home in religious discourses and perhaps why it has proven so intractable in the social sciences. When Stephen King said that it was by God's grace that he was alive, his mental calculus told him that given what might have happened on the rural road that day, he did not get what he deserved.

The problem, though, is that for many of us, a grace-filled worldview is difficult to sustain. The human mind contains mental tools that appear to work against the tendency to perceive grace. We are forgetful. We take things for granted. We have high expectations. We assume that we are totally responsible for all the good that comes our way. After all, we have earned it. We deserve it. When asked to pray at the family dinner table, son Bart Simpson offered the following words: "Dear God, we paid for all this stuff ourselves, so thanks for nothing." In one sense, of course, Bart is correct. The Simpson family did earn their own money. But on another level, he is missing the bigger picture. The grateful person senses that much goodness happens quite independently of his actions or even in spite of himself. We are the recipients of help from others, both past and present, and we need to be reminded of this. In his commencement address at Ithaca College, Ben Stein, whom I quoted at the beginning of this chapter, told graduating seniors, "We're all heirs and heiresses to a society of freedom and plenty that most of us did absolutely nothing to earn. It just fell into our laps." We can be proud of our accomplishments yet simultaneously realize they would have been impossible without help from others. This realization is the soil that permits gratitude to germinate.

Gratitude can also be a response to unmerited evilness. While we most often link gratitude in our minds with pleasant outcomes, gratitude is not an infrequent response even in the midst of horrendous trauma and tragedy. My work has led me to interview people who have suffered terrible illness and loss, including the events of

September 11, 2001, and the destructive hurricanes that hit the southeastern United States in 2005. Even in the face of such terrible adversity, it is possible to be grateful for a benefit one has received. And, more important, people who experience gratitude in such dire circumstances consistently report that they are happier than those who do not and are less susceptible to negative emotions and outcomes. It is this presence of thankfulness in trying times that enables us to conclude that gratitude is not simply a form of "positive thinking" or a technique of "happy-ology," but rather a deep and abiding recognition and acknowledgment that goodness exists under even the worst that life offers. That aspect of gratitude is one of the most intriguing to me.

WHY DOES GRATITUDE MATTER?

"Be grateful to those who do well to you. Be thankful for your blessings" is something that we teach our children at the youngest of ages. It is more than empty platitudes. Gratitude is an important dimension to our life as we interact with one another in our everyday affairs. It is impossible to imagine a world where individuals don't receive and give gratitude to one another on a regular basis. Binding people together in relationships of reciprocity, gratitude is one of the building blocks of a civil and humane society. Georg Simmel, a prominent early-twentieth-century Swiss sociologist, referred to gratitude as "the moral memory of mankind." He wrote that "if every grateful action . . . were suddenly eliminated, society (at least as we know it) would break apart." We need gratitude to function in relation to others.

To illustrate this connectional component, Roger, a man I interviewed, was on the verge of losing his home due to escalating medical bills and an extended period of unemployment. He wrote in his gratitude journal:

I was scheduled back to work August 7, 2000, and my coworkers and friends threw a benefit for me at a rock-n-roll club called "the Double Door." Located in an "upcoming" neighborhood the place was known as an opening stage for the Rolling Stones tour. My building manager spearheaded the effort organizing a raffle of restaurants' dinners, sports items, and free buffet and music. My wife, Sue, felt guilty about not having been part of the planning or promotion, we felt like this was asking too much of our friends and families but we weren't in charge so we sat back and just appreciated the effort and hard work being done on our behalf. Was it gonna be a bust? Or success? We didn't know but Sue, Brian, and the three boys were gonna show up to thank anyone who showed up. Well, the big day came after much anticipation. About two hundred people showed up, bought raffle tickets, drank, danced, partied, and ate till 1 A.M. closing! We went up on stage to thank everyone amid joy, tears, and hugs. My manager cut me a check for over $35,000 the next week! Without that check my house/car would have been on the market. Insurance picked up the majority of bills, but weekly tests and medication and follow-up ran into the thousands. We saw so many friends and coworkers it was truly a great night. The $1000 first prize was donated back to us by the winner (a stranger!). My doctor and nurse also attended and our priest stopped by for a few beers — I keep thinking of more highlights as I write. I truly felt like George Bailey in *It's a Wonderful Life!* I feel myself almost tearing up as I write. My heart warms as I see the people that attended. I also feel a need to help or reach out to others whenever I can help by speaking or just listening.

One needs simply to try to imagine human relationships existing without gratitude, as Simmel did in his thought experiment. By way of contrast, *in*gratitude leads inevitably to a confining, restricting, and "shrinking" sense of self. Emotions such as anger, resentment, envy, and bitterness tend to undermine happy social relations. But the virtue of gratitude is not only a firewall of protection against such corruption of relationships; it also contributes positively to friendship and civility, because it is both benevolent (wishing the benefactor well) and just (giving the benefactor his due). In gratitude, we show our respect for others by recognizing their good intentions in helping us. A grateful outlook can even dominate the life of an entire culture, as can be seen in certain Eastern cultures where individuals view themselves as recipients of endless ancestrally bestowed blessings.

But we can do better than thought experiments. Devotional writers have long assumed that an effective strategy for repositioning one's spiritual and emotional life is to count one's blessings. At the same time, current psychological dogma states that one's capacity for joy is biologically set. Our experimental research has begun to put these conflicting assertions to rigorous test. Preliminary findings suggest that those who regularly practice grateful thinking do reap emotional, physical, and interpersonal benefits. Adults who keep gratitude journals on a regular basis exercise more regularly, report fewer illness symptoms, feel better about their lives as a whole, and are more optimistic about the future. These benefits were observed in experimental studies when comparisons were made with those who were asked to chronicle their daily hassles or to reflect on ways in which they were better off than others. In daily studies of emotional experience, when people report feeling grateful, thankful, and appreciative, they also feel more loving, forgiving, joyful, and enthusiastic. These deep affections appear to be formed through the discipline of gratitude.

There is the short-term feeling of gratitude, but also the long-term disposition of gratefulness. Our groundbreaking research has shown that grateful people experience higher levels of positive emotions such as joy, enthusiasm, love, happiness, and optimism, and that the practice of gratitude as a discipline protects a person from the destructive impulses of envy, resentment, greed, and bitterness. We have discovered that a person who experiences gratitude is able to cope more effectively with everyday stress, may show increased resilience in the face of trauma-induced stress, and may recover more quickly from illness and benefit from greater physical health. Our research has led us to conclude that experiencing gratitude leads to increased feelings of connectedness, improved relationships, and even altruism. We have also found that when people experience gratitude, they feel more loving, more forgiving, and closer to God. Gratitude, we have found, maximizes the enjoyment of the good — our enjoyment of others, of God, of our lives. Happiness is facilitated when we enjoy what we have been given, when we "want what we have."

The significance of gratitude lies in its ability, as Ben Stein cogently noted, to enrich human life. Gratitude elevates, it energizes, it inspires, it transforms. People are moved, opened, and humbled through experiences and expressions of gratitude. Gratitude provides life with meaning by encapsulating life itself as a gift. Without gratitude, life can be lonely, depressing, impoverished.

So gratitude is a key to happiness, as I will argue from a scientific angle. And happiness itself is a good thing. An implicit assumption that many of us hold is that happiness depends on *happenings* — by what happens in our lives. We believe that success in life — whether in the boardroom or the bedroom — makes people happier. Yet a recent review of the scientific literature on happiness revealed that happiness yields numerous rewards for the individual and *precedes* these outcomes. This means that happiness makes good things happen. It actually promotes positive outcomes. The benefits of happiness include higher income and superior work outcomes (for example, greater productivity, higher quality of work, greater occupational attainment), larger social rewards (such as more satisfying and longer marriages, more friends, stronger social support, and richer social interactions), more activity, energy, and flow, and better physical health (for example, a bolstered immune system, lowered stress levels, and less pain), and even longer life.

Consider what this means in concrete terms. Two highly sought outcomes are longevity and affluence. We want to live long and prosper. Heavy cigarette smoking can knock off about six years from a person's life. Conversely, happiness can add as much as *nine* years to one's life expectancy. What about net worth? A longitudinal study of college students found that happiness levels in college predicted income sixteen years later. The most cheerful students earned $25,000 more per year than their more dour classmates.

But a long and comfortable life isn't everything, is it? The scientific literature suggests that happy individuals are also more creative, helpful, charitable, and self-confident, have better self-control, and show greater self-regulatory and coping abilities. Happy people, the facts clearly show, are flourishing and successful people. Therefore, interventions that increase people's enduring joy become even more desirable as happiness predicts changes in other positive outcomes, such as altruistic behavior, creativity, work performance, physical health, and social relationships.

Surely a deep and abiding gratefulness — the ability to relish the little pleasures that common occurrences afford — is a desirable human quality. Among the questions I will explore in this book are: How do we get there? How do we get from feeling gratitude to being grateful? Is gratitude one of those "unfair" gifts given to those who possess sunny dispositions, those who do not instinctively feel the anxiety, pain, and isolation of living in this world? Is this an emotion that comes from a chemical predisposition to optimism or are there choices we can make? Can we choose gratitude? I conclude that gratitude can indeed be cultivated in a positive way, and that it can become a critical component of human happiness. In the final chapter, I present a discussion of some of the exercises I recommend readers use to increase their gratitude and, consequently, to enrich their lives.

SOME RESERVATIONS ABOUT GRATITUDE

You may be already raising some objections about a grateful approach to life. I have heard the following protests lodged: Is not gratitude in today's day and age overly naive? Gratitude is fine for Hallmark sentimentality, but what of the harsh realities of life? Does it ignore tragedy and suffering? If I am grateful for my life, will my contentment lead me to avoid being an agent of change in the world? Are grateful people too satisfied with the status quo? Does gratitude undermine autonomy and self-initiated striving? Can I be justified in not feeling grateful even though others have been kind to me? What about people who have harmed me but also provided me with benefits? How do I handle this conflict?

For the inquisitive mind, these questions and others arise. One of my goals in this book is to provide some serious, thoughtful reflection on these objections, using science-based evidence where possible. Gratitude is a natural response to a particular situation when good things happen to an individual, but there may be times when it is an incorrect response. We may be so biased by good things that happen to us that we respond incorrectly to a particular situation. For example, we may feel gratitude toward an individual whose intentions do not deserve such a response. We may credit inanimate objects for saving our lives or bringing us luck to the point that we feel gratitude to the objects. We deceive ourselves into thinking that we should be grateful to things. We are grateful for our softball game not being rained out, for winning the lottery, or for finding a parking space in the mall lot at Christmas.

Part of the problem, I think, is that we lack a sophisticated discourse for gratitude because we are out of practice. The philosopher of emotion Robert Solomon has noted how relatively infrequently Americans talk about gratitude but how this emotion forms the foundation of interaction in many other cultures. Gratitude is a "hypocognized" emotion in America, meaning that collectively we typically don't give it much thought. On the other hand, anger, resentment, happiness, and romantic love tend to be overly scrutinized or "hypercognized." It has been argued that conventional males may be averse to experiences and expressions of gratefulness insomuch as they imply dependency and indebtedness. One fascinating study in the 1980s found that American men were less likely to evaluate gratitude positively than were German men and to view it as less constructive and useful than their German counterparts. Gratitude presupposes so many judgments about debt and dependency that it is easy to see why supposedly self-reliant American males would feel queasy about even discussing it. We don't like being reminded that we needed help. We don't want to be beholden to our saviors. Gratitude would seem to pose a challenge for this reason alone.

Gratitude can be a bitter pill to swallow, humbling us and demanding as it does that we confront our own sense of self-sufficiency. So we may avoid it as we avoid going to the doctor for the annual prostate exam. But it is also good medicine, and its side effects are few. Across cultures and time spans, experiences and expressions of gratitude have been treated as both basic and desirable aspects of human personality and social life. Gratitude is a virtue as well as an emotion, the possession of which enables a person to live life well and therefore must receive a hearing in any comprehensive treatment of the virtues. The Roman philosopher Cicero held that "Gratitude is not only the greatest of virtues, but the parent of all the others." Cicero's contemporary, Seneca, maintained, "He who receives a benefit with gratitude repays the first installment on his debt." "He is a wise man who does not grieve for the things which he has not, but rejoices for those which he has," wrote Epictetus. The theologian Dietrich Bonhoeffer wrote, "In ordinary life we hardly realize that we receive a great deal more than we give, and that it is only with gratitude that life becomes rich." Psychologists who have aligned themselves with positive psychology are quite interested in those psychological propensities that lead to a rich life, and my message is that gratitude is one of these essential propensities.

While gratitude is seemingly universally praised, ingratitude is universally condemned. Seneca called ingratitude an "abomination." The Enlightenment philosophers David Hume and Immanuel Kant, at odds on most heady philosophical issues, found common ground on ingratitude. Hume remarked that "Of all the crimes that human creatures are capable of committing, the most horrid and unnatural is ingratitude," while Kant contended that "ingratitude . . . is the essence of vileness."

Despite these powerful assertions, opinion concerning gratitude's status as a virtue is far from unanimous. In search for universal consensus, we should not overlook the ambivalence about the place of gratitude in the ancient world that is echoed by many of our contemporaries today. It was La Rochefoucauld who said, "Gratitude in the generality of men is only a strong and secret desire of receiving greater favours." Aristotle thought gratitude was a weakness. He found gratitude incompatible with magnanimity and therefore did not include it in his list of virtues. Magnanimous people, according to Aristotle, insist on their self-sufficiency and therefore find it demeaning to be indebted to others. Nietzsche believed gratitude was often a disguise for covert interests and that having a person's gratitude guaranteed that person's loyalty. Making the previous quotes generous by comparison, Dorothy Parker opined that gratitude "is the meanest and most sniveling attribute in the world."

Nowadays, it is not so much that we are strongly opposed to gratitude on philosophical and moral grounds, but rather that we simply don't think about it very often. In fact, we can be downright amnesiac when it comes to gratitude. The Reverend Peter Gomes, distinguished professor in the Harvard University Divinity School, wrote, "When I saw the Christmas lights being strung up across the city streets and the Santa Clauses in the store windows at Sears, I knew that Thanksgiving could not be far away." In Gomes's view, we have forgotten Thanksgiving in contemporary life, and more fundamentally, we have forgotten the very reason for Thanksgiving: expressing gratitude. Contemporary social science research will remind us that if we overlook gratitude, it will be at our own emotional and psychological peril.

One of the risks in writing a book on gratitude is that it might fall prey to the dual biases of sentimentality and sermonization. The sentimentalizing bias emphasizes the emotional aspect and personal benefits of gratitude: It feels good, so personal happiness becomes the ultimate motivation for gratitude. Gomes noted that "Once we have been liberated from the count-your-many-blessing-name-them-one-by-one routine, we will have made a significant step." The sermonizing bias stresses, on the other hand, the moral imperative nature of gratitude: We ought to be grateful, and wouldn't the world be a better place if everyone were more grateful? Although there is certainly a positive valence and moral imperative to gratitude, an exclusive focus on these two elements would fail to address the growing body of scientific scholarship on the topic. Besides, these assumptions are just flatly wrong. Far from being a warm, fuzzy sentiment, gratitude is morally and intellectually demanding. Similarly, feeling as if we *should* feel gratitude after being sermonized might produce resentment, not gratitude. This book, though, is based on scientific discoveries. However, although I strive for objectivity and accuracy in describing and explaining the benefits of grateful living, don't mistake objectivity for neutrality. I am not neutral about gratitude. I believe it to be the best approach to life.

GRATITUDE AS A CHOSEN ATTITUDE

From reading accounts of gratitude from people around the world and throughout history, I became convinced that gratitude is an approach to life that can be freely chosen for oneself. It does not depend upon objective life circumstances such as health, wealth, or beauty. Saying that gratitude is a choice means that we can select it from an array of responses to what life offers. The late Catholic priest, psychologist, and devotional writer Henri Nouwen knew this:

> Gratitude as a discipline involves a conscious choice. I can choose
> to be grateful even when my emotions and feelings are steep and
> hurt and resentful. It is amazing how many occasions present

themselves in which I can choose gratitude instead of a complaint. I can choose to be grateful when I am criticized, even when my heart responds in bitterness . . . I can choose to listen to the voices that forgive and to look at the faces that smile, even while I still hear words of revenge and see grimaces of hatred.

What does it mean to say that gratitude is a choice? It means that we sharpen our ability to recognize and acknowledge the giftedness of life. It means that we make a conscious decision to see blessings instead of curses. It means that our internal reactions are not determined by external forces.

That gratitude is a conscious decision does not imply that it is an easy decision. The ability to choose gratitude may not come easily, naturally, or effortlessly. While gratitude is pleasant, it is not easy. We have to work at it. It must be consciously cultivated. Albert Einstein admitted that he needed to remind himself a hundred times a day that his inner and outer life depend on the labors of other men, living and dead, and that "I must exert myself in order to give in the measure as I have received and I am still receiving." A number of personal burdens and external obstacles block grateful thoughts. A number of attitudes are incompatible with a grateful outlook on life, including perceptions of victimhood, an inability to admit one's shortcomings, a sense of entitlement, and an inability to admit that one is not self-sufficient. In a culture that celebrates self-aggrandizement and perceptions of deservingness, gratitude can be crowded out. It is also easy to see how gratitude can have a difficult time surviving in a culture that celebrates consumption. But in gratitude we recognize that we are not ultimately producers and consumers but, above all, the recipients of gifts.

2

GRATITUDE AND THE
PSYCHE

I would maintain that thanks are the highest form of thought,
and that gratitude is happiness doubled by wonder.

— G. K. CHESTERTON

ONE OF MOST PROLIFIC WRITERS of the past century,
G. K. Chesterton produced nearly a hundred books in the genres of
faith and philosophy, mystery, biography, poetry, and social and political commentary. In the course of his lifetime, Chesterton contributed to two hundred other books, wrote over four thousand newspaper essays, including thirty years' worth of weekly columns for the
Illustrated London News, and thirteen years of weekly columns for the
Daily News, and, at the same time, edited his own newspaper, *G. K.'s
Weekly.*

Chesterton was a deep thinker and had a knack for expressing profound truths simply and making simple observations sound
profound. One commentator wrote that Chesterton said something
about everything and said it better than anybody else. But to those
who knew Chesterton, even more notable than his sharp intellect was
his habitually positive demeanor. While we might expect that his
heavy workload would render him exhausted, Chesterton's friends
and acquaintances consistently described him as "exuberant" and
"exhilarated" by life. To what were these characteristics attributed?

To think of Chesterton, one commentator wrote, is to "think of gratitude." Gratitude and a sense of wonder and appreciation for life were consistently and constantly expressed in his life and in his writings. He delighted in the ordinary and was surprised and awed by his own existence and the existence of all else. Throughout his life, he set a conscious goal of remaining childlike in his sense of wonder and vowed not to succumb to the monotony and boredom that saps so many lives of joy and purpose. This sense of wonder at the ordinary is aptly illustrated in this letter to his fiancée, Frances, where he is apologizing for an ink stain on the letter:

> I like the Cyclostyle ink, it is so inky. I do not think there is anyone who takes quite such fierce pleasure in things being themselves as I do. The startling wetness of water excites and intoxicates me: the fieriness of fire, the steeliness of steel, the unutterable muddiness of mud. It is just the same with people . . . When we call a man "manly" or a woman "womanly" we touch the deepest philosophy.

So absorbed was he in the present moment, it was said that Chesterton lived in an almost mystical state of exaltation. Present-mindedness came at the cost of absent-mindedness, however, and his absent-mindedness was legendary. He rarely knew where he was supposed to be at any given hour. He did most of his writing in train stations, since he usually missed the train he was supposed to catch. He once hailed a cab to take him to an address that turned out to be across the street. On another occasion, he was sipping wine with his sister-in-law in a wine shop in London when he suddenly remembered that he was shortly due to be giving a lecture in another town. Once he sent a telegram to his wife that read: "Am at Market Harborough. Where ought I be?"

No doubt his ability to get into the flow of life, a state marked by total absorption and detachment from one's surroundings, contributed to his success as a writer and to his joyous affirmation of life. Many psychologists would argue that Chesterton was simply a naturally happy and engaged person, a man who won the genetic lottery at birth and whose brain was set up to experience pleasure and joy in even the most mundane surroundings. But there was another factor. In his best-known book, *Orthodoxy*, Chesterton wrote, "The test of all happiness is gratitude. Children are grateful when Santa Claus puts in their stockings gifts of toys or sweets. Could I not be grateful to Santa Claus when he puts in my stockings the gift of two miraculous legs? We thank people for birthday presents . . . Can I thank no one for the birthday present of birth?" In his autobiography, published the year of his death, he summarized his life's writings in saying that gratitude "if not the doctrine I have always taught, is the doctrine I should have always liked to teach." One is never lacking in opportunities to be happy, according to Chesterton, because around every corner is another gift waiting to surprise us, and it will surprise us if we can achieve control over our natural tendencies to make comparisons, to take things for granted, and to feel entitled.

Chesterton was raised without religious faith, yet he was filled with gratitude for his own life, for love, for beauty, for all that is. He was filled with an enormous sense of thankfulness and an enormous need for someone or something to thank. How can one be thankful, he wondered, unless there is someone to thank? This mystery became the fundamental philosophical riddle of his life and ultimately led to his conversion to Catholicism at age 48.

WHAT DETERMINES HAPPINESS?

If you ask most people what they really want out of life, what *really* matters, they will likely volunteer a variety of answers. Family, friends, health, and financial security are common responses. If pushed to go deeper by asking *why* these things are wanted, people will inevitably say it is because without these they cannot be happy. When Thomas Jefferson declared in the eighteenth century that Americans had the "inalienable right" to pursue happiness, little would he know that by the twenty-first century, happiness would become the ultimate aim of existence for most. The major decisions that people make in life — whom to marry, where to live, whether to start a family or not, whether to stay married — pivot upon options that will provide the greatest perceived happiness. Studies have shown that the majority of U.S. respondents rate personal happiness as very important and that people report thinking about happiness at least once every day. The scientists who do research on happiness have made significant strides in understanding who is happy and why. One of the more fascinating findings is that each person appears to have a set-point for happiness. Most people who diet are familiar with the notion of set-points. Despite their best efforts, weight loss is notoriously difficult to maintain as a metabolic pull of sorts encourages weight return to previous levels. There is a similar set-point for happiness levels: researchers suggest each person has a chronic or characteristic level of happiness. According to this idea, people have happiness set-points to which they inevitably return following disruptive life events. Getting that book published, moving to California, having the person of your dreams answer your personal ad — each of these may send the happiness meter right off the scale for a while but, in a few months, it will drift back to the set-point that is typical for that individual. What goes up must come down. Some researchers have argued that this tendency is so strong that trying to change one's happiness is futile because an individual inevitably returns to a predetermined state.

This process, in which we return to our characteristic happiness level a short time after we experience unusually good or bad events, is known as adaptation. Initially, people react strongly to changed circumstances, but, over time, their emotional reactions dampen and lose power. They adapt; in other words, they take good things for granted and overcome the obstacles life throws at them, returning to the happiness level that is natural for them. In one of the most famous adaptation studies, psychologists compared the well-being and reported happiness of two very different groups: those who had just won the lottery and those who had suffered devastating spinal-cord injuries. They concluded that lottery winners were less happy than most of us would expect (and, even more surprisingly, not significantly happier than a control group) and that individuals with spinal-cord injuries were happier than might be expected.

Where does this set-point come from? Our genes. Research has shown that about half of the variance in one's momentary feelings of well-being is determined by the great genetic lottery that occurs at conception and the other half depends on fortune's favors, good or bad (see Figure 2.1). The happiness set-point is genetically determined and is assumed to be fixed, stable over time, and immune to influence or control. One implication of this biological set-point is that people differ genetically in their variation around their happiness set-points. Some people are genetically programmed to be happy most of the time, while others are apparently doomed to go through life perpetually scowling. Compare and contrast, for example, the ever effusive Academy Award–winning actor and director Roberto Benigni (*Life Is Beautiful*) with the perpetually ill-tempered college basketball coach Bob Knight.

Together, these concepts and findings on set-points and adapta-

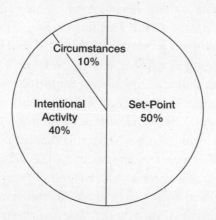

FIGURE 2.1. Three primary factors influencing the chronic happiness level.

Source: Lyubomirsky, Sheldon, & Schkade (2005). Reprinted by permission.

tion might suggest that trying to become happier may be as futile as trying to become taller. However, as in the case of weight, the biologically programmed set-point is not so much a fixed point but rather a range. While circumstances have a temporary effect that we adapt to, psychologists have identified a group of intentional activities that can work to move the set-point within its genetically determined range, up or down. These intentional activities take some degree of effort to enact: the person has to try to do the activity; it does not happen by itself.

There is good reason to believe that intentional activity can influence well-being. In fact, we perform these "intentional activities" all the time. Whether gardening, socializing, shopping, eating chocolate, or exercising, people choose activities that raise, at least temporarily, their moods. For example, faithfully engaging in a new exercise program positively boosts one's mood and vitality, and the gain can be maintained for as long as six months. Indeed, this point touches on one of the critical distinctions between the category of activity and the category of life circumstances — circumstances *happen* to people, and while there's not much we can usually do to change the circumstances except by adapting to them, we *can* change the ways we intentionally react to them. If circumstances are bad, we can speed the process of adaptation by seeking support from friends, exercising, prayer, or engaging other positive activity. We could also delay the process by engaging in negative activity: isolating ourselves, drinking too much alcohol, dwelling on our misfortune, or compulsively shopping. If circumstances are good, we desire the reverse: to slow the process of adaptation, though few of us know how.

Chesterton, with whom I began this chapter, did not attribute happiness to either nature or nurture but to the will — he firmly believed that one's capacity for joy can and must be trained. But little is known about which, if any, psychological interventions can tackle the problem presented by adaptation. While the way we react to life events can make them harsher or milder, depending on what we choose to do, for years I have researched the question of whether our reactions can, in fact, alter the process of adaptation itself and allow us to permanently improve our personal range of happiness.

IS GRATITUDE THE SECRET TO LIFE?

Think about a time when you felt grateful. What other feelings do you associate with this state? I sometimes begin public lectures with this question. If you are like others, you probably are thinking of words such as "peaceful," "content," "warm," "giving," "friendly," and "joyful." You'd be unlikely to say that gratitude makes you feel "burdened," "stressed," or "resentful." This simple thought experiment illustrates that gratitude is a positive, desirable state that people find enjoyable. Chesterton said that gratitude produces the most purely joyful moments that have been known to man. Many people describe an episode of gratitude as one of the best times in their lives. A 53-year-old man in our daily gratitude intervention study with persons suffering from neuromuscular disease wrote:

> In 1995 I became very ill with asthma and was in ICU for ten days. During that time I continually got worse and was finally transported to another hospital by private medical jet. I remember feeling that I would die and was panicking. Obviously, I did get well and came home after two weeks. When I walked into my home, I was so happy to see my children. I had thought I would never see them again. I was overwhelmed by feelings of thankfulness that I was alive. Although still very weak I was so happy to embrace the kids, have the dog cuddle with them, and generally to just see my home again. I cried tears of happiness. The experience gave me hope for the future so that I could eventually see grandchildren (kids marry) etc. During my follow-up visit with my Dr. I hugged him and expressed my thanks to him for helping to save my life. This experience was life-changing for me in that I opened my heart to God and I feel I also am a more sensitive, caring person.

A prevailing sentiment in both classical and popular writings on happiness is that an effective approach for maximizing one's contentment is to be consciously grateful for one's blessings. The great twentieth-century humanitarian, physician, theologian, and Nobel Peace Prize–winner, Albert Schweitzer, called gratitude "the secret to life." In one particular sermon he summarized his position by stating that "the greatest thing is to give thanks for everything. He who has learned this knows what it means to live. He has penetrated the whole mystery of life: giving thanks for everything." From ancient scriptures to modern devotional writers, counting blessings is frequently recommended as a strategy to improve one's life. The huge bestseller *A Simple Abundance Journal of Gratitude* advocates creating a life of gratitude and generosity and promises great rewards for those who do: "Whatever we are waiting for — peace of mind, contentment, grace . . . it will surely come to us, but only when we are ready to receive it with an open and grateful heart." Joel Osteen, the smiling preacher at Houston's Lakewood Community Church, advocates the following seven steps for living "your best life now": Enlarge your vision; develop a healthy self-image; discover the power of your thoughts and words; let go of the past; find strength through adversity; live to give; and choose to be happy. Developing a deeper appreciation for life and not taking things for granted are concrete, repeated recommendations he makes for progressing through these steps. "Reflect upon your present blessings of which every man has many — not on your past misfortunes, of which all men have some," wrote Charles Dickens, who surely knew a thing or two about human nature.

As an empirically minded scientist, I yearned to put these and other pronouncements on the importance and power of gratitude to the empirical test. I was thus led to probe the happiness-inducing nature of gratitude and to ask the following questions: Does the systematic counting of one's blessings impact happiness and well-being? If it does, why, in what ways, and for how long? Is gratitude simply an adaptation-enhancer in bad circumstances and an adaptation-delayer in good ones, or does it have a more permanent effect that actually moves the overall range of the set-point?

COUNTING BLESSINGS AND BURDENS

I have spent the last several years of my career trying to measure what, if any, discernible effect an "attitude of gratitude" can have on our happiness level. In my first series of experiments, my colleague Mike McCullough and I decided to look at the impact of a gratitude intervention on psychological and physical well-being.

In our first study, we randomly assigned participants one of three tasks, each of which created a distinct condition. We decided to encourage some participants to indirectly feel gratitude, encourage others to be indirectly negative and complaining, and create a third, neutral group to measure the others by. Every week, the study's participants kept a short journal. They either briefly described, in a single sentence, five things they were grateful for that had occurred in the past week (*the gratitude condition*), or they did the opposite, describing five daily hassles from the previous week (*the hassles condition*) that they were displeased about. The neutral group was simply asked to list five events or circumstances that affected them in the last week, and they were not told to accentuate the positive or negative aspects of those circumstances (*the events condition*).

The experiment lasted for ten weeks. The members of the gratitude condition reported that a wide range of experiences sparked gratitude: cherished interactions with other people, awareness of physical health, their ability to overcome obstacles, and simply being alive, to name a few. Examples of blessings that participants listed were:

- The generosity of friends
- The right to vote

- The God-given gift of determination
- That I have learned all that I have learned
- Sunset through the clouds
- The chance to be alive
- My in-laws live only ten minutes away

We wondered if some of the others would feel more grateful if their in-laws lived on the opposite side of the globe, but no one in the gratitude condition listed "my mother-in-law has moved to New Zealand" as one of their blessings.

Our second group was asked to do the opposite: to count their burdens instead of their blessings. They recorded a list of hassles or annoyances that bothered them each day. We found that these participants had no trouble listing a very original list of things that annoyed them. Some examples of these burdens were the following:

- Hard to find parking
- Messy kitchen no one will clean
- Finances depleting quickly
- Taxes
- No money for gas
- Our house smells like manure
- Burned my macaroni and cheese
- Doing favor for friend who didn't appreciate it

Before participants wrote about either blessings or burdens, they completed an extensive daily journal in which they rated their moods, physical health, and overall judgments concerning how their lives were going. Mike and I wanted to measure how happy these people were — in other words, what exactly their natural range of happiness was — both before and after they wrote in their journals. The moods rated included feelings such as interest, distress, excitement, alertness, irritability, sadness, stress, shame, and happiness. We assessed physical symptoms by having participants check off whether they had experienced any of the following sensations: headaches, faintness/dizziness, stomachache/pain, shortness of breath, chest pain, acne/skin irritation, runny/congested nose, stiff or sore muscles, stomach upset/nausea, irritable bowels, hot or cold spells, poor appetite, coughing/sore throat, or other. Participants were asked to rate how they felt about their life as a whole during the week, on a −3 to +3 scale, anchored with the adjectives "terrible" to "delighted." A second question asked participants to rate their expectations for the upcoming week, also on a −3 to +3 scale, with the endpoints labeled "pessimistic, expect the worst" and "optimistic, expect the best."

Although I expected that the gratitude group would show some positive benefits, I did not expect the results to be preordained or inevitable. Some aspects of gratitude might detract from its pleasantness. To be grateful means to allow oneself to be placed in the position of a recipient — to feel indebted and aware of one's dependence on others. For some, this acknowledgment of dependence might make them feel out of control and unhappy. Additionally, gratitude has an obligatory aspect. People are expected to repay kindnesses, and, sometimes, we rebel against expectations and dislike things we are "supposed to" do. Most people experience indebtedness as an unpleasant and aversive psychological state. Thus, making people aware of the things in their lives to be grateful for might actually increase their recognition of the need to reciprocate, and people may resent these obligations and even report strong negative feelings toward their benefactors, even as extreme as hatred.

We also expected that the natural happiness set-point of the experiment participants might affect the power gratitude had to change their moods. People assigned to the gratitude condition may be, by nature, ungrateful pessimists. Conversely, people in the hassles condition might be cheery optimists. If they were extreme enough, the disposition would trump the intervention. One female participant in the hassles condition listed the following in her account: "My cold is not going away; I really dislike my current living conditions; I'm really stressed about finals; my dad is too stubborn and strict; my roommate never cleans up her mess." Reading this list, one might assume that this person was a curmudgeonly, complaining, negative person, the nightmare person to find oneself sitting next to on a plane. But when asked about how she felt about her life as a whole, she circled the midpoint on the scale ("neutral"). When asked how she felt about the upcoming week, she chose the alternative "optimistic, expect the best."

We believed that this research represented a particularly strong test of the happiness-inducing potential of gratitude, and we hoped that if it was possible to demonstrate that there are significant effects of a brief intervention to induce gratitude, then the stage would be set for a longer, more sustained effort that could significantly impact long-term happiness and even alter people's set-points.

THE RESULTS

What did the first study reveal? At the end of the ten weeks, we examined differences between the three groups on all of the well-being outcomes that we measured at the outset of the study. Participants in the gratitude condition felt better about their lives as a whole and were more optimistic about the future than participants in either of the other control conditions. To put it into numbers, according to the scale we used to calculate well-being, they were a full 25 percent happier than the other participants. Those in the gratitude condition reported fewer health complaints and even spent more time exercising than control participants did. The gratitude group participants experienced fewer symptoms of physical illness than those in either of the other two groups. Lastly, there was a main effect for hours of exercise: people in the gratitude condition spent significantly more time exercising (nearly 1.5 hours more per week) than those in the hassles condition. This is a massive difference. Those in the neutral events condition fell somewhere in between the gratitude and hassles conditions.

Intrigued by these results, we increased the gratitude intervention to a daily practice over a three-week period in our second study. As in the first study, participants were randomly assigned to one of three conditions. In the second study, the gratitude and hassles conditions remained identical to those used in the first study, but we changed the events condition to one in which participants were encouraged to think about ways in which they were better off than others (the *comparison condition*). Subjects were told, "It is human nature to compare ourselves to others. We may be better off than others in some ways, and less fortunate than other people in other ways. Think about ways in which you are better off than others, things that you have that they don't, and write these down in the spaces below." We included this condition in order to have a condition that appeared to be positive on the surface but in reality might lead to different outcomes than the gratitude focus. The feelings rating portion of the daily mood and health report was nearly identical to the weekly report used in the first study. We also asked participants to indicate each day if they had helped someone with a problem or offered someone emotional support.

The gratitude condition still showed an impressive array of benefits, despite the fact that the comparison condition may have mimicked it and produced some grateful affect. Although the health benefits seen in the first study were not evident in the second study (perhaps because of the short duration of the intervention), participants in the gratitude condition felt more joyful, enthusiastic, interested, attentive, energetic, excited, determined, and strong than those in the hassles condition. They also reported offering others more emotional support or help with a personal problem, indicating that the gratitude condition increased prosocial motivation — and more directly supporting the notion that gratitude motivates people to do good. And this was not limited to what they said about themselves. We sent surveys to people who knew them well, and these significant others rated participants in the gratitude group as actually more helpful compared to those in the other groups (these friends were not aware of which experimental condition the participants were in).

Once again, the gratitude condition showed a significant effect on positive emotions as compared to the hassles condition, but produced no reliable impact on negative emotions. Additionally, we discovered that the frequency with which people practice gratefulness matters. Our second study produced evidence that the daily intervention led to greater increases in gratitude than did the weekly practice we had participants try in our first study.

In a third study, we replicated the benefits of grateful thinking in adults with neuromuscular diseases. With assistance from the Department of Physical Medicine and Rehabilitation at the University of California-Davis, we recruited adults with congenital and adult-onset neuromuscular disorders (NMDs). NMDs are estimated to affect approximately four million people in the United States. The majority of participants in our study had post-polio disease (PPS). PPS is a condition that can strike polio survivors anywhere from ten to forty years after recovery from an initial attack of the poliomyelitis virus, and it occurs in approximately 70 percent of persons infected with polio. It is characterized by a further weakening of muscles previously injured by polio infection. Symptoms include fatigue, slowly progressive muscle weakness, muscle and joint pain, and muscular atrophy. Some patients experience only minor symptoms, whereas others develop spinal muscular atrophy or what appears to be, but is not, a form of amyotrophic lateral sclerosis. PPS is a very slowly progressing condition marked by long periods of stability and an unpredictable course, although it is rarely life-threatening. Other neuromuscular diseases that were represented in our sample included Charcot-Marie-Tooth disease, limb-girdle muscular dystrophy, and facioscapulohumeral dystrophy.

Participants were randomly assigned to a gratitude condition or to a true control condition in which participants simply completed daily experience rating forms. Similar to the previous studies, results of the participants in the gratitude condition showed significantly more positive affect and satisfaction with life, while also showing less negative affect than the control group. Participants in the gratitude condition reported considerably more satisfaction with their lives as a whole, felt more optimism about the upcoming week, and felt more connected with others than did participants in the control condition.

Compared to those who were not jotting down their blessings nightly, participants in the gratitude condition reported getting more hours of sleep each night, spending less time awake before falling asleep, and feeling more refreshed upon awakening. Perhaps this is why grateful individuals feel more alive and vital during the day. When I began my study of gratitude, I was so exhilarated from being engaged in a new research program that I often had difficulty falling asleep at night. My mind raced with thoughts of the importance of the topic and puzzled over why it had been such a forgotten factor in the science of happiness. Perhaps I should have taken my own advice and spent more time counting my blessings instead of counting research findings.

This finding is enormous in that sleep disturbance and poor sleep quality have been identified as central indicators of poor overall well-being. People whose sleep is routinely disrupted have high levels of stress hormones and compromised immune function. Should these patterns persist, down the road the sleep-deprived face an increased risk for physical disease and premature mortality. Why is this? Sleep is a restorative process that serves to repair, maintain, and enhance our body's physiological capacities. Without such restoration, the wear and tear on our bodies' systems threatens our long-term health and even survival. It may sound simplistic, but the evidence cannot be ignored: if you want to sleep more soundly, count blessings, not sheep. A departmental colleague of mine, a developmental psychologist no less, told me that when her daughter was 6, she was afraid to be left alone at night and therefore had trouble falling asleep. Night after night, week after week, she would come into her parents' bed, a nightly routine that resulted in high levels of sleep disturbance for all three. One night my colleague suggested that her daughter make a mental list of the people in her life who had done something nice for her that day. This inadvertent thankfulness intervention had the intended result, no doubt one for which the parents themselves were overwhelmingly grateful.

Remarkably, not only did the reports of participants in the gratitude condition indicate increased positive feelings and life satisfaction, but so did the reports of their significant others. Spouses of participants in the gratitude condition reported that the participants appeared to have higher subjective well-being than did the spouses of participants in the control condition, indicating that the positive emotional changes that occur after practicing gratitude are not apparent to the participants alone.

One of the unique features of all of these research studies is that we randomly assigned participants to conditions. The research base on happiness is almost entirely grounded on surveys. Few studies have been able to successfully create interventions to increase happiness or well-being. It should be kept in mind that the manipulation used in these three studies represents, in our view, a rather minimal intervention. We asked participants to reflect, either once a week or once a day for two to three weeks, on what they have to be grateful for, yet we expected this limited request to have an immediate impact on well-being. Seen in that light, the results we obtained were rather noteworthy. After all, there are a myriad of influences on well-being, from personality factors to genetic influences to chronic and temporary life events, and thus any one factor by itself would not be expected to be particularly potent.

Will you become a grateful person by keeping a gratitude journal? It's possible, but may require a long-term commitment to practice gratitude. I am under no illusion that I was able to inculcate a deep sense of gratefulness as a fundamental life orientation or to instill the virtue of gratitude as a result of this short-term journaling study. As a personality psychologist, I am a firm believer in the long-term continuity of psychological dispositions. People's propensities to respond to the events of their lives and behave in characteristic ways do not change that much over time, even over decades. Therefore, you cannot expect that keeping a gratitude journal for a few days or even weeks will produce a deep and enduring change in the nature of grateful character traits. The momentary experience of gratitude is not the same as having a well-honed grateful disposition: although at one moment their emotional experiences might be identical, a person who always seems to have a deeply grateful heart no matter what the circumstance is very different from another who is simply appreciative of a gift he has recently received. That being said, if you want to dramatically improve the quality of your life, I would still highly recommend keeping a gratitude journal. In the final chapter, I'll describe additional methods for cultivating gratefulness.

WHAT GOOD IS GRATITUDE?

Expressing gratitude for life's blessings — that is, a sense of wonder, thankfulness, and appreciation — is likely to elevate happiness for a number of reasons. Grateful thinking fosters the savoring of positive life experiences and situations, so that people can extract the maximum possible satisfaction and enjoyment from their circumstances. Counting one's blessings may directly counteract the effects of hedonic adaptation, the process by which our happiness level returns, again and again, to its set-point, by preventing people from taking the good things in their lives for granted. If we consciously remind ourselves of our blessings, it should become harder to take them for granted and adapt to them. And the very act of viewing good things as gifts is itself likely to be beneficial for mood.

The Gifted Self

"Life is the first gift, love is the second, and understanding the third," wrote the novelist and poet Marge Piercy. And understanding the giftedness of life may be a prerequisite for emotional health. Gratitude contributes to happiness because of the additional emotional advantages one gains from a benefit when it is perceived to be a gift, that is, a favor that has been given to one for one's benefit. Speaking of the joy that moments of gratitude bring, Chesterton remarked, "All goods look better when they look like gifts." If one perceives a benefit to be a gift, are they indeed more likely to enjoy the benefit? Perceiving a positive experience as a gift may be a form of cognitive amplification that enhances positive feelings. When we amplify, we increase or make more powerful the object of focus. Our positive feelings become amplified when we see their source as a gift we have been given to benefit us. If good things really are better when perceived as gifts, this could be one way that gratitude directly contributes to states of happiness. Grateful people are more likely to perceive things in their lives as sheer gifts and to spontaneously use the language of being "blessed" and "gifted" by life.

In order to test this supposition, in one experiment we included a condition in which we tried to have participants focus their attention on gifts they had received, using the language of gifts in the broadest possible way. This procedure yielded benefits similar to instructions to list what one is thankful for. We asked participants to follow these instructions:

> Focus for a moment on benefits or "gifts" that you have received in your life. These gifts could be simple everyday pleasures, people in your life, personal strengths or talents, moments of natural beauty, or gestures of kindness from others. We might not normally think about these things as gifts, but that is how we want you to think about them. Take a moment to really savor or relish these "gifts," think about their value, and then write them down in the spaces below.

The results of this instructional set were fascinating. Nearly one-half of all the gifts listed fell into the "interpersonal" or "spiritual" categories, which is nearly 20 percent more than when the gift condition is not used in the experimental instructions. Significantly, it is precisely these categories of blessings that we have found to be related to superior well-being. On one occasion, one participant "received" the following gifts: "Weekly breakfast with son, always a pleasure, a fine gift," "Attended Peace Corps meeting and worked on quilts for Lutheran World Relief efforts," "Saw and visited with a number of dear people (at a funeral service)," "Gained strength from beauty of the church service, though my hearing loss deprives me of much." Faith, friends, and family were frequently mentioned gifts. There appears to be something inherent in relationships, whether worldly or transcendent, that encourages people to cloak them in the language of gifts and givers. So we must remember that people cannot be commanded to be grateful, any more than we can command people to love or to forgive. Rather, gratitude is a feeling that stems from certain perceptions and thoughts. Therefore, in order to become more grateful, we need to look at life in a certain way, and one tangible way we can do this is through the lens of gifts and giftedness.

In evaluating the conditions that produce gratitude, the literature suggests that three perceptions on the part of the gift receiver increase their experience of gratitude. First, the receiver must acknowledge the goodness of the gift. Research has shown that the more the receiver values the gift, the more likely they are to experience gratitude. Furthermore, when we perceive a good as a gift, we are more likely to protect it. I spent a great deal of time with my older son during his first two years of life when my wife was a full-time graduate student. When he was a few months old, I was making my way through an aisle at a local market with my son propped up in the shopping cart. An elderly man stopped us, took a good look at him, then at me, and then, as strangers often do, commented on the uncanny physical resemblance between Dad and his son. I'll never forget his next words. He looked me in the eye and said, "It goes fast when they're young. I didn't spend enough time with mine — now they're grown and gone," he lamented. There was a prophetic quality to this interaction. It's a cliché to say that children are gifts — we all know that they are — but taking this perspective seriously suggests that we invest in the gift, preserve and protect it, and cherish the time we have with it. This I have always tried to do with both my children.

Second, if the receiver acknowledges the giver behind the gift and the goodness of the giver, they are more likely to feel grateful. Gifts have givers attached to them. Several studies have shown that if the receiver thinks the giver is providing a favor intentionally for their benefit, the receiver is more likely to experience gratitude. Third, the receiver is more likely to feel grateful if the gift is thought to be gratuitous. The more a gift goes beyond the receiver's social expectations, the more likely gratitude is experienced.

Gratitude, Depression, and Pleasant Memories

In several studies, depression has been shown to be strongly inversely related to gratitude. The more grateful a person is, the less depressed they are. The more depressed a person is, the less likely they are to go around feeling thankful for life. Typically, depression is assessed in research studies by asking people a series of questions about their current levels of mood, attitudes toward themselves, and sleeping and eating habits. However, it is well known that self-reported questionnaires are inadequate measures of the clinical syndrome of depression because many of the statements on a depression questionnaire overlap with conditions found in other clinical states as well as with normal functioning (for example, who among us has not had occasional bouts of insomnia?). Philip Watkins, a clinical psychologist at Eastern Washington University, evaluated the gratitude status of individuals who were diagnosed with the use of a structured clinical interview. He found that clinically depressed individuals showed significantly lower gratitude (nearly 50 percent less gratitude) than nondepressed controls. Since depression is a pleasureless state, it follows logically that depressives would not be grateful as they don't experience happiness from blessings they experience and may be just less prone to noticing blessings in their lives.

Researchers have shown that gratitude enhances the retrievability of positive experiences by increasing elaboration of positive information. What does this mean? It means that when we are grateful, we are more likely to notice positive aspects in our lives, and this enhances the formation (or "encoding") of these experiences into memory. If at encoding we experience gratitude in response to a benefit, this by definition should increase the degree to which we think about the gift, the giver, and additional aspects of the situation (the effort expended by the person, how we felt at the time, how we expressed our gratitude, and so on). By elaborating the event at encoding, this will increase the retrievability of the event in our memory store. So, grateful individuals should be more likely to recall past benefits from their life and experience gratitude in response to these blessings. In other words, grateful individuals should be more likely to "count their blessings" spontaneously, not just when they are instructed to do so in a psychological experiment. People who are grateful do tend to show a *positive recall bias* (conjuring up many more pleasant memories than unpleasant ones) when asked about past life events, just as depressed individuals show a *negative recall bias* when asked to recall past events (recalling many more unpleasant than pleasant events).

A nurse who attended a gratitude workshop that I led told me that the day after the workshop her husband was laid off at work. She said he usually gets severely depressed when events of this magnitude happen. Every morning they have devotionals or "quiet time" together, and so she told him about the benefit of writing blessings. She wrote three and he wrote three and then they shared them with each other. After doing that for about three weeks, he began job hunting and his mood became much more optimistic. She couldn't believe the difference in him. Even their friends said to her, "What's with your husband — why isn't he depressed?" Shortly thereafter, he secured a good position.

How might gratitude prevent depression? If gratitude provides more focus on, and enjoyment of, benefits, this would seem to expel depression. To the extent that gratitude helps an individual direct their attention to blessings they have and away from things they lack, this should decrease the likelihood of depression. Perhaps the individual who lost his job became more grateful for his wife, his family, or the support of his friends during his unemployment period and this awareness of the support of others energized him enough to begin to look for a job. Stressful events appear to be important precursors of depressive episodes, so if gratitude proves to be an effective coping technique, this should also help to prevent depression. Also, in providing for increased access to positive memories, gratitude could help build more positive cognitions. While depression treatment approaches have historically emphasized correcting negative thoughts, recently some have encouraged more emphasis on building positive thoughts. A practice of gratitude could help develop a more positive way of thinking about life events and so assist in the prevention of depression. Various depression researchers have proposed that the lack of social rewards (and/or increased social punishment) is important in the etiology and maintenance of depression. If a grateful disposition actually provides for a more enjoyable social life, this should also help to keep depression at bay.

Grateful recipients of benevolence feel better about themselves. They feel esteemed and validated when they perceive that another person has provided them with assistance. This enhancement of self-worth can itself drive out feelings of depression by reducing feelings of hopelessness, itself a core feature in sustaining depression. A critical element in gratitude is the recipient's acknowledgment that the gift was given out of compassion, generosity, kindness, or love (and often, but not always, selflessness — always at least, though, some effort or loss or energy spent by the giver). One of the reasons gratitude makes us happier is that it forces us to abandon a belief that may accompany severe depression: that the world is devoid of goodness, love, and kindness and contains nothing but randomness and cruelty. Repeated patterns of perceived benevolence may lead the depressed person to reorganize his or her self-schema ("I guess I'm not such a loser after all"). By feeling grateful, we are acknowledging that someone, somewhere, is being kind to us, and therefore not just that we are worthy of kindness (as opposed to everyone else) but also that kindness indeed exists in the world and, therefore, that life may be worth living.

Similarly, gratitude might lessen depression by directing one's attention away from one's self. Research has shown that depressed individuals engage in self-focus that intensifies their gloominess. By practicing gratitude, attention is directed away from the self and more to others and what they are providing for us. In one experiment at the University of Virginia, participants wrote about several different situations in which they felt specific positive emotions. There were interesting differences between happiness responses and gratitude responses. When participants recalled something good that happened to them (the happiness scenario), the researcher Sarah Algoe found that they were "pretty much self-focused, not in a bad way, but they wanted to celebrate and tell people how great they felt." In contrast, participants who had something good done for them (the gratitude scenario) wanted to tell people about the other person's kindness and did not focus on themselves.

The Poverty of Affluence

One of the most frequent questions coming from experts of well-being seems to be "If we are so rich, why aren't we happy?" Well-being research has shown that happiness can't be bought. In the midst of our increasingly abundant culture, people don't seem to be getting any happier, and some have argued that in fact the misery index is rising (in terms of variables such as depression and suicide rate). One reason that increases in material blessings do not increase happiness is related to the principle of adaptation. Research from a number of different areas in psychology has shown how humans have an amazing ability to adapt to their ongoing circumstances. Yet one need not be a slave to the law of habituation. Adaptation to satisfaction can be counteracted by constantly being aware of how fortunate one's condition is. This is exactly what a practice of gratitude should accomplish, consistently reminding one of how good one's life really is.

As any advertiser knows, material strivings are fueled by upward social comparisons that promote feelings of deprivation and discontent. By focusing on blessings one is grateful for, attention can be directed away from making comparisons with others who have more. A number of studies have shown that upward social comparisons lead to less positive affect and more unpleasant feelings such as depression and resentment. When an individual is grateful for how green her own lawn is, she is not likely to be looking at the greener grass on the other side of the fence. I should note that the converse likely holds as well: if a person's attention is consistently devoted to things they do not have, they will be unlikely to focus on appreciating the blessings they do have. Research in our own lab has shown that grateful people are less likely to base their happiness on material possessions, are less envious of others, and are less likely to measure success in terms of material gain. Yet the relationship is not as simple as the "grateful people don't care about stuff" stereotype. They likely enjoy their material possessions as much as anyone. However, they also invest more in the protection of this "stuff." And they more readily acknowledge the contributions that others have made to their material well-being. When his car odometer reached the 200,000 mark, a friend of mine bought small gifts for the mechanics who had serviced his car since the time he bought it.

Grateful people are mindful materialists. Deliberate appreciation can reduce the tendency to depreciate what one has, making it less likely that the person will go out and replace what they have with newer, shinier, faster, better alternatives. The ability that grateful individuals have to extract maximum satisfaction out of life extends to material possessions. In contrast, there is always some real or imagined pleasure that stands in the way of the happiness of the ungrateful person. Consumerism fuels ingratitude. Advertisers purposely invoke feelings of comparison and ingratitude by leading us to perceive that our lives are incomplete unless we buy what they are selling. Here is a frightening statistic: by the age of twenty-one, the average adult will have seen one million TV commercials. By playing on our desires and fears, these ads fabricate needs and cultivate ingratitude for what we have and who we are. Human relationships are hijacked. Consumer psychologists argue that advertising separates children from their parents and spouses from each other. Parents are portrayed as uncool and out of touch with their teenage children, who are encouraged to reject the older generation's preferences and carve out their own identity around materialistic values. Gratitude for our spouses can have a difficult time surviving the constant parade of perfectly sculpted bodies exuding perpetual sexual desire. In a classic study conducted in the 1980s, researchers found that men who viewed photographs of physically attractive women or *Playboy* centerfolds subsequently found their current mates less physically attractive, became less satisfied with their current relationships, and expressed less commitment to their partners. Gratitude can serve as a firewall of protection against some of the effects of these insidious advertising messages. When a person wants what they have, they are less susceptible to messages that encourage them to want what they don't have or what others have. By the way, when women in another study were shown beefcake photos from *Playgirl,* they expressed no such changes of heart toward their husbands or boyfriends.

GRATITUDE STRENGTHENS SOCIAL TIES

Esther Summerson's strong attachment to John Jarndyce in Charles Dickens's *Bleak House* is born in gratitude. Jarndyce had taken in Esther as an adopted child and raised her. "From my childhood I have been," she says, "the object of the untiring goodness of the best of human beings, to whom I am so bound by every tie of attachment, gratitude, and love, that nothing I could do in the compass of a life could express the feelings of a single day." Bonds of attachment, like Esther's to John Jarndyce, are forged through benevolent actions between givers and their beneficiaries, and cemented and strengthened by the emotion of gratitude. Gratitude is based on the assumption that the other person wanted to do something good for me because it is good for me. He made *my* concern *his* concern. Esther reasons that Jarndyce's actions are motivated by kindness, and her gratitude is the inevitable outcome of this positive, trusting assumption. For her not to feel gratitude, she would have had to convince herself that he had not acted from genuine kindness, and she has no grounds on which to make this contrary assumption.

An unexpected benefit from gratitude journaling, one that I did not predict in advance, was that people who kept gratitude journals reported feeling closer and more connected to others, were more likely to help others, and were actually seen as more helpful by significant others in their social networks. The family, friends, partners, and others who surround them consistently report that people who practice gratitude seem measurably happier and are more pleasant to be around. We also have evidence that people who are high on dispositional gratitude, the habitual tendency to be aware of blessings in life, have better relationships, are more likely to protect and preserve these relationships, are more securely attached, and are less lonely. That grateful people are less lonely is a particularly key finding. Sigmund Freud wrote that the greatest fear in life is the fear of being alone and isolated. Contemporary social commentators have depicted this time in history as the "age of loneliness." Never before in history have so many people lived alone, never before have families been so geographically dispersed, or so small. People who have an easier time conjuring up reasons to be grateful are less likely to say that they lack companionship or that no one really knows them well. Our innate longing for belonging is strengthened when we experience and express heartfelt gratitude.

Why is gratitude good for our relational well-being? The University of North Carolina researcher Barbara Fredrickson, pioneer in the study of positive emotions, has argued that positive emotions broaden mindsets and build enduring personal resources. These resources function as reserves to be drawn on in times of need. Seen in the light of this broaden-and-build model, gratitude is effective in increasing well-being as it builds psychological, social, and spiritual resources. Gratitude inspires prosocial reciprocity and, indeed, is one of the primary psychological mechanisms thought to underlie *reciprocal altruism* ("You do something nice for me, and I'll do something nice for you"). Moreover, encouraging people to focus on the benefits they have received from others leads them to feel loved and cared for by others. So gratitude appears to build friendships and other social bonds. These are social resources because, in times of need, these social bonds are wellsprings to be tapped for the provision of social support. You can even think of gratitude as a form of love, a consequence of an already formed attachment as well as a precipitating condition for the formation of new affectional bonds, as those that occur between Esther Summerson and John Jarndyce.

GRATE-FUL OR GRAT-ING MARRIAGES?

Recent research suggests that chronically happy individuals experience approximately 4 times more positive emotions than negative emotions. University of Washington psychologist John Gottman, an expert in marital relations, predicts that unless a couple is able to maintain a high ratio of positive to negative affect in their interactions with each other (5:1 or greater), the likelihood that the marriage will dissolve is greatly increased. In a highly publicized study, he and his colleagues observed 73 couples discussing an area of conflict in their relationship. The research team measured positivity and negativity using two coding schemes: one focused on positive and negative speech acts and another focused on observable positive and negative emotions. Gottman has reported that among marriages that last and that both partners find fulfilling mean positivity ratios were 5.1 for speech acts and 4.7 for observed emotions. By contrast, among couples headed for break-up the mean positivity ratios were 0.9 for speech acts and 0.7 for observed emotions. Gottman has become so good at spotting the strengths and weaknesses of a marriage that he can predict with 90 percent accuracy whether the marriage will end in divorce or not, often after just three minutes of observation in his marriage lab.

What is the best way to create a positivity ratio? Gottman suggests practicing gratitude in marriage. In fact, the "thanksgiving exercise" that he recommends is the basis for one of the seven principles for making marriages work. In her book *The Second Shift*, Arlie Hochschild wrote about an "economy of gratitude" in marriages: "When couples struggle, it is seldom over who does what. Far more often, it is over the giving and receiving of gratitude. The struggle for marriage in the contemporary context is the struggle to cultivate gratitude between men and women." Troubled marriages are characterized by a significantly greater counting of complaints than counting of blessings. According to the positivity ratio, a desirable goal is at least five blessings for every one complaint (and some suggest a figure as high as eight to twenty blessings per every one complaint). The recipe is not complicated. I can appreciate and acknowledge kindness from my wife. I can consciously decide to focus on the blessings that she provides, rather than default to my tendency to criticize or focus on what is missing. When I notice and express gratitude for the kindnesses shown by her, it strengthens our relationship and makes additional kindness likely to happen. Failure to acknowledge gratitude gives rise to, at best, taking the other person for granted and, at worst, disrespect, resentment, and contempt.

GRATITUDE AND SUSTAINABLE HAPPINESS

From the results of our experiments we know that gratitude has at least a temporary power to improve emotional health, relationship satisfaction, and in some regards, physical well-being. But do any of these improvements survive the test of time? Strikingly, many of our participants with neuromuscular disease continued to keep gratitude journals long after the study ended, and when we contacted them, months later, they commented on the long-term benefits of being in the study. One individual told us that "Being forced, consciously to reflect, contemplate, and sum up my life on a daily basis was curiously therapeutic and enlightening. I was reminded of facets of myself that I very much like and others that could use improvement . . . I have tried to become more aware of my level of gratitude." Another wrote, "It is so easy to get caught up in the process of daily living that I sometimes forget to stop and remember the reason why I get up every morning. Your study helped me to form a pattern to take time each day to remember the beautiful things in life."

When the well-being of participants in the gratitude group was compared to the control group, a strong and consistent pattern appeared: the gratitude group was still enjoying benefits *six months later*. They were experiencing more positive emotions, were more satisfied with their lives, felt better about their lives as a whole, and continued to feel more connected to others. Even though the experiment they had participated in terminated nearly six months before, they maintained levels of overall well-being that were nearly 25 percent higher than persons in the control condition. The evidence contradicts the widely held view that all people have a set-point of happiness that cannot be reset by any known means: in some cases, people have reported that gratitude led to transformative life changes.

One of the joys of carving out a new line of research is to see how one's work inspires others to replicate and extend the original research in creative and novel directions. Replications and extensions have begun to pour in from other laboratories. In a six-week intervention, University of Missouri students were instructed to contemplate "the things for which they are grateful" either once a week or three times a week. They were told to make an effort to "think about the many things in your life, both large and small, that you have to be grateful about. These might include particular supportive relationships, sacrifices or contributions that others have made for you, facts about your life such as your advantages and opportunities, or even gratitude for life itself, and the world that we live in . . . You may not have thought about yourself in this way before, but research suggests that doing so can have a strong positive effect on your mood and life satisfaction. So, we'd like to ask you to continue thinking in this way over the next few weeks." Examples of "blessings" listed by students included "a healthy body," "my mom," and "AOL instant messenger." Control participants only completed the happiness assessments. The results again suggested that short-term increases in happiness are possible but also that optimal timing is important. Students who regularly expressed gratitude showed increases in well-being over the course of the study, relative to controls, but those increases were observed only for those students who performed the activity just once a week. Perhaps counting one's blessings several times a week led people to become bored with the practice, finding it less fresh and meaningful over time. This is why it is important for people to vary what they write about in the gratitude journals.

The Gratitude Visit

Additional evidence that gratitude can make a difference over the long haul comes from Martin Seligman's positive psychology laboratory at the University of Pennsylvania. In neither our experimental work nor in the University of Missouri study was a distinction made between experiences and expressions of gratitude. Our concern was with manipulating *felt* gratefulness. Yet emotions are multicomponent processes, consisting of eliciting conditions, physiological reactions, subjective experiences, and expressive behavior. Behavioral expressions are important in completing the action tendency associated with an emotion. Expression may be an especially critical aspect of gratitude. The concept of "thanksgiving," or the act of giving thanks, implies that there is one to whom thanks is given. The famed humanistic psychologist Abraham Maslow discussed the importance of expressing gratitude toward a benefactor, and the psychological tension that results from the unfinished business of failing to express thanks toward the one to whom a positive sense of indebtedness is felt. What if people were asked to explicitly communicate their appreciation toward a significant other? What might the effects be of a gratitude confrontation?

Fortunately, Seligman and his colleagues at the University of Pennsylvania arranged just that. Participants were given one week to write and then deliver a letter of gratitude in person to someone who had been especially kind to them or who made an enormous positive difference, who was still alive, but who had never been properly thanked. If you were going to make a gratitude visit, you did the following: First you'd write a three-hundred-word testimonial to that person — concrete, well-written, telling the story of what he did, how it made a difference, and where you are in life now as a result. Then you would call him up and say, "I want to come visit you." But you don't say why — it is supposed to be a surprise. About three hundred people have gone through the gratitude visit. This has turned out to be an extraordinarily moving experience for both the letter writer and the person to whom the letter was written. Everyone weeps.

For example, a big, tough, "hip" guy wrote a testimonial to his parents, setting forth how much they had sacrificed to raise him and his younger brother and how much the brothers appreciated and loved the parents — but he doubted he would ever read it to the parents as he would be too embarrassed. However, as fate would have it, over his Christmas vacation while the student was visiting back home, his little brother was seriously injured in an automobile accident and died in the hospital emergency room. After returning home from the ER that night, the parents and he were nearly inconsolable. The boy then decided that this was a fitting time to deliver his gratitude testimonial to the parents, describing how much he and his younger brother had cared for their parents who loved and cared for them so well over the years. He later confided that it capped off the most significant moment in the emotional life of the family, and it helped relieve his parents' grief over the younger brother's death. It seemed to provide a suitable epiphany and cherished capsule into which the family could pour their grief and cope with it.

At the immediate posttest (after one week of doing the assigned exercise), participants in the gratitude visit condition were happier and less depressed. In fact, participants in the gratitude visit condition showed the largest positive changes in the whole study. This boost in happiness and decrease in depressive symptoms were maintained at follow-up assessments one week and one month later. It turned out the gratitude visit was one of the exercises that, to Seligman's surprise, made people lastingly less depressed and happier than the placebo.

It may not be practical for individuals to schedule a formal gratitude visit on a regular basis, but most people can make time every day to express their appreciation for someone — elaborately and sincerely. The benefits extend beyond what we have observed for the gratitude journaling practice.

GRATITUDE BEGINS EARLY

We've conducted our gratitude research with people across the life span, from college age to late adulthood. Are there any groups that might be especially "gratitude challenged"? Consider children. Children are notoriously ungrateful. "Ingratitude! thou marble-hearted fiend, more hideous when thou show'st thee in a child than the sea-monster!" opined Shakespeare's King Lear. Envy and entitlement seem much easier developmental achievements than do gratitude and thankfulness. Research has shown that because of the perspective-taking that gratitude requires, children younger than the age of 7 do not reliably understand that gratitude requires giving credit to others for positive outcomes that happen to the self.

Yet much like gratitude's happiness-instilling qualities, these assumptions regarding children's presumed inability to feel gratitude have never been put to the experimental test. One recent study examined newspaper accounts of what school-age children said they were thankful for in the aftermath of September 11, 2001. The most common themes mentioned were family, friends, police, firefighters, other helpers, and freedom. Girls were generally more thankful than boys and were more thankful for family and friends, whereas boys were more grateful for material objects. One girl, age 9, wrote

> I am thankful for my mom and dad because they help me with my homework. I am thankful for myself because my hamster got his eye scratched by my cat and I took a damp rag and washed his eye that was bleeding. I am thankful for my grandma and grandpa because they give me money to get me a Christmas gift. I am thankful for my clothes because I would around tan naked [sic]. I am thankful for my cat because my cat eats mice from the field. I am thankful for miss long [sic] because she helps kids on math and other stuff. I am thankful for my hamster because he helps me know when I have homework.

The study did not examine the link between gratitude and outcomes such as happiness, well-being, or coping, however. It remains to be seen whether counting blessings impacts on children's well-being in a manner similar to that of adults.

With this in mind, Dr. Jeffrey Froh, a psychologist then at Candlewood Middle School in Dix Hills, New York, conducted a gratitude intervention with 221 students in grades 6 and 7. A quasi-experimental design was followed in which eleven classes were randomly assigned to one of three conditions (for example, gratitude, hassles, and control). Students in the gratitude condition were asked to list up to five things they were grateful for since yesterday, while the hassles group was asked to do the same, though focusing on irritants. The control group just completed the measures. Aside from the counting of blessings or burdens, all students completed the same measures. Data were collected daily for two weeks during class instruction time with a three-week follow-up.

Caring/supportive relationships were the most common theme for the gratitude group. Moreover, it was also very common for kids to report being grateful for their education, health, and activities (primarily sports). Both the gratitude and control condition experienced significantly less negative affect compared to the hassles condition at both post and follow-up. Moreover, the gratitude condition was significantly more optimistic about their upcoming week at follow-up compared to the hassles group. Within the school experience domain, the gratitude condition elicited greater satisfaction compared to both the hassles and the control condition at post. Concerning residency and life overall, the gratitude and control conditions were significantly more satisfied when compared to the hassles group at follow-up. There was also a tendency for kids in the gratitude group to be less sick as they reported being less bothered by physical problems. Finally, the gratitude and control groups felt more grateful toward others from whom they received assistance compared to the hassles group at follow-up. This suggests that gratitude makes us more sensitive to perceiving kindnesses from others. Gratitude thus seemed to have a gradual, yet significant, effect on both optimism and grateful feelings toward receiving aid. In sum, these findings suggest that gratitude has both immediate and long-term effects on positive psychological functioning. By fostering the positive emotion of gratitude, perhaps our children will experience an upward spiral of positive outcomes, creating a reciprocal interaction and giving them even more reason to count their blessings.

Even more encouraging is that the results of this study suggest that there may be better and longer-lasting ways of instilling gratitude in children than the obligatory thank-you note to relatives. The authors of children's books and articles in parenting magazines regularly encourage the cultivation of gratitude and thankfulness in children and offer strategies for parental inculcation. In the 1930s, the Swiss psychologist Franziska Baumgartner-Tramer suggested that parents emphasize the sense of community created or strengthened through gratefulness and diminished or destroyed through ingratitude, rather than appeal to its politeness function or its obligatory nature. Nearly eighty years later, this advice is at last being put into practice as parents and educators develop ways to more effectively guide their children's passage into responsible and grateful adulthood. The positive psychology movement, of which our gratitude research is an example, has called for increasing recognition of tools that enhance the psychological and physical well-being of children. In psychotherapy, education, and parenting, a strengths-based approach is slowly supplanting an exclusive focus on remediation for understanding how children develop. Childhood may be the optimal time to promote healthy attitudes and the prevention of problems, and gratitude training could play an important role in any program designed to foster well-being. As in adults, gratitude may be a very valuable tool that children can use to negotiate both the ups and the downs in their lives.

GLAD DEPENDENCE: GRATITUDE'S LINK TO HAPPINESS?

The degree to which children spontaneously feel grateful for what they receive in life and the degree to which this gratitude makes them happier and better citizens is surely an important issue for researchers, parents, and educators. Yet there is a more basic reality about gratitude that we can learn from children. When we were children, we had no illusion of self-sufficiency. We were aware of our dependence on our parents for survival, security, and comfort. As we grew, we were taught to look more and more to ourselves for the meeting of our needs. Eventually, we came to believe in the myth of our own self-sufficiency. For many people, it takes disease, disability, danger, or death to challenge this illusion of self-sufficiency. We all begin life dependent on others, and most of us end life dependent on others. In between, we have roughly sixty years or so of unacknowledged dependency. The human condition is such that throughout life, not just at the beginning and end, we are profoundly dependent on other people. And we are aware of this dependence. The moral philosopher Alasdair MacIntyre has referred to humans as "dependent rational animals." To be alive is to be in relationships with others, relationships that are vital to our well-being. The self, by itself, is a very poor place to find happiness or meaning in life. Gratitude takes us outside ourselves where we see ourselves as part of a larger, intricate network of sustaining relationships, relationships that are mutually reciprocal.

So gratitude is essential if we are to truly understand ourselves. In some respects this is a profoundly countercultural idea. Modern psychology has placed great emphasis upon individual autonomy and self-sufficiency. Gratitude requires, however, that we affirm our dependency on others and recognize that we need to receive that which we cannot provide for ourselves. Until this dependence is acknowledged, gratitude remains a potentiality at best.

The memory of the heart includes the memory of those we are dependent on just as the forgetfulness of dependence is unwillingness or inability to remember the benefits provided by others. I have tried to show in this chapter that gratitude is the best approach to life in that it leads to enduring happiness. I would also argue that it is the truest approach to life. Life is about giving, receiving, and repaying. We are receptive beings, dependent on the help of others, on their gifts and their kindness. As such, we are called to gratitude. Gratitude feels good and we gladly accept the dependence that it requires when we can reciprocate or "pay back" the kindness. Life becomes complete as we are able to give to others who are now in need of what we ourselves received in the past. A 33-year-old woman with spinal muscular atrophy expressed this dynamic between dependence and giving back:

> All of my life, people have been involved to assist me in getting dressed, showered, to work/ school, etc. It was my hope that one day, I would be able to do something really significant for someone else, like others have always done for me. I met a man who was married and very unhappy. He and his wife had a little boy born to them and then die at 7 months of age. For ten years they remained married, trying to have another baby. They were never able to have a child again. They divorced and he became my friend and lover. He told me of his life's dream of having another child. I got pregnant from him and had a miscarriage. I got pregnant again and had an ectopic pregnancy. (No loss of my tube, thank God!) A shot took care of the problem. I got pregnant a 3rd time; our beautiful son was born on 12/20/98. I have never felt as grateful for anything in my life. I was actually able to give something back to someone. Me, who was supposed to die before I was 2 years old.

It is gratitude that enables us to receive and it is gratitude that motivates us to repay by returning the goodness that we have been given. In short, it is gratitude that enables us to be fully human.

3
HOW GRATITUDE IS EMBODIED

↶ ON A RECENT TRIP to Washington, D.C., I visited the National World War II Memorial. Like other memorials, it is intended to foster remembering, in this case, the sixteen million men and women who served their country in the Second World War. A light rain fell on this cool fall morning, and I drifted through the central plaza, stopping in front of several of the semicircular granite pillars that are dedicated to a single state or commonwealth. A wreath had been placed at the foot of one. I bent down to take a closer look at it, but even before I could read the inscription I was suddenly overwhelmed with a mixture of different feelings — admiration, sadness, grief, but most of all, gratitude. Certainly gratitude is what one is expected to feel at places like this, but that did not make my feelings any less authentic. This emotional reaction propelled me to contemplate my own ancestral contribution to the "greatest generation."

Three of my uncles had served in the army during the conflict, yet I had never really stopped to recall and recognize the meaning of what they had set out to accomplish and the sacrifice that they and millions of their comrades had made. On the way out of the plaza, I stopped to look them up in the Registry of Remembrances, a computerized listing of Americans who contributed to the war effort. I remember one in particular, Uncle Ed (whom we affectionately called "Unky"), whom I was particularly close to when I was growing up.

My father had chronic health problems and was in and out of

the hospital repeatedly during my childhood. Unky became something of a surrogate dad. Physically imposing yet soft-spoken, he wore his hair in a crewcut befitting his military past. He had participated in the liberation of Dachau and received four different medals and the Bronze Star for his heroics. After the war, he served for over thirty years on the police force in the city that he grew up in, working his way up the ranks and eventually becoming captain, the second-highest-ranking position in his department. In retrospect, what struck me the most about him was his humility — he never spoke of his World War II experiences, nor did I know about the numerous honors he had earned in both the military and as a civilian. As a kid it never occurred to me to ask him about his war experiences, though knowing him as I did, I'm sure he would have deflected attention away from his contributions. By the time I was an adult, I had moved away and visits with Unky were few and far between. Today, I remember him gratefully.

The psychologist Jonathan Haidt has described the emotion of elevation, a warm, uplifting feeling that people experience when they see unexpected acts of human goodness, kindness, and compassion. A warm feeling in the chest, tears welling up, even chills and a lump in the throat characterize elevation, and it was these changes that accompanied seeing Uncle Ed's picture in the registry, reading his accomplishments, and reflecting back on his life as I knew him.

Although we associate tears with sorrow, positive emotions can also result in crying. Tears are a common response to profound gratitude. Tears have been referred to as "the most substantial and yet the most fleeting, the most obvious yet the most enigmatic proof of our emotional lives." Feeling an overwhelming sense of gratefulness, as I did on this occasion, can cause a person to overflow with tears. One man writes:

> There are times when I am driving my car, mentally reviewing some of the financial pressures I am under — two kids in college, debts piling up, no end in sight. Just when I start feeling

overwhelmed, I think about all that I have to be grateful for —
my health, the love of my wife, good friends who care about me,
and two wonderful children. I just feel so fortunate I want to
thank God, so moved sometimes I cry.

It was this feeling of being overwhelmed with gratitude that the
Catholic saint, Ignatius of Loyola, was well familiar with. His prayer
life was said to be so intense that during Mass he often had to pause
as his eyes filled with tears and he could not see. After a while, the
constant tearing began to adversely affect his eyes. He sought a special
papal dispensation to relieve him of some devotional duties so that
his health might be preserved. In his spiritual diary, he wrote, "because of the violent pain that I felt in one eye as a result of the tears,
this thought came to me: If I continue saying Mass, I could lose this
eye, whereas it is better to keep it."

THE EMBODIMENT OF GRATITUDE

Gratitude does not bring most of us to painful tears the way it did
Ignatius (I might say, gratitude does not always bring us to painful
tears. But most of us could, in an extreme situation, cry from gratitude). Yet gratitude, like other emotions, is embodied. It is felt and
expressed physically. When psychologists set out to study an emotion
such as gratitude, they are compelled to pinpoint several components. First, there should be something external that triggers the feeling — an elicitor. A cousin or a family friend could give us a much
needed present, or tell us that they were going to do us a big favor.
Second, we experience a particular perception of the elicitor that determines the subjective feeling and its corresponding intensity. Our
brain processes our cousin's announcement and realizes that they
are offering to help us out in a significant way. Third, the elicitor
should provoke a measurable, physiological response. We might feel
the welling in the throat, the warm, rising physiological feeling of

gratitude, as we process our cousin's offer. Then, the response — this feeling, in other words — should cause motivational and other changes to one's thinking. We realize our cousin is someone we can trust when we are in a tight situation. Finally, there is often an expressive component that allows us to communicate the emotion to others. This expressive component consists of ways in which we deliberately change our actions to reflect the fact that we feel grateful, as well as ways in which our facial expressions and physical body change, whether we want them to or not, to broadcast to our fellow humans the emotion we are experiencing. As we consider our cousin's offer, we smile and show that we are experiencing gratitude; we also decide on what we will say as a response to the offer.

These elements of a grateful reaction apply to other emotions as well. Consider anger. Anger arises in contexts where we perceive that an offense has been intentionally committed against us. We perceive the offender as blameworthy and therefore as deserving our ire. Our blood pressure and heart rate rise, and stress hormones such as epinephrine and cortisol surge throughout our body. The rate of our breathing increases and our muscles become tensed. Fists clenching and jaws tightening are also common signs of anger. As our thinking narrows and constricts, we find that our problem solving and other mental abilities are compromised, hence the lament, "I was so mad that I couldn't think straight." We may wish to see harm inflicted upon the target of our anger, either delivered by us or meted out by a third party. We may reveal our anger through movement or facial expression, and we may act on the emotion in ways we later regret.

The expressive component of emotions is extremely important, especially as to how we communicate our feeling facially to other humans. This expressive component is critical: if we do not look happy, angry, grateful, or sad, others find it hard to believe we are really feeling these emotions. Social interactions rely upon our ability to communicate emotion through the face, and if we can't express our emotions, our social lives become disrupted. Those who have facial disabilities can find that people do not react to them in the same way they do to those with normal facial expressions because their emotions are accompanied by a static, unnatural expression. Some persons, for example, those with right hemispheric stroke damage, are unable to recognize facial emotional expressions in others, which contributes to impaired social exchanges.

Researchers have documented that the basic emotions of anger, joy, disgust, happiness, and fear have universally recognizable facial displays. Around the world, whether in primitive or advanced countries, people can recognize when another person is angry, or disgusted, or happy, or surprised. For example, in the case of anger, lowered eyebrows are pulled together to form wrinkles in the skin of the forehead, lips are tensed and thinned, and a glaring look is achieved by the raising of the upper eyelids. The University of California researcher Paul Ekman and his colleagues have gathered evidence of the universality of seven facial expressions of emotion: anger, happiness, fear, surprise, disgust, sadness, and contempt. In every culture they studied — in Japan, throughout Europe and the United States, and among the nonliterate Fore tribesman of Papua New Guinea — a sizable majority could recognize the basic emotional expressions portrayed by people in other cultures, and others could recognize their own.

In contrast to the basic emotions, gratitude does not appear to have a distinct, recognizable expression. An exception may be most evident in the case of religiously inspired gratitude. In churches, temples, and shrines, worshippers prostrate themselves in grateful praise to their God or otherwise adopt a prayerful stance with closed eyes in a kneeling or standing position. More than any other part of the body, hands and arms express thanksgiving to God. For example, charismatics worship with hands raised, palms open, in a posture of receptiveness. This signifies gratefulness both for past blessings received and for God's continuing work in the believer's life. But apart from these religious contexts, it may be difficult to read a person's face or body language and determine if they are grateful, or happy, or relieved, or mildly amused, or not feeling anything at all in particular.

In his classic work on the expression of emotions, Charles Darwin attributed considerable importance to the voice as a carrier of emotional information. Oftentimes we do infer emotions and attitudes from not only *what* is said but also *how* it is said. There are acoustic cues — qualities such as loudness, pitch, and tone that provide information as to the speakers' emotional state. I sometimes notice that when a person is reciting what they are thankful for, their eyes water, they become choked up, and their voices shake a bit. Yet on many occasions, the sentiment of gratitude may be too subdued to reach the threshold for expression. Or there may be a time delay between the eliciting event and the grateful feeling. Many times we feel grateful only in retrospect, long after the original eliciting circumstance has passed. For example, it was not until I reached middle adulthood that I began to sense a deep gratefulness toward some of my college professors. This grateful acknowledgment resembles more a cognition than an emotion, and hence it would not be associated with a particular facial expression, vocal pattern, or visceral reaction.

Because gratitude is a secondary, more complex social emotion, we have learned ways to feign it when necessary and also to conceal it when needed. I recall the Christmas that my first wife's grandmother gave as a gift to all the men in our family the same plaid polyester cardigan. Try as I might, I could not visualize wearing this family uniform in public. Yet of course the correct thing to do was to express my thankfulness to Grandmother, which I dutifully did. There is evidence from research that observers have the ability to correctly infer true emotional state from the voice at a much better rate than chance. Across a number of studies and different emotional states, the average accuracy reported is about 60 percent. I can only hope that on that particular Christmas morning, my acoustic cues did not give me away.

To further deconstruct the physicality of gratitude, imagine yourself right now feeling a profound sense of gratefulness toward someone. Now, imagine that you are being observed or videotaped. Express how thankful you are to this person. Would an observer be able to tell from your face or from your body that you are grateful? Has your facial expression changed? If you are speaking, what is happening to your voice? Has your pitch, intensity, or intonation changed? Is your rate of speaking faster or slower? What about your posture? Has it shifted? You might be inclined to offer a gentle touch. If the feeling is strong enough, you are likely to notice other bodily sensations — perhaps your eyes will well up with tears, perhaps you will feel warmth in your chest, perhaps you will compress your lips slightly. It is likely that gratitude will be felt more from the neck down than in your face.

In an ingenious experiment conducted a number of years ago, groups of observers were shown videotapes of women who had either lied or told the truth about whether they were experiencing the emotion of "enjoyment" from watching a pleasant nature film. Half of them were actually watching gory films, but they were lying about both what they were seeing and how they were feeling. They claimed falsely that they were feeling positively about the nature film that they claimed they were viewing. The observers saw either the face or the body of the participants when they were being interviewed about how they felt but could not hear what was being said. Observers made more accurate judgments when they saw the body than when the saw the face, but only in the deceptive videos. Thus it appears that the body is a better source of information than is the face. Yet most people believe that the face is more diagnostic. The women who had been videotaped lying and telling the truth about what film they had seen were asked after the experiment what aspects of their behavior they had focused on controlling when they lied. Nearly all mentioned the need to conceal facial expressions; only a few referred to the need to manage their body movements. When we receive an appalling gift like a plaid cardigan, we may try to conceal our disappointment and work hard at conjuring up a sense of thankfulness, yet the lesson to be learned from this research is that we'd better pay close attention to managing the messages that our bodies are sending. And when it comes to figuring out what others are feeling, important information may be missed if we look only at their face.

Although our bodies may send certain messages to signal an inner feeling of gratitude, there is no direct, necessary relation between the subjective inner response of gratefulness and the body's outer display. Although we may have hunches based on our own personal experiences, research has yet to systematically examine the specific verbal and nonverbal cues that unequivocally lead us to infer that another person is experiencing heartfelt gratitude. We don't yet know how felt gratitude appears on the face; therefore we need to look creatively in other places to understand how gratitude is embodied.

A Grateful Heart Is a Healthy Heart

The University of Connecticut psychologist Glen Affleck likes a good challenge. His research studies have included patients with chronic pain disorders, parents of acutely ill newborns, developmentally disabled children, infertile couples, and victims of heart attacks. In an intriguing study, he and his colleagues showed that the explanation a person fashions for why he or she has had a heart attack has implications for future cardiac health. When an unexpected event happens, people try to figure out why. Why did my spouse, who expressed no dissatisfaction with me, leave? Why did the identity thief single *me* out? Why was I fired after thirty years of faithful service? Why did I get sick after eating a gourmet meal at that posh bistro?

Affleck and his colleagues at the Department of Community Medicine and Health Care asked patients to rate the degree to which various factors were seen as responsible for their heart attacks, and also asked whether or not they had seen any possible benefits, gains, or advantages from their illness. Cardiac patients who blamed their heart attack on others were more likely to suffer yet another heart attack within the next eight years! On the other hand, perceiving benefits and gains from an initial heart attack, including becoming more appreciative of life, was related to a reduced risk for subsequent attack. A substantial number of patients said that the heart attack caused them to reconsider their values and priorities in life and that they believed they had grown in their capacity to not take things for granted. Echoing these findings, one man in my study wrote:

> It is hard to put into words how many times I have felt grateful with such a great family and kids. Now grandkids. My daughter was in high school and knew the signs of a heart attack to call the ambulance when I had my first heart attack. My wife was always at my side when I needed her. When I had a cardiac arrest in New York she was there. Also the young man from California that did CPR to save me. When I came home from the hospital all my family of twelve was there to meet me. When I was waiting for my transplant my wife was there to take me to the hospital. Every time I went into heart failure, and three years ago I had a hematoma on the brain, my wife and family were there for me. Life just does not get better than that.

According to mind-body folklore, cardiac patients tend to be "hot-reactors" — they respond to everyday slights with reactions ranging from mild irritation to full-blown rage. Research has backed up this belief. People who are anger-prone are nearly three times more likely to have a heart attack than are emotionally calmer individuals. Anecdotal evidence suggests that heart attack victims often view their illness as their body's way of saying to them, "shut up, stop complaining, and count your blessings."

By the same token, counting blessings, itself an expression of gratitude, can be a coping strategy for dealing with the stress of cardiac procedures such as catheterization. Cardiac catheterization involves passing a catheter (a thin flexible tube) through an artery or a vein to the heart — usually from an entry point in the groin — and into a coronary artery. In most cases, this procedure is recommended when a partial or complete arterial blockage is suspected. It is used to evaluate how well the heart is functioning and to obtain information about blockages. If blockage is found, the procedure takes two to three hours to perform and patients are required to remain immobile for four to six hours following the cardiac catheterization. It is exceedingly stressful — it is simply unnatural to have sharp implements inserted into the groin.

A study conducted at the Duke University Medical Center compared nearly 3,000 patients that had significant levels of coronary artery blockage with patients that had less blockage. Among other forms of coping, the researchers asked patients the degree to which they typically "count their blessings" as a characteristic way of coping with stress. Patients with significant blockage *and* who were more socially isolated were substantially less likely to say they count their blessings by comparing themselves to less fortunate others. Social support influenced pain indirectly by encouraging the use of counting blessings as a coping strategy. Thus closeness to others might encourage the use of positive role models or otherwise facilitate the use of grateful thinking in persons undergoing stressful cardiac procedures.

A far more radical procedure than catheterization is transplantation. When asked to write about a time in which a profound sense of gratitude was felt, a transplant recipient in one of our studies recounts:

I'm not sure when it sank in that I had a heart transplant and a new lease on life. I do remember as an outpatient having choices and calling some of my shots again. I also remember when I got back home after two months as an outpatient. I remember being grateful for a new life. I remember driving to work again and hearing songs that connected me to my donor and crying happily. I remember meeting my donor's parents live for the first time and being beyond grateful and feeling some of the void in their life from the loss of their son. Then that weekend my donor's friends and family had a party in celebration of his life. I felt a little uncomfortable but glad to meet them all and connect. I had a new lease on life and he was gone. Even before being sick I was thankful and grateful for little to big things. But now it is way amplified.

In the context of receiving a new heart, what good is feeling grateful? Gratitude drives out toxic emotions of resentment, anger, and envy and may be associated with better long-term emotional and physical health in transplant recipients. In a study with 119 heart transplant patients conducted at the University of Pittsburgh, thankfulness and appreciation as an aspect of religious faith in heart recipients was positively related to their perceived physical and mental health at one year posttransplant. Thankfulness was also predictive of greater compliance with the medical regimen and of fewer difficulties with diet and medications.

A GRATEFUL LIFE, A LONG LIFE

The lengthening of the average American life span by twenty-seven years over the last century has led to efforts to understand the determinants of longevity. Although genes play a large role (if your Aunt Hilda lived to 99, then your chances for a long life increase), experts report that as much as 75 percent of longevity is related to psychological and behavioral factors. A number of recent studies have shown that attitudes and emotional predispositions are associated with a variety of indicators of poor health, including accelerated aging, increased illnesses, and even premature death. For example, chronic negative emotions — especially depression and pessimism — are linked to objectively shorter life spans. Pessimistic cancer patients do not survive as long as their more optimistic counterparts. Pessimists agree with statements such as, "If something can go wrong for me it will," "I hardly ever expect things to go my way," "Things never work out the way I want them to," and "I rarely count on good things happening to me." The underlying theme in all of these items is the expectation of a bleak future.

One of the most famous pessimists in history was the nineteenth-century economist William Jevons, who wrote a book called *The Coal Question* in 1862. In that book, he predicted the nation's supply of coal would soon run out. The coal age, as we know, went on for a hundred years or more after that, and it's continuing today. Jevons was also alarmed by the approaching scarcity of paper owing to deforestation and stockpiled such vast stores of writing and packing paper that fifty years after his death it had still not all been used up by his family. Jevons died at the ripe old age of 47. His brief life span might be contrasted with that of the legendary optimist Norman Vincent Peale, who was still writing and speaking about the power of positive thinking well into his nineties.

Hopelessness and despair can adversely impact the endocrine and immune systems, even hastening death. Conversely, being an optimist may help reduce your risk of dying from heart disease and other causes. A thirty-five-year longitudinal study of male Harvard students found significantly less disease at midlife in the optimists, after taking into account their health earlier in life. Even more compelling is a recent study conducted at the famous Mayo Clinic in Rochester, Minnesota. Here, researchers found evidence suggesting that pessimists have a shorter life span than that of their more hopeful counterparts. Researchers evaluated results from a personality test taken by participants more than thirty years ago and compared them to subsequent mortality rates. They found that people who scored high on optimism had a 50 percent lower risk of premature death than those who scored as being more pessimistic. A third study, with elderly Dutch men and women, found that people who described

themselves as being highly optimistic had lower rates of cardiovascular death and less risk of any cause of death than people who said they
were highly pessimistic. Those who reported high levels of optimism
had a 55 percent lower risk of death from all causes and a 23 percent
lower risk of cardiovascular death than people who reported high
levels of pessimism.

Optimism is related to gratitude, but it is not the same thing. We
have yet to establish whether gratitude can add years to one's life, but
there are clues that it might. Dr. David Snowdon is a professor in the
Department of Neurology at the University of Kentucky Medical
Center. He is the director of the Nun Study, a longitudinal study of
health and aging. The Nun Study has become famous for uncover-
ing factors associated with an increased risk for Alzheimer's disease.
Nearly seven hundred nuns of the School Sisters of Notre Dame order have participated in the project. Because of their homogeneous
lifestyle (same occupation), similar reproductive and marital histories (none), alcohol consumption (probably very little), this population offers a unique opportunity within which to examine health and
longevity. One of the most interesting findings to emerge from the
project came from linguistic analyses of autobiographies written by
the nuns in early life. This particular order has a tradition of requir-
ing brief, handwritten autobiographies of novitiates. The researchers
found that "idea density" — the number of distinct ideas expressed
in a writing sample — was predictive of which nuns would later develop Alzheimer's disease. Low idea density and low grammar com-
plexity in autobiographies written early in life were linked with poor
cognitive function and Alzheimer's disease later in life, some sixty
years after the autobiographies were written. From a one-page autobiography, the research team was able to predict with 85 percent accuracy who would get Alzheimer's disease sixty years later and who
would not.

Identifying cognitive risk factors that foretell dementia is a significant scientific accomplishment. But Snowdon and his colleagues

were stalking bigger game. The unique nature of their data allowed them to explore other factors that contribute to health and longevity. In a highly publicized study on positive emotions and health, Snowdon and the psychologist Deborah Danner examined the association between positive emotional content in autobiographies from 180 Catholic nuns written at age 22 and risk of mortality in later life. At the time these data were analyzed, participants in the study ranged in age from 75 to 107 years old.

Every word written in these autobiographies was coded for emotional experience. Several sisters, like 90-year-old Sister Genevieve Kunkel, flooded their autobiographies with grateful emotions:

> How thankful I am that He selected me to be one of a large family for now I realize there is no compensation for those who miss its joys and sorrows . . . the seeds of vocation were first sown when my oldest brother and special pal left at 16 to become a Jesuit . . . our visits each Thanksgiving and summer made a deep impression . . . His growth in physical health and spiritual peace made me reflect and it is to his example of courage and perseverance that I gratefully attribute my own following of Christ's call.

The results of this now classic study, published in 2001, were nothing less than startling. The more positive emotions expressed in the life stories of these nuns (contentment, gratitude/thankfulness, happiness, hope, and love), the more likely they were to still be alive six decades later. In fact, the astonishing finding was that there was nearly a seven-year difference in longevity between the happiest and least happy nuns! Stated another way, the nuns who used the fewest positive emotion words had twice the death risk at any age when compared to those who used the most positive emotion words. Now, nuns tend to have a much longer life expectancy anyway than that of the general population; even the least happy nuns in the study lived well into their eighties. The life-extending effects of autobiographical writing have received additional research attention. In an extension and partial replication of this study, Sarah Pressman and Sheldon Cohen, health psychologists at Carnegie-Mellon University, found that the longevity of famous psychologists could be predicted from their usage of social words in their autobiographies, as well as from word use indicating humor, interest, determination, and high activation (for example, excited, enthusiastic, alert). This adds more grist to the research mill on social integration and longevity.

HEART RHYTHMS AND THE RHYTHM OF GRATITUDE

"Close your eyes and relax. Shift your attention away from the mind to the area around your heart. If it helps you to focus, put your hand on your heart. Visualize your breath going in and out through the area of your heart and take very slow, deep breaths. Now focus on creating a genuine feeling of appreciation and care for someone or something positive in your life. Really try to feel the emotion of appreciation, not just the thought. Try to sincerely sustain those feelings of appreciation and love as long as you can."

You have just read an excerpt from instructions given by researchers at the Institute of HeartMath in Boulder Creek, California, to induce the positive emotion of "appreciation," a state similar to, though not identical with, gratitude. They call this the "heart lock-in" technique. It consists in consciously disengaging from unpleasant emotions by shifting attention to one's physical heart, which most people associate with positive emotions, and focusing on feeling appreciation toward someone, appreciation being an active emotional state in which one dwells on or contemplates the goodness of someone. Were you able to do it? Some people find that it is helpful to place their hand over their heart while they focus. Because it is pleasant, desirable, and focused in a specific area of one's life, appreciation is one of the most concrete and easiest of the positive emotions for individuals to self-induce and sustain for longer periods. HeartMath researchers believe that the heart communicates with the brain and the rest of the body through various communication systems and that through these systems, the heart has a significant influence on the function of our brains and all our bodily systems.

Rollin McCraty and the founder of HeartMath, Doc Childre, were pioneers in developing state-of-the-art technologies for examining heart-brain interactions and using these technologies to enhance human health, stress management, and performance. McCraty has developed analytic procedures for taking heart rate (normally measured in beats per minute) and mathematically converting it to a user-friendly index using something called *power spectral density analysis* (don't try this at home). This procedure produces a heart rhythm pattern that reflects a noninvasive or indirect test of "neurocardiac function" — basically, healthy or unhealthy communication between the heart and the brain. Heart rhythm patterns associated with appreciation differs markedly from those associated with relaxation and anger. Even when we are experiencing a desirable internal state of relaxation, our hearts may not be functioning in as efficient a manner as when we cultivate appreciation. These patterns are shown in Figure 3.1.

As we experience emotional reactions such as anger, frustration, anxiety, and insecurity, our heart rhythms become incoherent or jagged, interfering with the communication between the heart and brain. This jagged pattern is evident in the top panel. Negative emotions create a chain reaction in the body — blood vessels constrict, blood pressure rises, and the immune system is weakened. This kind of consistent imbalance can put a strain on the heart and other organs, and eventually can lead to serious health problems.

On the other hand, when we experience heartfelt emotions such as love, caring, appreciation, and compassion, the heart produces coherent or smooth rhythms that enhance communication between the heart and brain. This smooth, sine-like pattern can be seen in the bottom panel of Figure 3.1. Positive heart qualities produce harmoni-

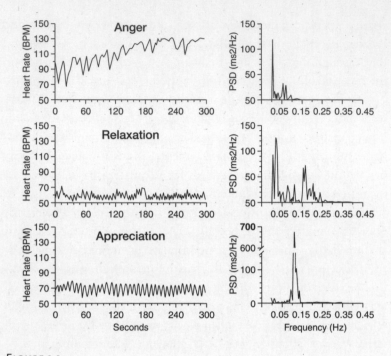

FIGURE 3.1

Source: HeartMath Research Center. Copyright © 2001 Institute of HeartMath. Reprinted by permission.

ous rhythms that are considered to be indicators of cardiovascular efficiency and nervous system balance. They've also been shown to produce beneficial effects that include enhanced immunity and hormonal balance. When people consciously experience appreciation and gratitude, they can restore the natural rhythms of their heart.

These findings would have come as no surprise to Robert "Butch" McGuire or to Richy Feinberg. Nearly every day for forty-four years, McGuire has owned and operated Butch McGuire's, an Irish pub and restaurant on Chicago's North Side. Two massive heart attacks and an eventual heart transplant provoked significant changes in McGuire's life: he quit smoking, lost over a hundred pounds, and has a whole lot more energy and a renewed appreciation for life. "I'm a changed man and no longer take a healthy heart for granted," he told a reporter. Similarly, at age 58, Richy Feinberg, an art teacher from New York, suffered a massive heart attack followed by quadruple bypass surgery. Two months later, he had another heart attack. For the first time in his life, he began to meditate for stress reduction. After twelve years, he has been given a clean cardiac bill of health and has attributed his 180-degree turnaround to emotional skills training that promotes appreciation, gratitude, and compassion.

McGuire and Feinberg, like those systematically studied by researchers from the HeartMath organization, showed measurable physical changes resulting from cultivating appreciation and other positive emotions. In one experiment, practice of the technique for fifteen minutes with a focus on appreciation resulted in a significant increase in levels of immunoglobulin A, the predominant antibody found in the nose and mouth that serves as the body's first line of defense against viruses. Other research has documented significant favorable changes in hormonal balance with these emotional restructuring techniques over a period of thirty days. In a study of thirty subjects, a 23 percent average reduction in the stress hormone cortisol and a 100 percent increase in a hormone known as DHEA (which reflects a state of physiological relaxation) were found after one month of practice. Increases in DHEA were significantly correlated with increases in "warmheartedness" (represented by kindness, appreciation, tolerance, and compassion), whereas decreases in cortisol were significantly correlated with decreases in perceived stress.

UNKNOTTING ONE'S EMOTIONS

There is a scene in the movie *City Slickers* when Curly, the grizzled trail master (played by Jack Palance in his Oscar-winning performance), stops his horse, shakes his head disapprovingly at Billy Crystal, and says to him, "You city slickers spend fifty weeks of the year getting yourself tangled up in knots, and then think you can come here and get untangled in two weeks. It don't work that way." Few viewers probably recall Curly's insight here into stress management (it's not nearly as memorable as his finger-raised, "one thing" lecture). But contemporary research in positive psychology has recently put Curly's hypothesis to the test.

The psychologist Barbara Fredrickson of the University of North Carolina reports that positive emotions are physiologically beneficial because they "undo" or "unknot" the harmful effects of negative emotions. Undoing means to replace one set of emotions (normally negative or unpleasant states that feel bad) with contrary emotions (positive or pleasant ones that feel good). Positive emotions thus correct the effects of negative emotions by restoring physiological and emotional balance.

The basic observation that positive emotions are somehow incompatible with negative emotions is not a new idea and has been demonstrated over several decades. Back in the 1950s, this basic principle of *emotional incompatibility* provided the basis of behavioral therapies designed to treat phobias and other anxiety disorders. One simply cannot be relaxed and stressed at the same time. Try it. You can't. Relaxation drives out anxiousness and vice versa. There is an ancient wisdom here that has been ratified by modern research. The Buddha said that "Hatred cannot coexist with loving-kindness, and dissipates if supplanted with thoughts based on loving-kindness." You cannot be grateful and resentful at the same time, or forgiving and vengeful. When we are savoring the moment, we cannot be regretting the past. Our brains are wired to prevent the emotional confusion that would result from the simultaneous activation of opposite emotional states. The parts of the brain that are active when positive emotions are experienced are not the parts of the brain that are active when the person feels depressed or anxious, and vice versa. Rather, each type of emotion is controlled by different hemispheres — the left prefrontal

region is more active in happiness, whereas the right prefrontal region is more active during negative emotions.

Fredrickson's strategy was the first to induce negative emotional
arousal in all participants, using either a fear-eliciting film clip (for
example, a scene from the movie *Cape Fear*) or an anxiety-eliciting
speech task. These sorts of tasks reliably speed up a person's heart rate
and elevate blood pressure. Next, into this context of negative emotional arousal, she induced amusement, contentment, neutrality, or
sadness, again using film clips. Again, it is relatively easy to evoke an
emotional state by this procedure. Sometimes we choose a comedy
because we feel blue and want to cheer ourselves up. Other times, say
if we have broken up with a romantic partner, we might choose a
weepy film in order to wallow in our hurt feelings. I have a friend
who could not pull himself away from the film *Ghost* after his wife
unexpectedly left him. Across three different experiments, the two
positive-emotion films — the amusement film and the contentment
film — each accelerated cardiovascular recovery relative to the neutral and sad films.

NO PAIN, NO GAIN?

It is estimated that forty-eight million people in the United States
suffer from chronic pain and twenty-two million Americans take prescription painkilling medications. These same persons spend $100
billion annually on pain care and nearly 4 billion workdays are lost
annually to pain. Medical science has known for years that there is
not a direct, one-to-one correspondence between physical damage
and felt pain, the latter influenced not only by the severity of the
painful stimulus but also by psychological and emotional factors.

Pain is both a physical and a psychological phenomenon. It is
generally believed that unpleasant emotional states intensify the experience of pain, whereas pleasant emotional states diminish it. There
are three things that I always do before I venture into my dentist's of-

fice. The goal is the same for each. First, I take two aspirin. Second, I avoid all caffeine for at least four hours before the appointment. Third, I try to make sure that I am in a good mood (or at least a non-negative one), for I know that the pain unintentionally inflicted upon me will be magnified by my mood state and my arousal level. Experiments have shown that fear and disgust, created by exposing subjects to slides depicting snakes and mutilated bodies, respectively, reduces tolerance for a painful stimulus. Pain tolerance is experimentally measured by the length of time a person is willing to keep his or her arm submerged in ice water, a procedure that is said to produce a "crushing" or "aching" pain. These same studies find that viewing humorous images increase pain thresholds and tolerance levels. A mind and body resonating with gratitude and other uplifting feelings provides an inhospitable dwelling place for pain. In a recent review of over two dozen studies, the Carnegie-Mellon health psychologist Sheldon Cohen found that through stimulating the release of endogenous opioids, positive emotions produce less sensitivity to pain and greater pain tolerance. Positive emotions may have analgesic effects, stimulating the release of the brain's own morphinelike substances.

Jeffrey Friedman is a physician in San Luis Obispo, California, specializing in the treatment of chronic pain. He conducted a study with chronic-pain patients in which he examined changes in subjective pain ratings over a four-week period. The treatment was feeling gratitude for things that were deeply appreciated in their lives. Ratings of depression and pain were obtained for each subject. Depression scores were pretty stubborn and were not affected by the gratitude meditation. But pain ratings did go down slightly.

When the average pain rating score pre-meditation versus post-meditation was compared, there was a highly significant drop in the rating scores as a result of the meditation. Did the twenty-eight days of meditation lead to improvement in pain? The average of the first three days' pain rating scores for each subject was compared with the last three days' scores; also compared were the average for the first fourteen scores against the average for the last fourteen scores. There was a hint toward declining post-meditation pain rating scores during the twenty-eight days of testing. This was a small study, but the results were promising and indicate that gratitude interventions might be helpful with chronic-pain patients.

A team of researchers in the pain prevention and treatment research program at Duke University recently tested an eight-week loving-kindness program for chronic low-back pain patients. Loving-kindness meditation has been used for centuries in the Buddhist tradition to develop love and transform anger into compassion. Meditation is often associated with solitary retreat, if not preoccupation with one's own concerns. How, then, does such a practice promote compassion for others? Taught by the Buddha himself, this form of meditation emphasizes feelings of love, happiness, and compassion. Basic meditative practices for cultivation of compassionate love, or *metta* in Pâli, have a long tradition. A widely used loving-kindness practice starts with engaging compassion toward the self, with the repetition of short phrases while in a meditative state:

> May I be free from suffering.
> May I find my joy.
> May I be filled with love.
> May I be at peace.

These phrases are then repeated, but with the focus shifted to others — first to a benefactor, then a good friend, then a neutral person, then someone with whom we experience interpersonal difficulties, or even an enemy, and finally to all beings in the world.

In this study, the intervention consisted of eight weekly ninety-minute sessions. Research and clinical observations suggest that loving-kindness meditation is related to a shift toward more positive emotions such as tranquillity and joy, and a decrease in anger, stress, and anxiety. Patients were randomly assigned to the intervention or to standard care. As it was employed in this study, there was also a specific gratitude component to the meditation. The protocol included a "body-scan exercise" that encouraged patients to accept their bodies as they are and feel gratitude for what their bodies have enabled them to accomplish in life. Standardized measures assessed patients' pain, anger, and psychological distress. Post and follow-up analyses showed significant improvements in pain and psychological distress in the loving-kindness group but no changes in the usual care group. Furthermore, more loving-kindness practice on a given day was related to lower pain that day and lower anger the next day. The researchers suggested that the loving-kindness program can be beneficial in reducing pain, anger, and psychological distress in patients with persistent low-back pain. This groundbreaking study was the first published demonstration of the clinical effectiveness of loving-kindness meditation, despite its use by thousands of practitioners over many centuries.

COUNTERFACTUALS AND BRAIN DYSFUNCTIONS

We are often told to always remember to count our blessings, to be grateful for what we have in life, and to avoid dwelling on what we lack. This mode of thinking can help us when we encounter the blows life throws at us, even when they are severe and bleak indeed. Psychologists refer to this as counterfactual thinking: the ability to imagine alternative, what-if scenarios to the world around us. When we imagine rosier scenarios than our current present reality, our emotional reactions are negative — we feel the emotions of envy and resentment. But when we use our counterfactual abilities to imagine darker scenarios to our current reality, the standard emotional reaction is gratitude. Gratefulness or thankfulness to someone who has done you a kindness may often be accompanied by a thought about how things could have gone differently: "He or she didn't really have to help me," or "I wonder what would have happened if that passerby hadn't been so helpful?"

Many survivors of Hurricane Katrina expressed gratitude despite losing all of their personal possessions in the devastating storm and ensuing floodwaters; they were simply grateful that they and their loved ones were still alive. Jessica Newman was a first-year law student at Tulane University who fled New Orleans at the height of the flooding. With a cell phone in one hand, she and a friend drove through flooded streets, being guided by her mother, who looked up maps online and told them where to turn. When one street was blocked, she tried another route, over and over again until they got out. In an interview, she recounted thinking about the ways in which her situation could have turned out differently. She might have ended up in the Superdome or at the convention center. "I could have been there," she said. "We made out very lucky. Not everyone I knew was so fortunate." Karl Teigen, a Norwegian psychologist, requested that his research participants tell a story about two occasions when they felt grateful and then later asked them if they had thought of what might have happened instead (that is, engaged in counterfactual thinking). He found that there was indeed a close relationship between gratitude and counterfactual thinking.

A recently published study in a leading neuroscience journal found a counterfactual deficit in patients with frontal lobe dysfunctions, so there may be a connection between ability to adopt a grateful attitude and ability to generate counterfactuals. To test the general conclusion that gratitude differentially relies on limbic-prefrontal networks, the neuropsychologist Patrick McNamara and I conducted a pilot investigation with individuals who evidence clinically significant prefrontal dysfunction — namely, individuals with mid-stage Parkinson's disease (PD). Brought into public awareness by such high-profile cases as Muhammad Ali and Michael J. Fox, PD is a brain disorder that results in the loss of smooth, coordinated function of the body's muscles and movement. PD is primarily characterized by tremors, slow movement, stiffness, and difficulty with balance; these symptoms are caused by the loss of dopamine production in the brain, particularly in key regions in the prefrontal cortex. Psychological and cognitive deficits that have been linked to prefrontal dysfunction include poor planning and poor problem solving, impaired working memory, and speech monitoring deficits. Bouts of depression are common in persons with PD as well, so that if an intervention such as gratitude training can alleviate depression and prevent future episodes, this will be an important discovery in helping PD sufferers to maintain a positive attitude.

We believed that measures of gratitude should correlate with measures of prefrontal brain function. In addition, we thought that individuals with prefrontal dysfunction should not display the normal benefit in mood that occurs when an individual conjures up a memory of an experience that induced gratitude. Normally if you ask an average person to remember a time when they felt grateful for something that someone did for them or for something that happened to them, their mood slightly changes into a more positive, happy one. If, however, gratitude and its beneficial effects depends critically on prefrontal networks, then we would expect no such mood improvement in persons with prefrontal dysfunction when they are asked to recall an experience involving gratitude. That is what we indeed found when testing PD patients. We compared a group of midstage PD patients to age-matched healthy controls on the mood induction procedure. We asked participants to recall either a gratitude memory or a "control" positive memory and then measured changes in their mood. While neither group reported a mood change when recalling a positive memory, there was a slight improvement in mood in the healthy controls after recalling a gratitude memory, but no such improvement in mood for the PD patients. We also found significant group differences in the time it took to recall a gratitude memory as well as the mean length (in number of words) of gratitude memories. Patients with PD took longer to retrieve memories that were also significantly more wordy or verbose than those of control subjects. Here is an excerpt from an interview with one of our patients with PD:

A: So now once again I'm going to ask you to try to remember something from the past month. All right, I want you to tell me about a specific event that happened when you felt grateful to someone. You can take as long as you want to remember.

P: Let me look at my calendar to see what I did this month, maybe it'll jog my mind. I can't think of anything specific in here. All I do is go to the doctor's and do my gigs.

A: So any time that you felt grateful toward a doctor or you felt grateful toward someone you . . .

P: I never feel grateful toward a doctor because he's always prescribing more pills.

A: Any time during a gig that you felt grateful toward someone?

P: Well, it's always nice when I finish the gigs, when I finish doing the hour show, when somebody . . . when I get the people in the audience to stand up and applaud. And that happens quite a bit.

A: So that happened in the past month?

P: Yeah.

A: And you feel grateful about that.

P: But as I say, I think that I mentioned this earlier, my speech is deteriorating. It's slower. My voice is softer. I have to use a microphone more extensively. So that's kind of nice when I finish a program, you know in my own mind I think I was slurring my words and not saying what I wanted to say, and they still applaud. And seem to mean it. So that makes me feel good.

A: Right. So you're grateful about that.

P: Yeah, I would say so.

A: OK. Now do you think that something else could easily have happened? Like do you think that maybe they wouldn't have applauded, do you ever think about that?

P: Well, that's possible. There's no reason why they should have to stand up and give me a standing ovation. But it's happened on several occasions.

A: And that would be pretty unpleasant.

P: That would bother me, that I had put my best out and maybe somebody didn't like it. But I haven't come across that.

A: Good, but do you ever think that way? Do you ever think when you go into a show, "Uh oh, they might not applaud for me to-night."

P: Oh sure, but lots of times it's only in my own mind.

GRATITUDE AND THE DOCTOR'S OFFICE

There is a ritual exchange that takes place every day in doctors' offices and hospitals throughout Hungary. Patients slip their physician an envelope containing payments known as "gratitude money." After some ceremonial dismissive protests, the doctor eventually accepts the envelope and discreetly deposits it in a desk drawer. Is this legal? No. Is it common? Yes. Is it ethical? Depends on whom you ask. Patients receive free medical care in Hungary but feel obliged to contribute money under the table in exchange for certain favors: to receive a hospital bed with a better view, to move up in the queue for a procedure, to be referred to a specialist, or just to get a little extra attention. Despite obvious moral difficulties (should the poor have to pay as much gratitude money as the well-off for similar services?), over 80 percent of physicians surveyed contend that so long as the state does not pay them accordingly, they have a right to accept gratitude money. Various medical procedures appear to merit different sums of gratitude money, from heart surgery (92 percent say they give money for this) to 50 percent for a pediatrician making a house call to a low of 8 percent for a routine x-ray. This system of gratitude money is not limited to Hungary, but occurs in other post-Socialist countries, including Romania, Bulgaria, Poland, and Russia. The payments are not always monetary; the same operation might cost a bar of chocolate, a bottle of vodka, or, for patients from rural areas, produce from their farm.

The accounts given by both physicians and patients are fascinating and provide a new, cross-cultural perspective on the dynamics of giving, receiving, and repaying and the link between status and gratitude. A patient replied, "It is a tradition to pay respect to a physician [with a gift] because he is looking after the most precious thing — health." A physician commented, "Among my patients there are prominent people, academics, but they would not consider [a gift]. . . . The ordinary people are more grateful usually. A driver will leave a much nicer present, respect your work, while the others will only say 'thanks.'" Several others surveyed also indicated that the most well-to-do people happened to be the most ungrateful.

This phenomenon of under-the-table payments for services illustrates that cross-cultural trafficking in gratitude can be risky business. Most people in the United States would be appalled by such a system. We would never think of inviting the surgical team over for dinner the night before a major operation or providing our surgeon with $27,000 worth of instruments as did one Russian cardiac patient.

Fortunately, gratitude money is unnecessary in the United States, where most physicians are compensated in a manner commensurate with their skills. Terms of exchange between patient and physician are not the same as they are in Hungary or Bulgaria. Gratitude is not the price paid by patients for the humanitarian services of a physician. But gratitude is still relevant to the practice of medicine. There is evidence that when people are encouraged to think about their health as a gift, they take fewer risks and engage in more health-promoting practices. Whether or not gratitude payments in the form of these highly ritualized gestures lead patients to adopt a grateful stance toward their health, though, is debatable.

Educating for Gratitude: The Role of Gratitude in Medical Training

A fascinating study, published in the journal *Academic Medicine* in 2003, assessed the full range of day-to-day emotions and the experiences that triggered them for medical trainees in hospital settings. Each emotion expressed by internal medicine and pediatric medical students and residents was coded from interviews and a weeklong observation period while they performed a variety of duties at the University of Washington Medical Center in Seattle. Gratitude, happiness, and pride were common positive emotions that were triggered by the joy of learning, the opportunity to practice medicine, emotional support from mentors, and recognition from patients. Resident "Sam" explained, "When all is said and done, I really do find it an honor to go and do this work . . . You're walking in the footsteps and tradition of service that goes back." Jane, a first-year resident in internal medicine confided:

> I was clearly struggling, and my senior resident basically just took me aside and kind of said, "How are you doing?" At which point I just went to pieces . . . We were on call that day, she said, don't think about us; don't worry about us, just go to sleep . . . I have been, and continue to be, very grateful for. Because when I really, really needed it, someone made it clear . . . what I needed to do for myself was just get the hell out of there . . . She made it clear that was not a problem for her.

Why is this study significant? Grateful physicians are better physicians. Physicians who are trained to recognize their own emotions and emotions in others are going to be more effective healers. Studies have shown that emotionally intelligent physicians facilitate patient satisfaction and they themselves have higher satisfaction. A recent experiment found that grateful emotions lead to better clinical problem solving in doctors. After having been given a small gift (a common procedure in mood induction research), internists made a more accurate diagnosis of liver disease in a hypothetical case than did doctors in a control group, who received no gift. Positive emotions such as gratitude lead to more efficient organization and integration of information, important cognitive tools in clinical assessment and diagnosis. Studies have also shown that these emotions improve decision making and creative problem solving in medical students and in physicians. Thus there are evidence-based reasons for educators to incorporate emotional competencies into medical training. Quite apart from the effect of gratitude and other positive emotions on clinical skills involved in patient care, there is the realm of personal development and physician well-being. Gratitude journaling can be an effective strategy that can be adopted as an element of self-care or stress management. Physicians may also be more likely to develop brief interventions such as gratitude journaling to help their patients if they themselves have benefited from the practice.

Illness Prevention: The Grateful Head

I live in Davis, California, a city that is purported to have the highest per capita bicycle ownership rate anywhere in the United States. When I cross campus between classes I am often struck by the small number of students that wear bicycle helmets, particularly in comparison to a community-dwelling sample. Every day on my campus there are accidents, sometimes serious. An informal observational survey on my part revealed that on an average day, fewer than one in ten riders wear helmets. This is despite evidence that helmets cannot only reduce head injuries (by as much as 85 percent) but also save lives. The Bicycle Helmet Safety Institute maintains a Web site replete with life-saving testimonies by helmet wearers. The pastor of my church sustained major injuries when his bike hit a patch of gravel and slid off the shoulder of a rural road during a race. Following the incident, he became a strong advocate for wearing helmets. Researchers at Appalachian State University in North Carolina investigated a social marketing intervention to increase the use of bicycle helmets on their campus. Focus groups of students developed a bicycle helmet program slogan and logo entitled "The Grateful Head." The authors trained student bicyclists who already used helmets as peer agents. These agents provided bicycle helmet information and asked fellow bicyclists to sign a pledge card to wear a helmet. They gave a coupon for a free helmet to those who pledged to wear a helmet. The authors received a total of 379 pledge cards and distributed 259 helmets. Bicycle helmet use nearly doubled: it rose from a baseline mean of 27.6 percent to a mean of 49.3 percent by the last week of the intervention. A comparison group at a comparable university showed no such increase.

An emphasis on gratitude can motivate us to take better care of our bodies. In public health situations, the mobilization of peer influences, safety information, pledge cards, and campaigns around catchy slogans can be noticeably effective in prompting healthy actions. A gratitude-based framing contains an implicit message that bodies, health, and even life itself is a gift and this gift-based construal can transform consciousness by increasing a sense of personal responsibility for these gifts. We tend to take better care of something if we see it as a gift, as opposed to believing we are entitled to it.

Do Physicians Yearn for Gratitude from Their Patients?

When I have given presentations on the science of gratitude to physician groups, I am pushed to think about how my work might be clinically useful. If it's an audience I feel particularly safe with, I'll daringly raise the question of whether doctors expect gratitude from their patients and the degree to which this desire motivates their practice. Psychoanalysts have held that a longing for something in return from patients is perfectly understandable and may be related to unconscious motivations for choosing a career as an analyst. Altruistic intentions may not account for everything. Whether this generalizes to other medical specialties is debatable, yet in the context of educating for emotional intelligence that I discussed above, it is an issue well worth pursuing in medical training. It is a rare doctor who is immune to patients' feelings of gratitude.

Several years ago, I presented my own primary care physician with a copy of a small inspirational book on gratitude that I had written. This was an appropriate and heartfelt gesture, not a bribe for a reduced fee or for a complimentary prescription refill. Though not being given to emotional displays — and wishing to maintain a professional doctor-patient relationship — he clearly found the gesture touching, which in turn I appreciated. I would not want a physician who was indifferent to my affirmation of his competence. Establishing and strengthening the bond between patient and physician is good medicine. Despite advances in medical technology, the patient-physician bond remains essential to quality health care. Appropriate displays of gratitude are an important element in any healing relationship and become increasingly so as medicine becomes more and more fragmented and techno-centered.

BEING ON THE RECEIVING END

"You know, it's an amazing feeling too — usually, as the pod's up front, we don't see the people as they're coming up on the hoist until they enter right there in the door, and to look around over your right shoulder and you see their face and the relief on their face, and the gratitude, that they just want to reach up and almost — some of them do — reach up and grab your shoulder and squeeze it and just tell you, 'Thank you.' There's not a better — probably not a better feeling in the world."

These words were spoken by Coast Guard lieutenant Jason Smith, whose team rescued nearly two hundred victims of Hurricane Katrina from their rooftops and out of floodwaters in the days following the storm's devastation. Smith's testimony reveals that being on the receiving end of gratitude — being the one to whom thanks is given — is itself a powerful experience. It feels good when our efforts are gratefully acknowledged and hurtful when our efforts are met with indifference, grudgingly offered thanks, or ingratitude. The effect of receiving gratitude goes beyond an emotional or cognitive satisfaction in knowing that we have contributed something useful, however. Modern research in the emerging field of neurocardiology suggests an intriguing physiological basis for why receiving heartfelt gratefulness is itself physiologically beneficial *for the receiver.*

Recall that researchers have shown that gratitude and the related positive emotions of love and appreciation are associated with a smooth, ordered, coherent pattern in the heart's rhythmic activity (see Figure 3.1). What was left unsaid earlier was that the heart itself generates an electromagnetic field. In fact, the heart is the most powerful generator of electromagnetic energy in the human body, producing the largest rhythmic electromagnetic field of any of the body's organs. The heart's electrical field is about sixty times greater in amplitude than the electrical activity generated by the brain. Furthermore, the magnetic field produced by the heart is more than five thousand times greater in strength than the field generated by the brain and can be detected a number of feet away from the body, in all directions, using a device known as a magnetometer. Prompted by findings that a person's cardiac field is modulated by his or her different emotional states, several studies have now documented that the electromagnetic field generated by the heart may actually transmit information that can be received by others.

For example, when two people are at a conversational distance, the electromagnetic signal generated by one person's heart can influence the other person's brain rhythms. When an individual is generating a coherent heart rhythm, synchronization between that individual's brainwaves and another person's heartbeat is more likely to occur. In other words, one person's brain waves harmonize with the other person's heart waves, an effect that has been measured between individuals up to five feet apart. This deep form of communication establishes a heartfelt connection between people, resulting in perceptions of, among other things, really being understood and appreciated by the other. So when a person expresses heartfelt gratitude toward us, there is the potential for us to experience all sorts of benefits, driven by this exchange of electromagnetic energy. What kicks this energy exchange system into gear is the coherent heart rhythm produced by grateful feelings. The flip side is that a force this strong may also repel, possibly explaining why we feel an immediate dislike for someone whom we barely know, as well as providing a physiological explanation for why perceptions of ingratitude are so profoundly aversive. This work is preliminary and has yet to see the light of day in rigorously peer-reviewed scientific journals, but it is intriguing to consider and does dovetail with common experience.

For millennia, the heart has been viewed as the primary source of the spirit, the seat of the emotions, and the window to the soul. Virtually all cultures around the world use the word *heart* to describe anything that is core, central, or foundational. Whoever gave us the French proverb "gratitude is the memory of the heart" may have known something that experimental research is now able to verify: gratitude is the way the heart remembers.

4

THANKS BE TO GOD:

GRATITUDE AND THE
HUMAN SPIRIT

Grace and gratitude go together like heaven and earth.

— KARL BARTH

If the only prayer you say in your life is "thank you," it would be enough.

— MEISTER ECKHART

To speak gratitude is courteous and pleasant, to enact gratitude is generous and noble, but to live gratitude is to touch Heaven.

— JOHANNES A. GAERTNER

ON NOVEMBER 19, 1997, the nation and the world were riveted by a drama unfolding at the Des Moines, Iowa, Methodist Medical Center. Bobbi McCaughey of Carlisle, Iowa, had completed thirty weeks of a high-risk pregnancy. Her doctors were astonished that she had made it this far. Defying scientific odds, the most improbable births in the history of the world were about to take place. The McCaughey septuplets were being successfully delivered. There had never before been a set of seven babies birthed that had survived.

At 12:48 P.M., the first baby, Kenneth Robert, was born. A girl, Alexis, followed one minute later. By 12:54, Joel, the seventh baby born in just over six minutes, was delivered. The new dad, Kenny McCaughey, a salesman at a car dealership in Carlisle, emerged from the delivery room moments later. After sharing the good news with all that had gathered in the waiting room, he tearfully joined his family and friends in singing the *Doxology,* a traditional Christian hymn of thanksgiving and praise to God.

Now instant celebrities, the McCaugheys endured media interview after media interview. Everyone wanted to know their story. These interviews were saturated with the language of blessings, gifts, thankfulness, and gratitude. Struggling to manage my own *one* newborn son, I would listen in awed amazement as they described these new lives and their new parental responsibilities. I was struck by how gladly dependent they seemed on so many others and how committed they were to expressing their thankfulness to the multitudes that provided help during the first days and weeks following the births. Hundreds of volunteers changed diapers, brought meals, and drove the McCaugheys back and forth to the neonatal intensive care unit. How did they find the time to acknowledge these efforts? A "thank-you note" committee was formed in their church to help them send out more than *four thousand* notes acknowledging gifts and help they received.

The McCaugheys' expressions of thankfulness to God did not go unchallenged. Controversy soon ensued. Some appeared offended that the parents would acknowledge a divine influence, saying that the children were an act of science because of the use of fertility drugs. Others maintained that given the incredible odds against them, the babies were indeed a miraculous gift from God. Notably, the McCaugheys did not take an either-or approach in apportioning credit for their new family. Even though they had strongly sensed God's hand at work throughout the pregnancy, they were not any less likely to give credit to the staff at Iowa Methodist who had performed nothing short of a medical miracle. Their thanks extended in many directions — to God, to the hospital staff, to their church family, and to strangers they had never met. Kenny and Bobbi McCaughey did not see these various sources as mutually exclusive, and their perspective mirrors those who maintain that scientific and religious perspectives are fully compatible. Giving glory to God did not preclude their acknowledging the efforts of all the medical personnel involved, from the nurses in the neonatal intensive care unit to the hospital delivery team to their fertility specialist with whom it all began. Mom Bobbi later wrote how the ordeal taught her about dependency — on others and on God — and shattered her illusion of self-sufficiency. In both extraordinary circumstances such as these and in more mundane affairs, we are dependent on countless others. Insomuch as we value our own autonomy, acknowledging dependence can be intimidating. But it is absolutely essential in order to feel gratitude.

The McCaugheys' gratitude was not just a privately felt emotion. It served another important function, hearkening back to scriptures written over three thousand years ago. Within Judaism, for example, the proper response to divine gifts is a public proclamation of praise and thanksgiving for God's steadfast love and faithfulness. There is a strong communal aspect to expressions of thanksgiving to God, in which public testimony calls attention to the grace of God in the life of the believer. The McCaugheys believed that God had heard and responded to their prayers for the safe births of their newborns. Their expression of thankfulness was a reflection of their own inner gratefulness and a witness of God's goodness and steadfast love to others. This declaration is the testimonial function of gratitude that serves to draw in and incorporate a larger community in joyful celebration of what has happened in one's own life and in one's experience. In the local paper, a reporter wrote, "Religious leaders could not have asked for a better public relations campaign on the power of faith. Doctors, family members, the community, even the governor spoke often of God as the story unfolded." President Clinton called to offer his congratulations, telling the McCaugheys, "I have been so happy about this. All of us have just been grateful that it came out all right."

THE SPIRIT OF GRATITUDE

There is the story of the fifth grader who, when asked to tell the origin of Thanksgiving Day in America, gave this politically correct account: "The Pilgrims came here seeking freedom of you-know-what. So, when they arrived, they gave thanks to you-know-who. Because of them, we can now worship without fear each Sunday at you-know-where." Though the Pilgrims were surely thankful people, the tradition of thanksgiving did not begin with them. Giving thanks is a tradition that is widely shared and has deep historical roots. Where one finds religion, one finds gratitude. As long as people have believed in God, they have sought ways to express gratitude and thanksgiving to this God, the ultimate giver. The great religious traditions teach that gratitude is a hallmark of spiritual maturity and a quality to be cultivated through spiritual disciplines. Gratitude is thus a universal religious sentiment, evident in the thank offerings described in ancient scriptures and in both traditional hymns and contemporary praise and worship choruses. The German theologian Karl Barth once said that the basic human response to God is not fear, not guilt, but thanksgiving. "What else can we say to what God gives us but to stammer praise?" Barth asked. And what better way to stammer than with hymns such as "Come Ye Thankful People Come," or "We Gather Together to Ask the Lord's Blessing," or "Now Thank We All Our God, with Heart and Hand and Voices," which the late Stanford University professor Robert McAfee Brown once declared to be the best general-purpose hymn, suitable for every significant occasion — birth, baptism, wedding, or funeral.

What does modern research tell us about the link between gratitude and religion/spirituality? People who describe themselves as either religious or spiritual are more likely to be grateful than those who describe themselves as neither. A Gallup survey reported that 54 percent of adults and 37 percent of teens said they express thanks to a God or Creator "all of the time." Two-thirds of those surveyed said they express gratitude to God by saying grace before meals, and three out of four reported expressing thanks to God through worship or prayer. One of our research participants, a 48-year-old male with spinal muscular dystrophy, wrote:

I am daily thankful to God! Most of the time it is very difficult to be weak. However, being weak keeps my perspective in line and keeps me closer to God. I know that God has a plan for me. Part of it is to be weak so that others can be strong. Part is that my faith can speak stronger to others because they can see me struggle. I am afraid of the future and at the same time I know that no matter how scared I might get that somehow God will get me through it. I am not afraid to die. Day to day struggles are scarier to me than the thought of going to heaven. I keep hanging in there looking to do what God wants me to. I am grateful each day.

In a classic study conducted over a half-century ago, gratitude was one of the main motivations for religious conversion in college students. In our research, we have found that those who regularly attend religious services and engage in religious activities such as prayer or reading religious material are more likely to be grateful.

Whether or not a person is religious, there is a fundamental spiritual quality to gratitude that transcends religious traditions. This spiritual quality is aptly conveyed by the late Fredrick Streng, a scholar of world religions: "In this attitude people recognize that they are connected to each other in a mysterious and miraculous way that is not fully determined by physical forces, but is part of a wider, or transcendent context." Gratitude is a universal human experience that can seem to be either a random occurrence of grace or a chosen attitude to create a better experience of life; in many ways, it contains elements of both.

For a person who has religious or spiritual beliefs, gratitude sets up a relationship to the Divine, the source from which all good comes. It is a relationship that recognizes the gift of life from the Creator. Choosing to live in that space of recognition repositions one into a heavenly sphere of humility, awe, and recognition of how blessed one is to have the opportunity to learn, grow, love, create, share, and help others. The response to these gifts can be an over-whelming sense of humility, wonder, and desire to give thanks and to pass along the love that is activated within. There is a looking up and then out. Grateful people sense that they are not separate from others or from God. This recognition itself brings a deep sense of gratefulness.

BLESSED BE THY NAME

For a person of faith, gratitude is a glad acknowledgment of God's generosity. Gratitude is an ethic that is deeply rooted in Judeo-Christian doctrine and worship. The word *thanks* and its various cognates (*thankful, thankfulness, thanksgiving*) appear over 150 times in the Old and New Testaments. The imperative to "give thanks" appears thirty-three times. The Jewish and Christian scriptures insist that God's people, whoever they are and wherever they are and whatever they face, are to be a grateful people, a people filled with praise and with thanksgiving to God. The idea that one should reflect upon the abundance of God's gifts and express that in thanksgiving and praise is a theme that permeates texts, prayers, and teachings of Biblical faith. There are spiritual traditions that say that prayers of gratitude are the most powerful form of prayer, because through them people recognize the ultimate source of all they are and all they have in life. The reformationist Martin Luther referred to gratitude as "the basic Christian attitude" and the theologian Karl Barth remarked that "grace and gratitude go together like heaven and Earth; grace evokes gratitude like the voice and echo."

Gratitude in the Hebrew Scriptures

Religious Jews are people of the Bible. They know about ancient Israel's harvest festival, how Israel, at the end of a successful harvest, thanked God for the bounty of creation — and also for delivering them from their captivity, giving them their freedom as a people. In

Judaism, gratitude is a vital component of worship and permeates every aspect of the worshiper's daily life. In the Hebrew Scriptures, the poetry of the Psalms is saturated with thanksgiving to God: "O Lord my God, I will give thanks to you forever" (Ps. 30:12) and "I will give thanks to the Lord with my whole heart" (Ps. 9:1). Private and congregational liturgical prayers remind the observant Jew of the beneficence of God as creator, sustainer, and redeemer. In the worship of ancient Israel, special instructions were given concerning the offering of thanks to God (Lev. 7:28–29). Many of the sacrifices offered on altars and, later, in the Temple in Jerusalem were infused with the sentiment of gratefulness and thanks, as was the elaborate ceremony of bringing the "first fruits" — *bikkurim* — to the priests, the representatives of God in the Temple. Biblical prayers of thanksgiving take a particular form, in which human distress and a cry to God is met with deliverance from the situation. "Give thanks to the Lord, for his steadfast love endures forever" (2 Chron. 20, Jer. 33:11, Ps. 107).

The Jewish prayers begin with the *Shema,* in which the worshipper recites from the Bible, "You shall love the Eternal, your God, with all your heart, with all your soul, and with all your might" (Deut. 6:5), and the concluding prayer the *Alenu,* which thanks God for the particular destiny of the Jewish people. In addition to these daily prayers, the observant Jew recites more than one hundred *berakhot* (blessings) throughout the day. Thankfulness for everything is appropriate in Judaism because all things come from God in the Hebrew worldview, and Jewish life is filled with thankfulness. The sentiment of gratitude is central to the very relationship between Yahweh and the people of Israel. God is acknowledged as the source from whom all goodness comes. Rabbis have taught that "It is forbidden to a man to enjoy anything of this world without a benediction, and if anyone enjoys anything of this world without a benediction, he commits sacrilege." Thus, for example, a prayer may be said upon hearing either good or bad news, and God is praised for everything. In this way, a divine perspective on life is kept.

This spirit of constant gratitude is well illustrated in the life of the revered Jewish rabbi and author Abraham Joshua Heschel after he suffered a heart attack from which he never fully recovered. A friend who visited him in the hospital found him weak and barely able to talk. "Sam," Heschel whispered, "when I regained consciousness, my first feeling was not despair and anger. I felt only gratitude to God for my life, for every moment I have lived . . . I have seen so many miracles."

Gratitude in Christian Theology and Scripture

"A true Christian is one who never for a moment forgets what God has done for him in Christ, and whose whole comportment and whole activity have their root in the sentiment of gratitude," wrote the Scottish minister John Baillie in his 1961 Gifford Lectures. The idea that gratitude is not only central among Christian virtues but is also at the heart of the faith has a long history in classical writings and is a theme in modern devotional writings. Understanding God to be the giver of all gifts and the ultimate foundation for thankfulness, Christians gratefully acknowledge their dependence on him and rejoice in the gifts that only he provides. Gratitude in this account is not merely a sentimental feeling in response to a gift but is a virtue that entails an obligation or sense of indebtedness to the benefactor. Indebtedness to others enables followers of Christ to share a common bond, which shapes not only emotions and thoughts but also actions and deeds.

Furthermore, entire theologies have been built around the concept of gratitude. The founder of Methodism, John Wesley, stated, "True religion is right tempers toward God and right tempers toward man. It is, in two words, gratitude and benevolence — gratitude to our Creator and supreme Benefactor, and benevolence to our fellow creatures." Wesley and his contemporary Jonathan Edwards led revivals in piety that were amplified by intense emotions and a "warming of the heart," where God's love and power ignited strong feelings of grateful devotion to saints and sinners alike. Jonathan Edwards, the renowned eighteenth-century New England pastor and theologian, wrote of the "gracious stirrings of grateful affection toward God" in his theological classic *A Treatise Concerning Religious Affections*. Edwards was so struck by the evidentiary force of emotion that he made it a cornerstone of his theology, as exemplified in this quote: "The Holy Scriptures do everywhere place religion very much in the affections; such as fear, hope, love, hatred, desire, joy, sorrow, gratitude, compassion, and zeal." For Edwards, and for those who cut their spiritual teeth on American evangelicalism, what one believed *about* God was far less important than the feelings one held *toward* God. Gratitude and other emotions were the sign of true spirituality and the yardstick by which authentic faith could be measured.

Gratitude and thanksgiving are central motifs in the New Testament writings of the apostle Paul. Paul begins nearly every letter with expressions of thanks to whomever he is writing. There is also a strong imperative component of gratitude in Paul's letters where the phrases *be thankful* or *give thanks* occur multiple times in multiple contexts. Christians are called on to live lives of thanksgiving as a glad acknowledgment of God's generosity, which then provides a model for how Christians are to deal with each other. Christians are urged to "give thanks in all circumstances" (1 Thess. 5:18), "give thanks to God the Father for everything" (Eph. 5: 19–20), present prayers and petitions "with thanksgiving to God" (Phil. 4: 6–7), and separate themselves from those who have been ungrateful ("For although they knew God, they neither glorified him as God nor gave thanks to him . . . their thinking became futile and their foolish hearts were darkened" Rom. 1: 21–22).

Of all the gifts that God provides, for the Christian nothing compares with the gift of eternal life made possible by the atoning sacrifice of Christ on the cross. The central message of the gospel — and therefore the cornerstone of the Christian faith — is that God the father provides the gift of salvation through his son, Jesus. "Thanks be to God for his indescribable gift" (2 Cor. 9:15) writes Paul in his letter to the church at Corinth. The human condition is such that people desire to be close to their Creator and live forever with him. On the other hand, we know that our own present imperfections will not permit us access into God's presence. This paradox is resolved through the gift of the Savior, Jesus Christ, the only sinless one, who paid for the sins of humanity by his death on the cross. This is the "amazing grace" that has been sung about in the Christian church for over two centuries. As a gift that is freely given, there is nothing a person can do to merit salvation. It is completely and totally unmerited. This reminds us that true gratitude stems from the willingness to recognize what is unearned or undeserved. Grace is love freely shown to undeserving sinners.

In Paul's writings, there is a strong link between the awareness of grace and the resulting experience of gratitude, in that a theology of grace that emphasizes God's unmerited favor cannot fail to lead to an ethic whose basic motive is gratitude. Some have argued that what makes Christianity distinctive from other world religions is the emphasis on the grace of God. It is commonplace to call Christianity a religion of grace. Paul himself uses the term *grace* more than one hundred times. The Greek New Testament word for grace, *charis*, means gift. But not just any gift — gifts that have their foundation and source in God, the ultimate giver.

The dynamic between divine grace and human gratitude has been the foundation of entire systems of theological ethics, as in the Presbyterian reformer John Calvin's Eucharistic theology. The Greek word *eucharistia* means "giving thanks to God." A major metaphor that Calvin uses for God is the fountain, referring to the One who is near, life giving, the spring and source of all that is good. The highest human good is to know the God that lavishes benefits upon his children and to glorify him forever.

Gratitude in Islam

The Holy Koran, which is divided into chapters called *suras*, repeatedly asserts the necessity for gratitude and thankfulness to God throughout the suras. For instance, in Sura fourteen it is written:

"The gift of eternal life? How am I gonna return _that_ the day after Christmas?!"

Reprinted by permission from http://www.CartoonStock.com.

"If you are grateful, I will give you more" (14:7). A traditional Islamic saying states, "The first who will be summoned to paradise are those who have praised God in every circumstance." The prophet Mohammad also said, "Gratitude for the abundance you have received is the best insurance that the abundance will continue." Performance of the daily Islamic prayers is considered to be one of the pillars of the religion. The essence of the prayer is not to ask or petition God, but to show everlasting praise and adoration to God for life and mercy. This is apparent in the opening lines of _Sura Al-Fatiha_ (the opening chapter) of the Koran, which begins each of the five daily prayers (1:1–5):

> In the name of God, most gracious most merciful.
> Praise be to God, the cherisher and sustainer of the worlds;
> Most gracious, most merciful; master of the day of judgment.
> Thee do we worship, and Thine aid we seek.

Another tenet of Islam is fasting during the month of Ramadan. This period is prescribed as leading to a state of gratitude. "He wants you to complete the prescribed period and to glorify him that he has guided you, and perchance ye shall be grateful" (Koran, 2:185).

In treatises on Sufism, the mystical tradition of Islam, entire chapters have been devoted to exploring the meaning and importance of gratitude. Gratitude often is divided into different ranks or stages. First is gratefulness for the gifts received from God, for one should be grateful for receiving any gift. But an even higher state is attained when one becomes grateful for not receiving gifts or at being delayed in having a hope fulfilled. In this state of gratitude, one sees the blessings that are veiled in affliction, and this is considered an insight into the wisdom and workings of God. The final state of gratitude is recognizing that no amount of worship is sufficient to express gratitude to the Creator and that even feelings of gratitude are a gift from God. There is gratitude for the capacity to feel grateful, literally a thanking for the thanking.

GRATITUDE TO AN UNKNOWN GIVER

Do only the monotheistic religions commend gratitude? Stated differently, does one have to believe in a personal God in order to be grateful? In religions of the East, such as Hinduism, Buddhism, and Shintoism, does not gratefulness pose a problem, in that it would tend to presuppose a Supreme Other to whom thanks should be given? These are not "God" religions. There are, however, Buddhist, Hindu, and Shinto notions of gratitude. In each case, the importance of leading a good moral life is stressed and, therefore, the ethic of gratitude inculcates moral and domestic virtues, such as loyalty, thankfulness for all favors received, philanthropy, justice, truth, and honesty. The Buddha, for example, is purported to have exhorted his followers in this fashion: "Let us rise up and be thankful, for if we didn't learn a lot today, at least we learned a little, and if we didn't learn a little, at least we didn't get sick, and if we got sick, at least we didn't die; so, let us all be thankful."

One variation of Buddhism, Nichiren Buddhism, teaches that

there are four debts of gratitude. The first is owed to all living beings, the second to one's mother and father, the third to the ruler of one's country, and the fourth to the "three treasures": the Buddha, the Law, or Dharma, and the Priesthood, or Sangha. In each case, it is imperative that one repays one's debt of gratitude to each source. Of these, gratitude to one's parents (what is sometimes referred to as "filial piety") is the supreme duty and cornerstone for ethics that is shared here with other Eastern philosophies, most notably Confucianism. In *Regarding the Debt of Gratitude to One's Parents,* the Buddhist teacher Nichiren Daishonin writes:

> The mother is pregnant for 270 days or 9 months. During this time she experiences terrible pain, the pain is enough to cause one to die 37 times. Upon delivers the baby, the pain is unbearable, but upon the birth of the child, the feeling transforms into the bliss of heaven. After the baby is born, it will drink more than 180 Koku of the mother's milk. The child will play on the parents' knees for three years. If we are born as human beings and believe in Buddhism, we should recognize our debt of gratitude to our parents. The height of one's gratitude toward one's father is higher than Mt. Sumeru. The depth of one's gratitude toward one's mother is deeper than any great ocean. Be resolved to repay your debt of gratitude to your parents.

There are some knotty philosophical arguments as to whether gratitude toward Buddha is properly considered to be understood as an expression of gratitude toward an ultimate reality, the spiritual equivalent to thankfulness to God in theistic traditions. There are terms, though, that approximate the meaning of gratitude and thankfulness in various Buddhist traditions. One is *anumodâna,* translated as "a thankful joy experienced in receiving benefits from others." In this sense, it has a rather specific context and is not used in the "developing the virtue of gratefulness" sense that we are familiar with. Another term used in some Buddhist traditions is *krtaveda,* and it is often linked with *pratikara,* which carries with it a sense of reciprocity and repayment. Similarly, the Chinese experience of gratitude is expressed in two characters, *pao-en. Pao* includes such meanings as to return, to repay, and to respond and constitutes an essential basis for social relations. The failure to repay signifies an incomplete experience of gratitude.

In these Eastern perspectives, a positive affirmation of life comes from a deep sense of gratitude to all forms of existence, a gratitude rooted in the essence of being itself, which permeates one's every thought, speech, and action. Gratitude, in this profound sense, is not just a mere attitude, a deep feeling, or even a desirable virtue. It is as elemental as life itself. In many world ethical systems, gratitude is *the* compelling force behind acts of compassion, because life is seen as a vast network of interdependence, interpenetration, and mutuality that constitutes being.

THE HAPPIEST PEOPLE ON EARTH

In his powerful role in the movie *The Apostle,* Robert Duvall plays Sonny E. F. Dewey, a Southern Pentecostal preacher who is "on fire" for the Lord. In a fit of rage that follows the discovery that his wife, played by Farrah Fawcett, has been carrying on an affair with the youth pastor of Sonny's church, Sonny beats the man senseless. He then flees to another state, where he establishes a new identity and his road to redemption begins. Duvall's character is a compelling one — an intense, charismatic preacher who carries on continuous conversations with God. Throughout his ordeal, he feels led by God, seeks to discern God's will for his life, and experiences and expresses constant gratitude toward God. Despite the fact that he is on the lam and has lost his church, his wife, and his children, constant expressions of "Thank you, Lord" and "Thank you, Jesus" continually flow from his lips. The worship scenes in the movie, filmed with local townspeople and real preachers, not actors, offer a glimpse of the power of gratitude in rural, poor, Southern religion. In inspiring and emotionally moving scenes, these dirt-poor faithful, rallying around the church that Sonny has built in their town, are constantly thanking God for answered prayer, physical healing, and the restoration of fractured relationships.

The connection between religion and emotion seen in this film is an intimate one. Religion has always been a source of profound emotional experience, and there is no greater exemplar of this than in the Pentecostal movement depicted in *The Apostle*. Some thirty years ago, a Pentecostal leader hailed this denomination as "the happiest people on Earth." Today, Pentecostalism is the most rapidly growing religious movement in the world, now claiming over four hundred million adherents. While attendances at mainstream churches have declined over the past decade, Pentecostal congregations are up 30 percent. By the year 2040, it is estimated that there could be as many as one billion Pentecostals, at which point Pentecostal Christians will outnumber Buddhists and will enjoy roughly equal numbers with the world's Hindus. The hallmark of Pentecostalism is the believer's dynamic and personal relationship with God, a mutuality that nourishes a dynamic of grateful dependence in the believer. Historical narratives of Pentecostal women from the early twentieth century indicated that gratitude was one of the central emotions that the Pentecostal movement sought to evoke and sustain in believers.

In Pentecostal holiness circles, the story of Carrie Judd is a familiar one. In 1877, a young woman confined to bed wrote a letter to a Mrs. Edward Mix, an African-American woman in Wolcottville, Connecticut. Mrs. Mix replied in her letter that Carrie should discontinue her medicine and on a Wednesday when Mrs. Mix and friends would be praying at a distance, Carrie was to get up from her bed, something she had not done for two years. Following these instructions, Carrie stood, walked, and began to recover. Little did she know that due to bad weather, no one other than Mrs. Mix and her husband had attended the Wednesday meeting, but nonetheless their prayers proved effective. The greatest joy, she later wrote, "was of a spiritual nature, as my soul which had been so hungry for God, was now filled with a satisfaction hitherto unknown, and inexpressible worship constantly arose in my heart . . . my mother and father were filled with unbounded joy and gratitude to God." The sociologist of religion Marie Griffith stated that an important function of these testimonies of gratitude, praise, and exuberant joy were to solidify membership in the group and separate Pentecostal insiders from others.

Gratitude to God for healings still occurs today. Here is a narrative written by a 66-year-old woman I interviewed, who had contracted poliomyelitis at the age of 7:

> Our family was on vacation in Miami, Florida. My brother and I had been playing in the waves along the beach when I became very chilled and was shivering. My parents took me back to the hotel. There I became very sick with a high fever of almost 107 degrees. I barely remember my father carrying me in his arms — wrapped up in a blanket — through the hotel lobby to a car. By the time we reached the hospital, I was unconscious.
>
> The doctors told my parents that I would not live, and they should prepare themselves for my death. For several days and nights, everyone expected me to die. Suddenly my fever broke. My Mother said that the bobby pins in my hair rusted from the sweat when my fever broke.
>
> I clearly remember Mother telling me this, and also the gratitude upon her face and in her voice that I had lived. The experience of listening to her made a profound impression on me. I think this is why I have always felt that life is a gift — and that my life is from God.
>
> Most people do not realize that life is a gift until much later in life. I feel I am very fortunate to have known even as a child that life is indeed a gift to be cherished. So that is another gift: to have this awareness of life being a gift.

Knowing that I almost died — and was expected to die — has made me exceedingly grateful to be alive. I thank God for this gift of my life! And I like to share my experience with others, in the hope that they too may become aware of how precious the gift of life is.

GRATITUDE, AGENTS, AND COSTLY SIGNALS

Stop and think about some of the things that religious people (including perhaps you) believe in. These may include some pretty strange and peculiar beliefs — in unseen spiritual beings, heavenly streets paved with gold, virgins giving birth, lakes of fire, the dead coming to life, and so on. Anthropologists tell us that there has never been a known culture without religion in one form or another. Scientific scholars of religion have offered a variety of explanations to account for the ubiquity of religious beliefs and rituals. Sigmund Freud, among others, espoused the best-known position when he promoted the "religion-as-consolation" hypothesis. According to this notion, religious beliefs and rituals bring comfort to the believer and are a way of seeking security, certainty, and control. Freud believed that we human beings are afraid of the unfriendly powers of nature and of our own dark urges, so we invent a "Big Daddy" in the sky, a supernatural superman who will protect us and also keep us in line. Like other stereotypes, Freud's theory contains a grain of truth. Many religious beliefs are comforting. But also like other stereotypes, it is too simplistic. Religious doctrines can be as disconcerting as they are comforting. Consider, for example, the apocalyptic images in the book of Revelation or the fundamentalist doctrine that unbelievers will be swept from God's presence for eternity ("And shall cast them into a furnace of fire: there shall be wailing and gnashing of teeth," Matt. 13:42). I imagine it was scriptural passages such as that that led the famed anthropologist of religion, Clifford Geertz, to conclude that "over its career, religion has probably disturbed men as it has cheered them; forced them into a head-on, unblinking confrontation of the fact that they are born to trouble as it has enabled them to avoid such a confrontation."

Yet another approach that attempts to explain the origins of religious belief and ritual comes from the cognitive sciences, which attempts to understand them as normal offshoots of the way in which the mind and brain work. Belief in God(s) requires no special parts of the brain. Belief in God(s) requires neither special mystical experiences or coercion, brainwashing, or special persuasive techniques. Rather, belief in God(s) comes from the operation of the same mental tools that the vast majority of our beliefs come from. This belief in God(s) does not amount to anything strange or peculiar after all; on the contrary, such belief is nearly inevitable.

Justin Barrett, in his book *Why Would Anyone Believe in God?*, contends that it is the design of our minds that leads us to believe. An important mental tool that we all use is what Barrett calls the "hyperactive agency detection device" (HADD). People have a strong bias to interpret ambiguous evidence as being caused by an agent. We constantly scan our environment for the presence of other people and nonhuman agents. It is HADD that makes us suppose that our computers are deliberately trying to frustrate us, or that crop circles are produced by extraterrestrial beings. But more relevant to religion are situations in which a sheet on a clothesline or wisp of mist gets recognized as a ghost or spirit. This function of HADD, identifying objects as agents, has begun to receive a fair amount of attention from cognitive scientists.

An example of an event that may trigger agent detection is the following true story: Doug was in a grain silo when a propane explosion occurred. Surviving the first blast that buckled the doors and blasted out the windows, he resigned himself to die in the subsequent blast. Instead, he heard a voice say "Not yet" and felt himself lifted up through a second-story window and deposited on the ground outside. Moments later the silo and barn exploded into rubble. Given that his body moved in a way that was not readily explained by the nonreflective beliefs of his naive physics system, and his life-saving movement out of a window seemed goal-directed, Doug's HADD detected agency at play and registered the automatic belief that the event was caused by an unseen agent. Moving this automatic belief to a reflective one involving supernatural agents was perfectly natural given the circumstances.

Crop circles, intricate geometric patterns mysteriously left in fields around the world, would be an example of a "trace" that HADD might identify as being caused by agents. People do not look at crop circles and say, "Hmm, it looks like those were made by chance." No, they tend to believe they were caused by agents — human or superhuman. The more unusual an event is from a natural perspective, the more people are likely to attribute it to the hand of God, especially if the event is a positive one and if they tend to see God as the giver of all gifts. Recall the McCaughey parents.

From this theoretical framework, then, it is easy to understand why people would believe that the good things that they have in life — those blessings that they are grateful for — were intentionally given to them for their benefit. Our mental tools support such an inferential process. It would be far more unnatural to see these blessings as randomly occurring or to attribute them to luck or fate. This being the case, gratitude is a nearly inevitable outcome of how our mind works. When the blessings that we have cannot be attributed to human benevolence, attributions to God's goodness become all the more likely. Therefore, people are more likely to sense a divine hand in cherished experiences that cannot easily be attributed to human effort — the birth of a child, a miraculous recovery from illness, the restoration of an estranged relationship — for which gratitude to God is the apt response.

A related contemporary theory that may be especially useful in understanding the function of religious gratitude is a perspective known as *costly signaling theory.* According to this theory, both public and private religious behaviors (for example, ritual activities such as fasting, prayer, worship, and tithing) can be regarded as "costly" in that they incur significant effort without prospect of immediate returns. In their roles as signaling devices, these religious rituals and behaviors can become reliable indicators of commitment (of the person enacting them) to the religious community. By engaging in these religious practices, the religious adherent is saying, in effect, "Look, I would not be devoting so much time to these irrational and useless activities unless I was truly committed to the group." No "free rider" (a person who takes more than they give) would be willing to consistently engage in apparently useless ritual activities; thus you can separate the truly committed from the lukewarm by looking at their willingness to comply with all of the ritual obligations of the community. For example, parents may benefit by sending their children to Sunday school activities, but if those parents are asked to give up drinking, smoking, and renting "mature" movies, their commitment may wane. Those who are willing to embrace these "costly signals" will become more committed and less likely to ride for free. Identifying who is and who is not in compliance with the rules facilitates group cohesion and cooperation, as you can have confidence that you are not being exploited by free riders.

Theologians and church leaders have recognized the effectiveness of public expression of compliance with ritual forms. A public religious expression, such as a public testimony of thanksgiving in response to answered prayer, can authenticate commitment to one's God and to one's faith community. This testimony, if it is repetitive and sincere, provides concrete evidence of one's commitment that not only reinforces and strengthens one's faith but also signals to other believers the level of one's commitment to the group and to their shared ideology. For instance, a family ritual of saying grace before meals is a simple example of how thanksgiving practices can be inculcated within groups and lead to increased cohesiveness. In his book *They Cried to the Lord,* the Princeton University theologian

Patrick Miller documented the communal character of praise and thanksgiving in Biblical theology. When an individual corporately testifies to God's gracious beneficence, the faith community becomes a "circle of thanksgiving to God" and the resultant effect is the enhancing and strengthening of communal ties and a powerful reminder to the individual that he or she is not autonomous and self-sufficient. Recall the McCaugheys' testimony after the birth of their septuplets or Carrie Judd's following her healing. These expressions of gratitude are not easily faked and serve as signals to the community of one's commitment to the group.

GRATITUDE AND THE MAKING OF MEANING

A woman with post-polio syndrome whom I interviewed wrote:

> One of my most profound experiences of thankfulness came at the birth of my first child. I had wondered, all my growing up years, as to whether I would be able to have children, whether I could care for children with only one arm, and whether God would choose to bless me in that way. When my daughter was born, all the nursing staff showed distrust of my ability as a caretaker. However, I realized that God had chosen to bless me with a child and he would bless me with the physical needs to care for her. Since God had not chosen to spare me from polio, I knew my having a baby was no sure thing. Therefore, when she was born, I praise God for allowing my husband and I to share the joy of molding a new human being into a blessing to God. We were excited about the magnitude of our job and I felt expectant and hopeful. What greater purpose could I ever have than to raise another human? None, and that was the joy in my thankfulness. The joy of meaning and purpose in life.

For most people, religion serves as a lens through which reality is perceived. It grows out of the need to understand or to find something comprehensible in the existential problems that humans face.

Religion guarantees that whatever happens to the individual, no matter how good or bad, it will make sense. This framework of meaning is particularly important in interpreting and responding to the most challenging aspects of life, such as childbirth, suffering, death, tragedy, and injustice, but religion provides a way of understanding mundane occurrences as well as extraordinary ones, both pleasant and unpleasant.

The psychologist Kenneth Pargament described the power of religion to transform the meaning of events in this way: "When the sacred is seen working its will in life's events, what first seems random, nonsensical, and tragic is changed into something else — an opportunity to appreciate life more fully, a chance to be with God, a challenge to help others grow, or a loving act meant to prevent something worse from taking place." It is in these times of greatest stress and of searching for meaning that religion seems to exert its most pronounced influence. Many religious traditions emphasize the necessity of, and possible good outcomes of, enduring the difficulties in life. Most religions provide ways of understanding, reinterpreting, and adding value to difficulties and suffering as well as ways to see the work of a loving God. For people experiencing injustice, suffering, or trauma, a religious belief system may be the most unfailing way to make meaning from their experiences.

The same event can be viewed quite differently depending on an individual's specific views, including their religious beliefs. Religious beliefs provide many options for understanding the meaning of an event, including the notion that there is a larger plan, that events are not random, or that personal growth can arise from struggle. Some individuals may believe that God would not harm them or visit upon them more than they could handle, whereas others may believe that God is trying to communicate something important through the event or that the event is a punishment from God. For example, a study of hospice caregivers found that some caregivers appraised their situation as part of God's plan or as a way to gain strength or understanding from God, while others viewed their situation as a punishment from God. Specific religious beliefs can lead directly to understanding of particular events. Death and bereavement, for example, could be appraised very differently depending on beliefs about the afterlife. Many people believe that the deceased continue to exist, that they will be reunited with the deceased after death, and even that they can currently continue to interact with the deceased, albeit in a different way. One study of bereaved elders in Japan found that those with positive afterlife beliefs reported lower blood pressure. Some denominations have specific views on death that influence adherents' understandings of it. In another study of bereavement, a sample of Spiritualists and Christian Scientists completely denied the importance of death; to them, therefore, the situation did not call for grief, and they did not experience grief.

The Episcopal priest John Claypool's reflection on the death of his 10-year-old daughter from leukemia shows the power of gratitude in the midst of grief:

> It makes things bearable when I remember that Laura Lue was a gift, pure and simple, something I neither earned nor deserved nor had a right to. And when I remember that the appropriate response to a gift, even when it is taken away, is gratitude, then I am better able to try and thank God that I was ever given her in the first place.

In addition to explicitly religious beliefs, such as the existence of God and the possibility of an afterlife, religion can inform and influence other beliefs that are less explicitly religious, such as beliefs in fairness, control, coherence, benevolence of the world and other people, and vulnerability. Psychologists have argued the notion of a just world: that people tend to believe they get what they deserve and deserve what they get. While some religious concepts are consistent with the just world notion (the Hindu idea of karma), other theological understandings turn this assumption upside down. Once, after I gave a talk on my research to a local church group, a man in the audience commented that it is a good thing that we humans do not get what we deserve. Otherwise, in his view, we would have a difficult time explaining why so many fortunate things come into our lives, seemingly independent of our own actions or worthiness. Although there is the problem of evil — why bad things happen to good people — there is the reciprocal problem of goodness — why good things happen, even to "bad" people. The Christian conception of grace is that God in his goodness generously dispenses unmerited favor — favor that is not earned or deserved.

Although religion commonly facilitates the making of more positive meanings, religious reinterpretations are not always positive. For example, people sometimes come to believe that God has harmed them, either through deliberate action or through passivity and neglect. These negative conclusions in the search for meaning can lead to mistrust, anger, hurt, and disappointment toward God, or even doubt regarding God's existence. Consider the following narrative from one of my research participants, a 64-year-old female with neuromuscular disease:

> My feelings of gratitude are fleeting and few and far between. I suffer from post polio sequella and have a great deal of anger toward this disease. It's robbed me of my ability to continue my career, which I truly loved, and to continue to roller skate (another activity I truly loved) and has a deleterious effect on my everyday life. There is a lot of physical pain involved, to say nothing of the emotional stress. Almost any activity I want to do (i.e., shopping, traveling) is no longer a spontaneous happening. I use a walking stick around the house and a wheeled walker otherwise. My feelings of gratitude are that I am still ambulatory and considerably more mobile than a lot of other PPS victims.
>
> At this point in my life, I have an estranged relationship with God. I get no comfort from being in a church or praying. At some point that may change — however, that's the reality at this time. I have no intention of taking my own life, but there are days when I feel that I'd just as soon not be here.

Viktor Frankl, the Viennese psychiatrist who survived the Nazi concentration camps, described the "will to meaning" as the primary and basic human motive, arguing that the main goal in life is not to gain pleasure or power, but to find meaning and value in life. After the loss of his wife in the Holocaust, he remarried, wrote another twenty-five books, founded a school of psychotherapy, built an institute bearing his name in Vienna, lectured around the world, and lived to see his book *Man's Search for Meaning* reprinted in twenty-three languages and over nine million copies.

Frankl reminds us that gratitude is a quality that can be a permanent part of our lives. No person or circumstance can take this from us. He writes:

> We who lived in concentration camps can remember the men who walked through the huts comforting others, giving away their last piece of bread. They may have been few in number, but they offer sufficient proof that everything can be taken from a man but one thing: the last of the human freedoms — to choose one's attitude in any given set of circumstances.

A spiritual perspective on gratitude reifies the central thesis of this book: those who live under an aura of pervasive thankfulness — the G. K. Chestertons, Viktor Frankls, and Kenny and Bobbi McCaugheys of this world — reap the rewards of grateful living. Conversely, those who fail to feel gratitude for life's blessings cheat themselves out of their best experience of life.

RITUALS OF REMEMBRANCE

Though experienced for the most part as a pleasant affective state, a felt sense of gratitude can require, at times, considerable effort. This is precisely where a religious framework is so valuable. Making the personal commitment to invest psychic energy in developing a personal schema, outlook, or worldview of one's life as a "gift" or one's very self as being "gifted" is a motif that is encouraged and nurtured by religious traditions. Indeed, numerous groups have absorbed this insight. For example, many religiously oriented events such as reflection days or scheduled weeklong retreats have as a recurring theme the idea of "gift" (for example, those influenced by Jesuit spirituality) as do many self-help groups and organizations (such as Alcoholics Anonymous). All in all, setting aside time on a daily basis to recall moments of gratitude associated with even mundane or ordinary events, personal attributes one has, or valued people one encounters has the potential to interweave and thread together a sustainable life theme of highly cherished personal meaning just as it nourishes a fundamental life stance whose thrust is decidedly positive. On this point, a grateful outlook does not require a life full of material comforts, but rather an interior attitude of thankfulness regardless of life circumstances.

As I have emphasized throughout this book, an important aspect of gratitude is remembering. Litanies of remembrance encourage gratitude, and religions do litanies very well. Ceremonies of remembering include daily prayer and less frequent observances such as communion and holy days. Every religious tradition has them. For Christians, the Eucharist or Communion centers on remembering the Last Supper, where Jesus instructed his followers to "do this in remembrance of me." When Christians eat the bread and drink the wine (or juice), they are reminded of sharing and participating in the death of Christ.

The high holy days of Judaism are occasions for remembering. One of the holiest times for Jews is the Passover, a memorial to God for passing over the houses of the children of Israel, sparing the lives of their firstborn children. The Biblical book of Deuteronomy encourages the people of Israel to remember their exile in Egypt, and the Israelites are to remember God by giving the first fruits of their harvest. The greatest holy day in the Jewish faith is Yom Kippur, a day that is set aside for remembering the sins one has committed against

God and against others. Rabbinical writers have also stressed that Yom Kippur can be an occasion for great gratitude over being forgiven.

Days of remembrance are not necessarily religious. The most notable in the United States is the holiday of Thanksgiving, where we reenact another feast, that of the Pilgrim settlers celebrating their first harvest in the New World. Even atheists and agnostics are likely to use their annual Thanksgiving dinner as a brief occasion to pause and remember to be thankful for family, friends, and food. Yet people who are religiously active are more likely to observe traditional Thanksgiving holiday rituals. According to a survey of over a thousand adults, one out of every eight people either planned a nontraditional Thanksgiving or did not observe the holiday at all in 2004. Who were those least likely to head over the river and through the woods to gather for the annual family feast? People who are nonreligious. The study found that people who have no religious preference or who had not attended church services recently were more than twice as likely to skip the traditional observances compared to those with stronger ties to religion. A number of other holidays — especially Veteran's Day, Memorial Day, and Mother's and Father's Day — also are designed to have us pause and remember gratefully.

GRATEFUL IN ALL CIRCUMSTANCES?

There is a final element of religious gratitude that bears mention here. Thankfulness to God often occurs not only within the shadow of suffering, but also, paradoxically, is made possible through it. The Harvard theologian Harvey Cox includes the "recognition of tragedy" as one of the defining features of religious celebrations. The sense of festive happiness and celebration that is evident in customs and rituals of thanksgiving is juxtaposed, in many instances, with loss and adversity. The harvest celebration is joyous in view of the effortful activity that it required; the sadness of the loss of a loved one is transposed by thankfulness for their memory.

We need look no further for exemplars of grateful living in the midst of trials than the lives of the Pilgrims. More than half of those courageous souls who crossed the Atlantic died after one year in their new home. All but three families had dug graves in the rocky soil of New England to bury a husband, wife, or child. But they knew about ancient Israel's harvest festival: how Israel, at the end of a successful harvest, thanked God for the bounty of creation — and also for delivering them from their captivity, giving them their freedom as a people. And so they did the same. They understood their God to be a God who is to be thanked and praised when times are good and when times are tough. Their gratitude was not a selective, positive thinking façade, but rather a deep and steadfast trust that goodness ultimately dwells even in the face of uncertainty. Their thanksgiving was grounded in the actuality that true gratitude is a force that arises from the realities of the world, which all too often include heartbreak, sometimes overpowering heartbreak.

Surely this was also the worldview under which the McCaugheys, whom I began the chapter with, also operated. Despite their hopeful, thankful orientation toward life, they were fully aware of the potential risks and complications associated with multiple births. They had all of the normal fears and worries of expectant parents, times seven. This sentiment is expressed in the stanzas of the contemporary worship song "Blessed Be the Name of the Lord," sung in the nation's megachurches every week:

> Blessed be Your name
> On the road marked with suffering
> Though there's pain in the offering
> Blessed be Your name.
>
> Every blessing You pour out
> I'll turn back to praise
> When the darkness closes in, Lord
> Still I will say
> Blessed be the name of the Lord
> Blessed be Your holy name.

You give and take away
You give and take away
My heart will choose to say
Lord, blessed be Your name.

GRATITUDE WITH A CAPITAL G

In March 1999 I had the privilege of attending the Thanksgiving World Assembly, a gathering of religious and spiritual leaders from over thirty nations. This three-day event took place at the Center for World Thanksgiving at Thanks-Giving Square in Dallas, Texas. Yes, there is such a place. It was the brainchild of a Dallas businessman, Peter Stewart, who in the 1960s saw a need for a place where people of all faiths and creeds could gather and express their common humanity. The plaza is located on a sloping three-acre triangular site in the heart of downtown Dallas, with the chapel at the highest point on the site. The shape of the chapel is often described as symbolic, even mystical, with the concept of gratitude being expressed in an ascending circle.

In 1997, through the efforts of Thanks-Giving Square, the General Assembly of the United Nations passed a resolution proclaiming the year 2000 the International Year of Thanksgiving. In a ceremony in 1999 commemorating the UN stamp issued for that year, the United Nations emphasized that "thanksgiving is basic in human nature and is observed worldwide. It ties human communities together and encourages brotherhood and sharing."

The celebratory banquet for the World Assembly gathering was held at the glitzy Fairmont Anatole Hotel grand ballroom. I arrived early, in the hopes of finding someone I knew to sit next to. To my horror, I found that seating had been preassigned, which upon reflection made sense. You simply cannot have religious dignitaries scrambling for seats in a game of musical chairs. After locating my table, I met my dining companions for the evening. On one side of me sat Brother David Steindl-Rast, a Benedictine monk and one of the world's foremost teachers on the subject of gratefulness. Brother David has written several books on the contemplative life and has given lectures and workshops in the United States, Europe, and Asia. Born in Vienna, he studied art, anthropology, and psychology and now lives in a monastery in upstate New York. Dr. Jaswant Singh Neki, a Sikh and professor of psychiatry at the India Institute of Medical Sciences in New Delhi, sat to my left. Mike Rediker, a graduate student at the Southern Baptist–affiliated Dallas Theological Seminary, rounded out the foursome. It would be hard to imagine a more theologically diverse foursome than those seated at our table.

As an admittedly opportunistic researcher, I saw this as a once-in-a-lifetime chance to search out some ideas for the research proposal on gratitude I was preparing to submit for funding. Most of the evening I spoke with Steindl-Rast, who was seated beside me. The minute you meet him, you understand why, even if he were not a monk, that the title "Brother" would still suit him. He immediately feels like a beloved family member. I probed Brother David's mind for ideas about the meaning of gratefulness and its association with humility, which he reminded me comes from the Latin root meaning *humus,* or dirt. I later learned that Emanuel Swedenborg, an eighteenth-century Swedish scientist and theologian, wrote that those who feel love toward their neighbor and a blessedness toward God are in a grateful sphere or heavenly state, and are thus in heaven. Therefore, it is through gratitude we have the ability to live in a joyful, peaceful state; in its paradoxical, elusive way, gratitude is the door to many heavenly gifts. But the door is low, and Swedenborg reminds us that we must humble ourselves to enter.

If I had to pick one person to go to for advice on how to live, it would be Brother David. His advice is simple, but profound. Wake up, be alert, be open to surprise. Give thanks and praise — then we will discover the fullness of life — or rather, the *great-fullness* of life. It is a message that he lives. Now 80 years of age, he has eyes that sparkle with the fullness of life.

As the evening wore on, I gradually let my scientific guard down.

When I did, I was able to experience the moment as a rare opportunity to appreciate the others' diversity and humanity. I cannot remember the exact point at which this happened, but what I experienced was a flow-like state in which I was able to lose my self-consciousness and awareness of surroundings even while in this ballroom overflowing with five hundred bodies. It was at this point that I believe I experienced the difference between what some have called "gratitude with a small *g*" and "gratitude with a capital *G*." Pulitzer Prize–winning poet Edward Arlington Robinson wrote that there are "two kinds of gratitude: the sudden kind we feel for what we take; the larger kind we feel for what we give." Gratitude with a small *g* is the gratitude we feel for the benefits we have been provided — for what we get from others. Gratitude with a capital *G*, on the other hand, is gratitude for the contribution that we make. It is the giving of thanksgiving. This illustrates a profound truth about gratitude. When we give the gift of gratitude, with the right spirit, genuinely from our heart, we get as much or more in return for giving the thanks as the receiver gets from receiving it. When we are truly grateful, we are led to experience life situations in ways that call forth from us an openness to engage with the world in order to share and increase the very goodness we have received. It is the feeling of connection with humanity emerging from a sense of wonder and joy that participating in an intricate network of existence brings.

It was this larger form of gratitude that I was feeling as the evening wore on. This kind of gratitude has less to do with the exchange of benefits and more with an emotional relationship that is associated with love, bonding, and empathy. One discovers this larger sense of gratitude in a stellar moment when the heart opens and one sees clearly the great blessings of life. Awareness breaks through and we understand gratitude as a spiritual force throughout the world. When I returned to my hotel room, I had the palpable sense that something special had occurred that night. It was an occasion that I would not soon forget.

This link between gratitude and love cannot be more elegantly cast into words than through this poem written by a 54-year-old lung transplant recipient who participated in our project on gratitude and quality of life in organ recipients. He read it as a prayer at the Thanksgiving meal following his operation:

My best friend
As I struggled for my life
My days becoming few
You reached out to help me
My best friend I never knew.

Each day had become a burden
While I clung to my only hope
My family suffered with me
My back against the ropes.

God had a plan for me
A plan for you my friend
Our paths would cross in time
As our lives came near the end.

The Father needed you in heaven
The angels a helping hand
That is why you were chosen
Only you, in all the land.

My God, my God your family cried
As you were taken from this earth
There was a price that had to be paid
But oh, what angelic worth.

You showed your love to others
Before they even knew
Your love is a living testimony
I am alive because of you.

Your love for me, my love for you
I wish it could be known
So few on this terrestrial ball
Will know the love you've shown.

That someone would give their life to another
There is no greater love
How can I ever repay the debt
As you soar with the angels above.

So as I wake each morning
I thank the Lord for you
I've been blessed by you and your loving family
My best friend I never knew.

5

AN UNNATURAL CRIME: INGRATITUDE AND OTHER OBSTACLES TO GRATEFUL LIVING

〜 HURRICANE KATRINA SLAMMED into the Gulf Coast in late August of 2005. The storm was the second deadliest and financially costliest natural disaster in the history of the United States. Federal disaster declarations blanketed 90,000 square miles of the United States, an area almost as large as the United Kingdom. Over 80 percent of the city of New Orleans flooded. More than 1.5 million people were displaced. Unlike the city's inhabitants, most of us had the luxury of watching Hurricane Katrina on television rather than fighting for survival amid the destruction the storm unleashed. Yet we were still overcome by the images of desperation and despair broadcast from the Gulf Coast. Response to the devastation by Americans was swift and strong as Katrina set another record, this time in the area of charitable contributions. Whether giving time, provisions, perspiration, or cash (an 11-year-old girl donated $6,000 raised from her lemonade stand), record donations poured in and totaled five billion dollars by five months after the disaster. This represented a more than doubling of the amount given after the tragic events of 9/11.

Like many Americans, Tanya and Tracey Thornbury of Montevideo, Minnesota, felt it was their duty to do something following the destruction caused by Katrina. Over the Internet, they made an offer to open their home to hurricane refugees. E-mailing a shelter in Baton Rouge, they were subsequently contacted by Nicole Singleton, an impoverished 33-year-old-single mother of six who saw the e-mail posted on a bulletin board. Tanya and Tracey welcomed Ms. Singleton, her six children, ranging in age from 3 to 16, and her mother, Dot, to their Victorian home in rural Minnesota, 1,300 miles from New Orleans.

Things seemed to go smoothly at first. The three Thornbury children welcomed the six Singleton children with open arms, sharing their rooms and their lives. On the way to the airport to welcome her guests, Tanya stopped at a Wal-Mart and bought Nicole a bathrobe, pajamas, and sandals. She helped Nicole find a job and offered to help her make financial decisions regarding the federal aid funds she was receiving. She loved the six Singleton kids as if they were her own. She accepted the costs of a growing household, which included a doubling of electricity costs and a tripling of her natural gas bill. Tanya, a painter, gave up her sunlit office, where she kept her easel and canvas, so that Dot and Nicole's youngest child, Juju, could room together. Although they were helped somewhat by donations, the Thornburys paid household costs out of their own pocket.

This blending of families soon proved to be much more difficult than either could have foreseen. Merging families is often fraught with difficulties, let alone families from wildly different cultures. Shortly after she arrived, Ms. Singleton mentioned she had a boyfriend who was incarcerated in Louisiana. She refused to divulge the reason he was imprisoned, admitting only that he "was a bad boy." The Thornburys were understandably nervous about the prospect of having a convict in their home, but Nicole began a surreptitious correspondence with him anyway and informed him where they were living. Nicole's mother, Dot, refused to live by the rules of the house and allowed her grandchildren to watch violent, inappropriate movies in the presence of the Thornbury kids. Finding there were no local radio stations that played rap and hip-hop, Nicole and her oldest daughter,

Helen, wanted to download music from the Internet. Tanya said no, partly to protect the computer from viruses and partly to preserve a tiny area of private space. Tensions built. Disputes and quarrels became more and more frequent. Police and family services had to frequently intervene. Eventually, the daily drama was too much for either family to bear. Six weeks after it began, the merger was over when the Singleton family moved to a donated house in Minneapolis. In opening their home and their hearts, the Thornburys made significant sacrifices, yet their good deeds had been met, largely, they felt, with ingratitude from the Singletons. They felt taken advantage of. Tracey Thornbury vowed, "I won't help anyone [again] for the rest of my life."

Sometimes, as this example shows, people receive gifts and, for complex reasons, they react with ingratitude. The act of giving and receiving a gift can be fraught with a widely diverging assortment of perceptions, psychological states, and conflicting emotions. The dynamics of giving and receiving, the relationship between donor and recipient, perceived motivations of each, and their prior histories in similar situations influence the degree to which gratitude is felt, as well as the way in which gratitude is expressed. Sometimes gifts bring joy, at other times they come with pride, and, if certain circumstances are present, they can also bring envy, hatred, greed, and jealousy.

One reason for this arises from the fact that the promise of gifts, or the threat of their being withheld, can act as potent tools of social control. Sometimes this is benign: I strongly doubt that my wife and I are the only parents in the world who attempt to keep their children in line through the annual exploitation of Santa Claus's power to give and withhold. Perhaps the Singletons viewed the charity of the Thornburys as oppressive and sabotaged their goodwill in order to assert their personal autonomy and freedom. Their saga reminds us that receiving a gift can place one in a position of inferiority. The Singletons at first accepted the gift of housing but then eventually insulted the givers as they grew to dislike them, disregard house rules, and came, apparently, to question the motive for their generosity. Sensing not unconditional acceptance, it was impossible for Nicole Singleton to believe that the Thornburys sincerely cared about their plight. Perhaps she felt weighed down by a sense of obligation and ingratitude removed any future need to reciprocate. If a recipient believes that a motive for a gift is to make the giver feel generous and munificent or that the gift was intended to put him in his place, to render him unable to challenge the society that allowed him to be destitute because such a "generous" gift had come his way, then right or wrong, such a perception destroys gratitude. Whatever the dynamics in this case were, the intensifying resentment on the part of the Singletons toward their benefactors undercut any opportunity for true gratitude.

Gratitude requires that a giver give not only a gift but also a gift dear to himself — a "pearl of great price," as it were. For the recipient to be grateful, in an emotional sense, he must know that the act of giving caused the giver to lose something, to forgo some opportunity, to part with something of value, or, at the very least, to make a real effort.

This is why the amount of gratitude we feel when we receive a gift has next to nothing to do with how much the gift cost. The wealthy businessperson who asks their assistants or personal shoppers to buy expensive gifts and then send them on to various recipients won't generate significant gratitude from those on their gift list. The recipients simply know the gift cost nothing in terms of effort and that the loss of money involved meant nothing to the giver. They may actually feel more grateful to the harried, underpaid assistant who chose the gift than the actual giver, a judgment that the assistant's effort cost him more than the money and supervision cost the "generous" donor.

The degree to which we feel gratitude always hinges on this internal, secret assessment of cost. It is intrinsic to the emotion, and perfectly logical, that we don't feel all that grateful for the gifts we receive that cost little or nothing to the giver. Yet, there is another important factor: our degree of gratitude is influenced by our perception of the motives that underlie the gift. Given the pleasure that accompanies gratitude, it may seem that ingratitude is a denial of pleasure, an anhedonic act, presumably motivated by the urge to punish or harm the self and the other. A desire to harm the self and the giver through ingratitude is a significant obstacle to feeling and expressing gratefulness. But there are other, less psychologically complex impediments to gratitude.

OBSTACLES TO GRATITUDE

I have never found it easy to be a disciplined practitioner of gratitude. When I examine my life, I become painfully aware of powerful elements that work against gratitude. A number of personal burdens and external obstacles can block grateful emotions, grateful thoughts, and grateful actions. In order to reap the benefits of grateful thinking, these obstacles must be recognized, confronted, and overcome.

The Negativity Bias

In some respects it may be natural to ignore one's blessings, or even to complain about them. This might come as a surprise to most people, in that most of us believe that we are grateful for the benefits we have received. This should not be unexpected, though, given that psychologists have identified a natural tendency of the mind to *perceive an input as negative.* This "negativity bias" means that incoming emotions and thoughts are more likely to be unpleasant rather than pleasant. Furthermore, the negativity bias appears to be a very real phenomenon with a solid neurophysiological basis. In layman's terms, this means that for some of us being a grouch comes naturally.

At the risk of overcomplicating matters, I should point out that there are actually two opposing tendencies at work. Scientists studying emotional processes have concluded that there is a general tendency for us to evaluate neutral events, objects, and people as slightly positive. A "positivity offset" is a slight positive bias in mood state that characterizes most of the people most of the time. In other words, when no significant events are impinging on them, most people walk around in a somewhat positive mood. But our emotional systems are poised to react negatively when something of significance occurs in our environment. The negativity bias provides for a cautious appraisal and, if need be, a quick withdrawal that undoubtedly has some survival value. There are also differences between people in these tendencies. For those with a tendency toward a large negativity bias, a substantial impediment to feeling grateful exists. Some of us simply wouldn't know how to manage our lives without complaints and resentments. We've been accustomed to a pattern of negativity. We wonder if we can afford the luxury of gratefulness.

In our experiments on gratitude described in chapter 2, I contrasted a *hassles writing* condition with a *counting blessings* condition. Instead of focusing on what they were thankful for, the hassles participants were asked to write down their complaints — what was going wrong in their lives. We have never found a research participant who has had any difficulty in understanding what we were asking for or coming up with a list of problems. When I define hassles in the talks I give, there is invariably chuckling and much head-nodding among audience members. The truth is that, in the absence of conscious efforts to build and sustain a grateful worldview, we lapse into negative emotional patterns, including taking goodness for granted. The upshot is that this natural default tendency must be overridden by conscious processes. Without a conscious intervention, we are held hostage by an information-processing system that appears bent on maximizing our emotional distress and minimizing positive experience.

Although "bad is stronger than good," help is on the way in the form of aging. Exciting recent neuroscience research reveals that areas of the brain responsible for processing negative information show decreased activity with age while maintaining or even increasing re-activity to positive information. Whereas it may be a blessing that there is something to look forward to as we grow older, my hunch is that we would prefer to gain control over our negative thoughts and emotions earlier in life.

The Inability to Acknowledge Dependency

Charles Dickens's novel *Great Expectations* is a timeless story where gratitude and ingratitude are set in bold relief as central elements in the human condition. For most of the novel, Pip, the protagonist, takes for granted the benevolence of Joe Gargery, his brother-in-law who has been his constant friend and protector throughout his life. Any smattering of thankfulness that Pip might have is driven out by his selfish ambition. Toward Magwitch, Pip's secret benefactor, Pip has nothing but contempt. Even in the scene of profound revelation when he learns the truth about Magwitch, his initial response is not one of gratitude but one of disgust and disappointment:

> I could not have spoken one word, though it had been to save my life. I stood, with a hand on the chair-back and a hand on my breast, where I seemed to be suffocating — I stood so, looking wildly at him, until I grasped at the chair, when the room began to surge and turn. He caught me, drew me to the sofa, put me up against the cushions, and bent on one knee before me: bringing the face that I now well remembered, and that I shuddered at, very near to mine . . . The abhorrence in which I held the man, the dread I had of him, the repugnance with which I shrank from him, could not have been exceeded if he had been some terrible beast . . . he took both my hands and put them to his lips, while my blood ran cold within me.

Like Pip, many of us live under the illusion of self-sufficiency: the tendency not to acknowledge how much we need others. This tendency undercuts gratitude. Why should we be hesitant to admit that we feel and should feel indebted to someone who is our benefactor and has helped us in some way? We (especially in this society) do not like to think of ourselves as indebted. We would rather see our good fortunes as our own doing (whereas the losses and sufferings are not our fault). Like the emotion of trust it involves an admission of our vulnerability and our dependence on other people. Like Pip, though, we sometimes have the opportunity to learn who our true benefactors are before it is too late.

In his famous essay entitled *Gifts,* Ralph Waldo Emerson wrote,

> The law of benefits is a difficult channel, which requires careful sailing . . . It is not the office of a man to receive gifts. How dare you give them? We wish to be self-sustained. We do not quite forgive a giver. The hand that feeds us is in some danger of being bitten . . . We sometimes hate the meat which we eat, because there seems something of degrading dependence in living by it.

In the 1980s, the late social psychologist Shula Sommers studied attitudes toward gratitude (and other emotions) in American, German, and Israeli societies. She asked subjects a series of questions concerning their emotional lives, gauging which emotions they most like to experience, which they most dread having, which they prefer to "keep in," and which they view as constructive and destructive. She found that Americans in general ranked gratitude comparatively low in desirability and constructiveness, and that American men, in particular, tended to view the experience of gratitude as unpleasant. Some, in fact, found gratitude to be a humiliating emotion. Older men found it difficult to express this emotion in an open way, and over one-third of American men reported a preference for concealing feelings of gratefulness. In contrast, not a single woman in the study said that it was difficult for her to openly express gratitude. But uncomfortable though it may be for men, we need to recognize that none of us is wholly self-sufficient and without the need of help from others. To deny that obvious truth is not just to be self-deceived. It is to be a person of poor character, whatever one's other virtues, for expressing gratitude is giving someone their due for providing a benefit.

How might one handle dependency issues in a way that enhances rather than inhibits gratitude? The psychologist Charles Shelton tells of a middle-aged woman who had moved into a new apartment. She recounted:

> As I stood there looking around, I realized that almost everything in that apartment had been given to me by others. Much of it was from my family but some things were from friends, coworkers, and the families of students I had taught. What I saw (looking around my apartment) were material things, but those material things got me to remember all the nonmaterial gifts that I had been given by these same wonderful people. I thought back on my childhood and how the only way I could have grown was if others had helped me and provided for me along the way. I was truly grateful to God and all those people for everything they had given to me and done for me. I looked at myself in a new way also. I realized my interdependence with others and that I couldn't and hadn't lived life on my own. I think it made me less egocentric. It was easier to say to myself that I didn't need to do everything for myself, though I still struggle with that sometimes.

What this woman teaches us is that interdependence is not the same as dependence, but rather a glad sense of reliance on others that nourishes a heartfelt gratefulness. For her, dependence is akin to trust where reliance is embraced and it expands, rather than diminishes, the self.

Internal Psychological Conflicts

Closely related to an inability to admit that we are not self-sufficient are internal conflicts that we experience over expressing intimate, positive emotions. As the research by Sommers suggests, this is more an issue for men than it is for women, at least in American culture. Given our culture's general emphasis on the containment of emotional expression, coupled with a natural tendency to seek expression, it is not surprising that individuals become ambivalent over emotional expression. A number of years ago, Laura King and I noted the prevalence of internal conflicts in people's emotional lives. We reasoned that although the natural course of an emotion requires expression, because of perceived negative consequences people are often inhibited from expressing their feelings. We developed a questionnaire to measure ambivalence over expressing emotion, which included items such as "I try to show people I love them, although at times I am afraid that it may make me appear weak or too sensitive," "I can recall a time when I wished I had told someone how much I really cared for them," and "It is hard to find the right words to indicate to others what I am really feeling." In our research, we found that people who scored high on this measure of ambivalence reported greater levels of psychological and emotional distress compared to persons who were comfortable with their levels of expressiveness.

Yet there are occasions when these deeply contained feelings can come gushing to the surface. A 59-year-old male heart-transplant recipient, another participant in my research group, recalls his childhood and the death of his father when he was 26. I will present the narrative in its entirety because it is so poignant:

> As a young boy/man, I had grown up with a sense of "real men don't cry" and prided myself on controlling my emotions, never showing any tears. Even falling in love and getting married with a growing family didn't change this stoicism. It was the way of the strong man.
>
> When Dad died of heart failure in 1969, I was the oldest male in the family and supported my mother in making the funeral arrangements. Even in this new experience, my sense of pride in

having no feelings continued. There were no tears despite the loss. Dad was 50 at the time of his death. I had been at his hospital bedside just hours before he passed, feeding him and shaving him, seeing for the first time his vulnerability. He had always been very self-sufficient, showing us all a healthy, vibrant lifestyle of "can do" in everything he did. He enjoyed the emotions of being truly human and wasn't afraid to show that side of himself, although in retrospect, I can't recall being hugged or told, "I love you." This was a generation that didn't express themselves in that way, but rather in many other ways.

On the morning of Dad's funeral, I was equally stoic, feeling a sense of manhood in being there for Mom during such a trying moment without showing tears or emotions. As the religious burial service drew to a close in the old church, I led the procession with Mom on my arm, as we slowly preceded Dad's coffin down the aisle.

It was that moment that Dad's greatest gift was bestowed on his son (and I find my eyes tearing up even as I write these words, thirty-three years later . . .) as the moment welled up from deep inside, emotions of sorrow never acknowledged before. Tears came to my eyes for the first time in my life and I accepted them without restraint, letting the drops run down my cheeks and fall to the church floor. A very strong sense of pride came with those tears and I found myself holding my head up higher than I had ever done before, with Mom on my arm, making no attempt to wipe away or hide those tears.

Clearly this was Dad's legacy to his son. From that day on, I have found great joy in both feeling and sharing my human emotions, yes, even the tears — tears of sorrow, tears of joy, tears of uncontrolled laughter. I have come to see the sharing of tears as one of the greatest gifts two humans can give each other. Every time such emotions are now accepted in my life, I offer silent prayers of gratitude to a father who gave this gift at his own death.

Another type of conflict involving gratitude occurs in cases where the giver has both helped and harmed the recipient. Feelings alternating between warm acceptance and stony resentment will likely be common in any enduring, psychologically significant relationship. What is the appropriate response when one is both angered by and feels indebted to the same person? If, say, a parent or trusted person did something terrible to cause us significant harm, but also gave us valuable gifts, our feelings will be conflicted and confused.

Sometimes we may feel a conflict over expressing gratitude because of the message that it may convey (for instance, "I condone the harm you have caused as long as you keep the goodies coming"). The child psychiatrist John Bowlby noted that "love, anxiety, and anger, and even sometimes hatred, come to be aroused by one and the same person. As a result, painful conflicts are inevitable." A woman in my research group illustrated this point. The 60-year-old female polio survivor wrote about how, at age 32, she summoned the courage to look up her biological father, whom she had never met:

> I wondered what would he be like. Would I be glad to meet him or would I hate him? Could I love him? We went to his hamburger place in Kentucky "unannounced" and saw my half-sister working with her mother at the restaurant. Sharon drove us up to my father's trailer. My father was cutting grass — a small, short, little elflike man in cowboy boots and cowboy hat. My aunt pulled up and said, "Hey, Fred, long time no see. Would you like to see your grandchildren and your middle daughter for the first time?" He came down to the car and looked at all of us with smiles [and] with tears in his eyes. He asked us to come in for tea or cokes. He said he never knew he was divorced until after it was over. I asked him why in eighteen years he never looked us up. His response was that we were better off with our grandmother, that he loved wine, women, and song too much. When we left, he cried and said, "Don't let it be so long next time." My thought at the time was "You jerk. I made my first and last move. Goodbye."

I've never had so many emotions over this adventure: love, hate, sadness, excitement, pride, joy, sorrow. But mostly gratitude. I'd finally have a face to put with my father, which I didn't have for thirty-two years. I was very, very grateful to fill my empty space. My mother nearly disowned me for looking him up, but I'm thankful.

In long-standing relationships where partners inevitably hurt each other, one of the greatest gifts that partners can give each other is the gift of forgiveness. One participant wrote, "Not too long ago, I did something which I'm sure caused my wife much heartache. It took me a while to admit what I had done and ask for her forgiveness. What amazed me was her willingness to forgive and say 'Let's just put it behind us.' The gift of forgiveness is indeed one of the greatest gifts one can receive."

Inappropriate Gift Giving

Another obstacle lies not in the mind of the receiver but in that of the giver. The gift relationship has been referred to as one of the most morally laden relationships that human beings have. Gift exchange is governed by the law of reciprocity, and gratitude calibrates the desire to make an appropriate return. Gifts have many meanings, and the risk for unintended outcomes is high. Gifts can be unwelcome burdens. Gifts may be used to control the receiver and to guarantee his or her loyalty. A gift that is lavishly disproportionate to what is appropriate to the relationship between giver and receiver will produce resentment, guilt, anger, a sense of obligation, or even humiliation. Boundaries may be violated when a gift exchange occurs between people of vastly different status levels. The secretary of a physician who had saved a man's life received a sheepish call from the patient's wife, asking what might make an appropriate gift to express their gratitude. The physician suggested that a bottle of single malt Scotch would be fitting; it never materialized. His relationship with the couple was never the same after that. Because of the ethical complexities involved, psychiatrists and other physicians routinely refuse to accept their patients' gifts.

Writing in *The New Yorker,* Caitlin Flanagan describes what has become the hazardous ritual of classroom holiday gift giving. Whereas at one time a plate of homemade cookies or a lovely Christmas tree ornament would have more than sufficed, the ante has now been upped considerably. One teacher at a school in Malibu, California, was presented with a cache of $800 from her class (she graciously gave $200 to her student assistant and kept the rest). But the parents weren't yet finished with her: she also received a cashmere designer sweatshirt, a watch, and a Gucci cosmetic bag. Many unconscious motives are involved in the choice of a gift (although some are likely quite consciously strategic). Is there a better way to ensure that little Caleb or Kaitlyn is given the benefit of the doubt on the next placement test than with a gift certificate to the local Lexus dealership?

Comparison Thinking

In one experiment on gratitude conducted in my laboratory, we actually created a *comparison condition* to gratitude by asking participants to write down each day five things that they didn't have that they wished they had. Over time, this group experienced significantly less gratefulness and joy than those who were assigned to other conditions. In another research study, participants were randomly divided into two subgroups. Both groups were asked to write several endings to an incomplete sentence. One group was to finish the sentence "I wish I was ___." The other was asked to complete the sentence "I'm glad I'm not ___." When individuals rated their sense of satisfaction with their lives before and after this task, those who completed the "I'm glad I'm not ___" sentence were significantly more satisfied than before. It is human nature to make judgments. We constantly evaluate situations, events, other people, and ourselves against a standard of one type or another. Certain types of these comparisons impede gratitude. When we look around and we see students with harder bodies, coworkers with larger retirement portfolios, relatives whose children are more grateful, neighbors whose SUVs are larger, we feel resentment and envy, not gratitude. We find ourselves employing the language of scarcity, focusing on what we do not have, rather than the language of abundance, appreciating what we do have. The lesson here is that we need to choose our comparisons wisely. Epicurus wrote, "Do not spoil what you have by desiring what you have not; but remember that what you now have was once among the things only hoped for." Gratitude is the realization that we have everything that we need, at the moment.

Perceptions of Victimhood

In a scathing critique of the field of professional psychology, Tara Dineen (herself a licensed psychologist) wrote that a segment of the psychological industry had "manufactured victims," encouraging clients to think of themselves as damaged goods who have fallen prey to victimization at the hands of others, be they parents, spouses, coworkers, or society at large. Her thesis is that the therapeutic culture within which we live encourages finger-pointing for one's problems while minimizing personal responsibility. Without dismissing the truly horrific cases of many people, I believe the perception of being victimized has become an identity frequently adopted in contemporary culture. The tendency to blame others can be a strong resistance against gratitude. A sense of victimization leaves one wounded and mired in resentment and desires for retaliation. People who think of themselves as victims are unable to conjure any appreciation for what life has to offer them. When one's identity is wrapped up in the perception of victimhood, the capacity for gratitude shrinks.

Many now realize, however, that the psychology industry has gone too far and have begun to introduce correctives. The resurgent positive psychology movement has countered the prevailing victim mentality by focusing on concepts such as resilience, self-determination, and personal responsibility. It is becoming less acceptable to blame one's parents or one's genes, and the notion that we are all prisoners of our pasts has proven to be a psychological canard. Still, victimhood is a lens through which significant segments of the population continue to view their lives. With it comes the impossibility to sense the giftedness of life.

A History of Suffering

There are, of course, real victims. There are people who, due to no fault of their own, have suffered atrocities at the hands of others or other cruel twists of fate. In these instances, suffering can trump gratefulness and it becomes difficult to find any reason for gratitude. In my research on the quality of life in individuals with neuromuscular disease, one participant was a 25-year-old single white male who had suffered a spinal cord injury at age 18. He scored lower than anyone else on our questionnaire measure of dispositional gratitude. When asked to write a story about a time in his life when he felt a sense of gratitude, he wrote only a single sentence that read, "Sorry, but I honestly can't think of or remember a time I felt any sense of gratitude for anything or to anyone." I was shocked when I read this, for he was the only respondent out of over two hundred individuals who did not describe at length a personal experience of gratitude. Among his personal goals were "try to be happy," "try not to be a loser," "try to be good at something," and "try not to be like my brother." Here was an individual in deep psychological pain. In the midst of his brokenness, he was unable to recognize and affirm any goodness at all in his life. Yet we know there are also inspiring examples of individuals who are able to discern blessings in the midst of personal suffering. The fact that most people recover emotionally from catastrophic events in a relatively short period of time is testimony to the resilience of the human psyche. As mentioned earlier, a classic study showed that even individuals who suffered disabling spinal cord injuries returned to their prior levels of positive emotions within six months of their accidents.

Witnessing how others deal with suffering in their lives may have the unintended effect of increasing one's own gratitude for life. One woman in my research group expressed her gratitude for someone she knew who had "crippling arthritis." However, she noted that instead of wallowing in self-pity and constant complaining, this man displayed a "joyful spirit" and "humility." She stated that his display of nobility in the face of adversity had what she described as a "spillover effect" on her. His response to his infirmity had offered her a "steppingstone," enabling her to open her eyes and see what she referred to as the "unbounded generosity" of others for which she was profoundly grateful.

The Business of Life

Consider these eye-popping statistics: In 2005 it was estimated that 779 million cell phones would be sold, on which 1.7 billion people would be logging some 5.6 trillion minutes. By the year 2010 this number would more than double to 12.6 trillion minutes. Over 5 million iPods were sold during the first three months of 2005 alone, and over 15 million personal digital assistants were expected to be shipped worldwide during that year. All of which makes for harried, distracted individuals with little discretionary time to invest in everyday civilities like saying thanks to one another, let alone for more urgent matters. A newspaper story reported that passersby stepped over a blood-soaked shooting victim as he lay on a New York sidewalk. A witness was quoted as saying, "People were just walking by with their iPod headphones on. That was tripping me out, that they kept on walking."

Gratitude requires taking time out to reflect on one's blessings. As daily life is increasingly frantic, frazzled, and fragmented, gratitude can be crowded out. Events, people, or situations that are apt to evoke gratitude can easily be taken for granted or shunted aside as one contends with life's daily hassles and struggles to regulate intense negative feelings such as anger, shame, and resentment.

AN UNNATURAL CRIME

> Nothing more detestable does the earth produce than an ungrateful man.
>
> — DECIMUS MAGNUS AUSONIUS

> I hate ingratitude more in a man than lying, vainness, babbling, drunkenness, or any taint of vice whose strong corruption inhabits our frail blood.
>
> — SHAKESPEARE

> Ingratitude is treason to mankind.   — JAMES THOMSON

> Of all the crimes that human creatures are capable of committing, the most horrid and unnatural is ingratitude, especially when it is committed against parents, and appears in the most flagrant instances of wounds and death.
>
> — DAVID HUME

> Ingratitude is the essence of vileness.   — IMMANUEL KANT

Whereas gratitude is an emotion, ingratitude is an accusation. A person does not feel ingratitude but exhibits it through word and deed. It is a vice that represents, as the above quotes illustrate, a profound moral failure. Ungrateful individuals are universally excoriated. Shakespearean plays in particular are hotbeds of ingratitude. In his texts, Shakespeare uses the terms *ingrate, ingrateful,* and *ingratitude* some forty times, often modified by the adjectives *monstrous, hideous,* or *grotesque.* The above quotes are strong indictments that in

TABLE 5.1. Gratitude Contrasted with Nongratitude and Ingratitude

GRATITUDE	NONGRATITUDE	INGRATITUDE
Recognize the benefit	Failure to recognize benefit	Find fault with the benefit
Acknowledge receiving it	Fail to acknowledge receiving it	Impugn motive of benefactor
Return the favor	Fail to return the favor	Return evil for good

no way can be smoothed over. Throughout the history of ideas, I could find only one person who tried. The curmudgeonly writer H. L. Mencken, far ahead of his time in political incorrectness, saw in unthankfulness a sign of "healthy independence and strength."

Ingratitude is not the same as forgetfulness, or what I am calling "nongratitude." The table above illustrates the differences between gratitude, nongratitude, and ingratitude. The main difference between the latter two is that in cases of nongratitude, the person fails to do something — fails to respond to a gift with an appropriate feeling and display of thankfulness. Nongratitude is essentially forgetfulness. In the inaugural Thanksgiving Day proclamation of 1863, President Lincoln warned against forgetfulness:

> We have been the recipients of the choicest bounties of heaven; we have been preserved these many years in peace and prosperity; we have grown in numbers, wealth and power as no other nation has ever grown. But we have forgotten God. We have forgotten the gracious hand which preserved us in peace and multiplied and enriched and strengthened us, and we have vainly imagined, in the deceitfulness of our hearts, that all these blessings were produced by some superior wisdom and virtue of our own. Intoxicated with unbroken success, we have become too self-sufficient to feel the necessity of redeeming and preserving grace, too proud to pray to the God that made us.

Whereas nongratitude is an omission, an absence, a type of forgetting, ingratitude is the presence of something negative. It is a form of punishment. When a person is ungrateful, they respond with hostility, resentment, or in some other way choose to willfully disparage the gift and the giver. When I forget to write a thank-you note, I am showing nongratitude. If I say to my mother upon opening a gift she has given to me, "Gads! What a hideous sweater," then I am ungrateful. In the latter case, my intention is hurtful (keep in mind this is purely a hypothetical example). Of course, I might express my ingratitude more indirectly, say, by putting the sweater out in the driveway with other items for a garage sale. Failing to acknowledge gratitude is not morally equivalent to responding to another's benevolence with hostility or resentment.

Admittedly, the line between forgetfulness and ingratitude in practice can be fuzzy. If I send my unpublished book manuscript to a colleague preparing a talk on gratitude and he uses my ideas without giving credit, is this ingratitude, or forgetfulness? He has not responded with hostility or resentment. He has not been cruel or mean. The judgment of whether I attribute his behavior to ingratitude or forgetfulness depends on many factors, particularly our history together, current life circumstances, and my perceptions of his intentions. If he has a neurological deficit that causes memory lapses, I will cut him some slack. If, on the other hand, he suffers from a deficit in character, ingratitude will more likely be the accusation (and this would then raise the question of why I helped him in the first place!).

Consider a recent example of blatant ingratitude. The Iraqi soccer team was the surprise of the 2004 Summer Olympics. Finishing fourth in the soccer competition, they just missed out on a bronze medal. Bringing home a medal would have been a tremendous accomplishment. To put it mildly, Iraq has never been an Olympic power. Iraq has won only one medal in Olympic history: a weightlifting bronze in 1960. In the midst of the rebuilding of their nation, and against all odds, the soccer team qualified for the Athens games. In 2004, the Iraqi team was competing without the prospect of having to face the former Olympic Committee head Odai Hussein, who was killed four months after the United States–led coalition invaded Iraq in March 2003. It was the brutal Odai, who, according to human rights groups, was responsible for the torture of hundreds of athletes and at least fifty deaths.

Now competing without fear of torture — or worse — the Iraqi team stunned commentators with their apparent ingratitude. Not only were they not grateful for the liberation from the former Iraqi regime, but they did not mince words in expressing their disapproval as well. One team member, Ahmed Manajid, was quoted as saying this about President George W. Bush: "How will he meet his God after having slaughtered so many men and women? He has committed so many crimes." He went on to say that if he were not playing soccer, he would be fighting as an insurgent against coalition forces.

Regardless of one's political stance toward the war in Iraq, the ingratitude of the Iraqi soccer team was difficult to digest. It seemed clear to foreign commentators that whatever their feelings about the invasion, the Iraqis should at least have expressed gratitude for the removal of a chairman who had tortured and killed their members, and threatened to do so to them. Why were Americans so outraged by this profound expression of ingratitude? In some respects, all expressions of ingratitude are met with contempt. I think it was because at the core of the Olympic ideal is the spirit of sportsmanship, which includes being humble in victory and gracious in defeat, without hostility, resentment, or retaliation toward one's competitor. Thus ingratitude in this instance was especially hard to swallow.

In contrast is the story of 5-year-old Noor Abd Al-Hady, who needed surgery to repair a birth defect that caused her to have a hole in her heart between her two ventricles. This condition is easily corrected in the United States, but doctors in her native Iraq were unable to perform the surgery. Through connections with the

Utah Army National Guard, arrangements were made to bring Noor to the United States to Maine, where the state's only pediatric heart surgeon would perform the operation. Her father, Abdul Al-Hady Hassan Hesab, describes himself as a fortunate man, who because of the kindness of American soldiers stationed in Iraq and the generosity of surgeons at the Maine Medical Center saw his daughter's heart repaired. "If Noor stayed in Iraq, the prospect for an operation would have been very difficult," he said. He said that the doctors and hospital staff became his family, and although he and his daughter returned to Iraq following the successful surgery, that Maine had become his home. "Somewhere in the back of my mind," he said emotionally, "this place belongs to me."

Whether we are personally involved or not, we expect people to acknowledge the good that has been done for them; ingratitude is the refusal to acknowledge this good. Why is ingratitude such a profound moral failure? The principle of reciprocity, upon which human societies are based, states that one has an obligation to help others who have helped us, while at the same time not harming others who have helped us. Directing ingratitude toward our benefactor is a way of inflicting harm upon that person. The moral rule underlying reciprocity is violated when one is not grateful for the benefit received. While occasionally each of us responds to a benefit in a manner that may be interpreted as an ungrateful response by our benefactor, there is clearly a psychological disturbance in the personality that habitually responds to benefits with indifference, resentment, or ingratitude. This is a flagrant violation of natural law.

When we level a charge of ingratitude against someone, we are making a moral claim. Violations of this type elicit what the social psychologist Jonathan Haidt has called "moral disgust." Moral disgust is triggered by actions that reveal an absence of normal human decency, actions such as ingratitude, which show the lower, darker, and more "monstrous" side of human nature. Haidt argues that moral disgust makes people shun those that trigger it. It certainly tends to be the case that we are motivated to avoid people who are ungrateful, and this shunning contributes to their self-centered misery.

Religious writings provide some pointed examples of ingratitude. In some spiritual traditions, ingratitude toward God is considered the worst sin and the source of all human misery. Ignatius of Loyola wrote:

> In the light of the Divine Goodness, it seems to me that ingratitude is the most abominable of sins and that it should be detested in the sight of our Creator and Lord by all of His creatures who are capable of enjoying His divine and everlasting glory. It is a forgetting of the graces, benefits, and blessings received, and as such it is the cause, beginning, and origin of all sins and misfortunes.

Historical examples of ingratitude are found throughout scripture. In the Hebrew Bible, the Israelites, rather than thanking God for redeeming them from slavery and for the manna from Heaven that sustained them in the wilderness, complained: "The people spoke against God and against Moses, 'Why have you brought us up out of Egypt to die in the wilderness? For there is no food and no water, and we detest this miserable food" (Num. 21:5). Perhaps the most famous instance of ingratitude in religious literature is found in the New Testament gospel of Luke. Jesus heals ten lepers of their physical afflictions, yet only one returns to express thankfulness. Jesus asked, "Were not all ten cleansed? Where are the other nine? Was no one found to return and give praise to God except this foreigner? Rise and go; your faith has made you well." Commentaries on this passage imply that by "faith" Jesus was referring not to faith in a generic sense but rather to *gratefulness,* as in "your *gratitude* has made you well."

But perhaps history has been too judgmental on this gang of nine. Norms dictate that a decent interval of time should pass before a gift is reciprocated. If I invite you over for dinner, it would be a show of ingratitude on your part if, at the end of the evening, you pulled out your checkbook to settle up. Maybe the lepers had planned to purchase a gift certificate for Jesus, have him over for dinner, or at the very least send a thank-you note. We do know, however, that even a delayed expression of gratitude would have led to Jesus's sorrow. A gift as significant as a complete physical healing demands an immediate response. This parable reminds us of just how common ingratitude is and how easy it is to take blessings for granted.

The Dynamics of Ingratitude

Several forms or degrees of ingratitude can be distinguished, ranging from the slap in the face by the Iraqi soccer players toward the U.S. government to the forgetfulness behind a lack of written thank-you note to one's host following a dinner party. While we might overlook the latter case, or perhaps even come to not be surprised by it, the former display of ingratitude is much more difficult to accept. Why would people be ungrateful? How can we come to understand such a "horrible and unnatural crime?" Being "ungrateful" is clearly the mark of a vice, whether in a single instance or as a long-term defect of character. Whereas gratitude is appropriate, even mandatory, being ungrateful is a sign or symptom of lack of socialization, whether the inability to appreciate what others have done for you or, worse, the grudging resentment of one's own vulnerability and the refusal to admit one's debt to others.

There are both conscious and unconscious reasons why people might refrain from expressing appreciation for the benefits they receive. For example, they may impugn the generous motives of their benefactor in order to feel better about themselves or to avoid future reciprocation. Or to protect a fragile self-esteem they cannot recognize that other people would intentionally provide a benefit to them. If we view ourselves as unworthy of benefits, we would not recognize benevolence when it happens to us and therefore not feel gratitude, for gratitude can be felt only when there is recognition of goodness.

When something good happens, the recipient may reflect, at

least briefly, on why it happened. If the recipient him or herself is the cause, the emotion experienced is pride. Psychologists have documented that a self-serving bias permeates most explanations of why good things happen. We tend to take more credit for our successes than is warranted. Conversely, when we fail, we are apt to blame others. When a group of workers completes a project and each person estimates the percentage of success he or she was individually responsible for, the percentages substantially exceed more than 100 percent. This pattern easily encourages ingratitude. If we see ourselves as the causes of our own success, then there is no "other" to give credit to and to be grateful toward.

In some cases of ingratitude, deeper underlying motives may be involved. A psychodynamic perspective, emphasizing unconscious intrapsychic processes, suggests at least four motives for ingratitude. First, this view proposes that attitudes of ingratitude are aggressive attempts at covering up basic feelings of inferiority and inadequacy. Being provided with a benefit puts us in a position of dependence relative to the giver. The Singleton family with whom I began the chapter either did not want to feel inadequate by accepting the hospitality of the Thornburys or did not wish to feel obligated to them. Whichever the explanation, their perceived ingratitude was a defense against feelings of inferiority. Second, the giving of a gift can be seen as an "infinitesimal" installment on an old debt, either real or imagined. "You owe me so much, and this is just a drop in the bucket," laments the ungrateful recipient. In this case, the ingrate is never satisfied by what he receives, because the amount owed is so large it can never be repaid. Third, by doing a good deed, the benefactor may be seen through some neurotic distortion in the mind of the beneficiary as weak. This perception in turn justifies, in the ungrateful mind, hostile and aggressive behavior toward the perceived weaker person as the ingrate hates weakness. Last, beneficiaries may misjudge the motives of their benefactors. If I am an ungrateful recipient, I might assume that a person was kind in order to feel better about him or herself, to garner publicity, or to make me feel humiliated. Skeptics often tried to explain away Mother Teresa's sacrificial behavior by accusing her of "trying to win favor with God."

Whatever its root causes, there are serious negative consequences to ungratefulness. Because providing benefits and creating bonds of gratitude tie people together in society, ingratitude weakens our bond to others. The Roman philosopher Seneca said that "no other vice is so hostile to the harmony of the human race as ingratitude." Ungrateful people are unable (or unwilling) to partake in the cycle of giving and receiving and thus risk being alienated from society. From a personal standpoint, they are unable to experience the joy and fulfillment that grateful living brings and are instead mired in complaint and negativity. I believe certain personality traits may predispose certain people to ingratitude, and these traits are, unfortunately, hard to change.

I Did It Myself, So Thanks for Nothing

> All of the women on *The Apprentice* have flirted with me — consciously or unconsciously. That's to be expected.
>
> — Donald Trump

By the end of his life, the prominent industrialist Armand Hammer, CEO of Occidental Petroleum, had alienated virtually all of his friends and family, driven his corporation into financial ruin, and tainted his public reputation. Nevertheless, he seemed quite pleased with himself: "There has never been anyone like me, and my likes will never be seen again . . . the brilliance of my mind can only be described as dazzling. Even I am impressed by it."

Since at least the time of Seneca, a prevailing view has been that an overly high opinion of oneself is the chief cause of ingratitude. My work has shown that the ungrateful person appears to be characterized by a personality not unlike that of Armand Hammer: one that manifests narcissistic tendencies, characterized by a sense of excessive self-importance, arrogance, vanity, and an unquenchable need for admiration and approval. Narcissists are profoundly self-absorbed people: they lack the empathy needed for entering into deep, satisfying, mutually enhancing interpersonal relationships. Like Hammer, they have a strong need to broadcast their assets and successes to themselves and others. Given this constellation of characteristics, being grateful in any meaningful way is beyond the capacity of most narcissists. Without empathy, they cannot appreciate an altruistic gift because they cannot identify with the mental state of the gift giver. Narcissism is a spiritual blindness; it is a refusal to acknowledge that one has been the recipient of benefits freely bestowed by others. A preoccupation with the self can cause us to forget our benefits and our benefactors or to feel that we are owed things from others and therefore have no reason to feel thankful.

Consider the following pairs of statements:

A. I expect a great deal from other people.
B. I like to do things for other people.

A. I will never be satisfied until I get all that I deserve.
B. I take my satisfactions as they come.

These items come from the Narcissistic Personality Inventory, developed in the late 1970s by Robert Raskin and Calvin Hall of the University of California, Santa Cruz. Which of the statements in each pair do you most identify with? If you selected A's, chances are that you are going to find it difficult to be grateful. High expectations and a sense of deservingness can undermine the ability to feel grateful for life's blessings.

The paramount characteristic of narcissism is a sense of entitlement. People with narcissistic tendencies erroneously believe they are deserving of special rights and privileges. When they are given a gift, they believe it is their due or right. They are highly invested in asserting their own rights and collecting on debts owed to them. Their exaggerated sense of deservingness leads them to expect special favors without assuming reciprocal responsibilities. The sense of entitlement combined with their insensitivity to the needs of others engenders, whether consciously or unconsciously intended, interpersonal exploitation. In short, if one is entitled to everything, then one is thankful for nothing.

Perhaps even more egregious than the lack of felt gratitude is the inability to express genuine gratitude. Expressions of gratitude are acknowledgments that one is dependent on other people for one's well-being, and therefore one is not self-sufficient. Given this reality, such individuals find expressions of gratitude to be highly unpleasant and to be avoided. The narcissist says, "I owe nothing to anyone." Trying to gain evidence, then, of a narcissist's gratitude in order to feel accepted is likely to be a frustrating experience. Furthermore, because narcissists possess a distorted sense of their own superiority, they might be reluctant to express gratitude in response to benefactors whose generosity or kindness they dismiss as little more than attempts to curry favor.

Expressions of gratitude in narcissistic persons, when they are forthcoming, may be nothing more than attempts to ingratiate themselves with their benefactors. Instead of experiencing or expressing gratitude in situations when it would be expected, narcissistic people choose other means of responding to those who have helped them, such as (a) expressing approval; (b) feigning indifference or even suggesting that by receiving the benefit conferred upon them, the narcissist was allowing the benefactor to meet the benefactor's needs; (c) denying that he or she deserves the benefit; or (d) offering gratitude so excessive that it could not possibly be sincere. Finally, narcissistic people may be capable of a distorted form of gratitude — distorted because it is centered not on the giver but rather on them. So it was with the proud Pharisee who prayed, "Thank God, I am not a sinner like everyone else" (Luke 18:11).

There seem to be convincing reasons to believe that narcissists, on average, are going to be less grateful. But this has proven to be a difficult proposition to support with research data. Robust relationships between gratitude and narcissism have not been established. Besides, isn't there the story of Donald Trump expressing gratitude to the unemployed auto mechanic who stopped to help repair his limo by sending the man's wife a bouquet of flowers and then paying off their mortgage? Narcissistic people evidently can be grateful at times and can express this gratitude in appropriate ways. Perhaps narcissists are grateful in different ways or for different sorts of things than are nonnarcissists.

With this in mind, I went back to the daily gratitude journals and examined the nature of the "blessings" recorded by the most and least narcissistic participants. I discovered two things: first, in daily gratitude journals, narcissism is correlated with *gratitude span*. Gratitude span refers to the number of life circumstances for which a person feels grateful at a given time. Someone with a strongly grateful disposition might be expected to feel grateful for their families, their jobs, their health, and life itself, along with a wide variety of other benefits. Someone less disposed toward gratitude, however, might be aware of experiencing gratitude for fewer aspects of their lives. On average, narcissists list fewer daily blessings than do nonnarcissists.

Second, narcissists also differ from nonnarcissists in the nature of what they are grateful for. In these journals, narcissists are less likely to cite the benevolence of others and more likely to mention material possessions and self-attributes. One of the more narcissistic persons in the study included these among his gratitude blessings: "my health, strength," "my mind and thinking rationally," "my strong will and desire," "my football team," "receiving money from my Grandma," and "that a person found me attractive." In contrast, here is a sampling of gratitudes from one of the lowest scorers on the narcissism scale: "my family, especially my child to come," "the support I receive from those around me," "God's help through difficult times," "my caring husband," "having food on the table," and "able to pay taxes."

In a questionnaire study, we also found that narcissistic persons have a lower *gratitude density*. Gratitude density refers to the number of persons to whom one feels grateful for a single positive outcome or life circumstance. When asked to whom one feels grateful for a certain outcome, say, obtaining a good job, someone with a strongly grateful disposition might list a large number of others, including parents, elementary school teachers, tutors, mentors, fellow students, and God or a higher power. Someone less disposed toward gratitude might feel grateful to fewer people for such a benefit. Narcissists take more credit for positive outcomes, tending to attribute them to innate ability or effort and giving less credit to others.

Were narcissism a condition that afflicted only a small percentage of humankind, then there would be little cause for concern. Indeed, psychiatrists estimate that only one percent of the general population meets the clinical criteria for narcissistic disorders. However, narcissistic characteristics are found in all individuals in varying degrees. Psychoanalysts have observed that narcissism is a normal stage of human development. As such, it is part and parcel of the human condition. We are born narcissists. Thus, we must be constantly on guard for narcissistic thoughts and attitudes that oppose genuine gratitude. The failure to outgrow narcissism results in a spiritually impoverished life, the chief casualty of which is the inability to feel grateful for what life provides.

GRATE-FUL EXPECTATIONS

> Act with kindness, but do not expect gratitude.
>
> — CONFUCIUS

A final obstacle to feeling grateful is expecting gratitude from others. When we provide a benefit to others, it is pleasant to be acknowledged. But all of the obstacles that I have identified in this chapter work in concert to thwart grateful emotions and grateful expressions. Our acts of kindness are likely to be forgotten or overlooked. So if we come to expect gratitude from others, whether from our children, students, or spouses, we are bound to be disappointed. Gratitude is a duty that ought to be paid, but that none have a right to expect, said Rousseau. True generosity that comes from the heart comes from not expecting rewards. A gift is not a gift when strings are attached.

Hans Selye was a physician and endocrinologist at McGill University. Born in Vienna in 1907, he established himself as the world's foremost authority on stress, emotional and physical responses to stress, and physical disease. His contributions were so pioneering that some authorities referred to him as "the Einstein of medicine." Believing that gratitude played a pivotal role in the human stress response, he wrote, "Among all emotions, there is one which, more than any other, accounts for the presence or absence of stress in human relations: that is the feeling of gratitude." Selye was not bashful in using his stature as a leading scientist as a pulpit for espousing his beliefs about how humans live, as well as how they *should* live. In his classic book, *The Stress of Life,* and in the sequel, *Stress Without Distress,* he spent significant sections of several chapters identifying what, in his view, were the basic elements of a fulfilling life. It was in this context that he wrote about gratitude. Gratitude, for Selye, "was the awakening in another person of the wish that I should prosper, because of what I have done for him . . . by inspiring the feeling of gratitude, I have induced another person to share with me my natural wish for my own well-being." It was a conscious striving for other people's gratitude that served as Selye's guiding philosophy of life and that he believed was the ultimate aim of existence. Think about this for a moment. Why do people do what they do? What motivates them? According to Selye, most people do what they do in order to make other people grateful. And gratitude from others is tied to their approval of us. By gaining the approval of others, we have an indication of how grateful they are to us, for they perceive that we have benefited them in some way.

As a scientist, Selye was hardly alone in wishing for the approval and even admiration of his peers, his pupils, and the public. It is not my purpose here to undertake an extensive psychobiography of Selye, but similar to other narcissists, this need for approval seemed to consume him, especially in his later years. What developmental experiences could have produced this strong and insatiable drive for validation? In his autobiography, he recalled, "I don't remember my mother ever hugging me, although she must have, especially when I was a baby . . . she never cried, and she could not tolerate little boys with tears in their eyes. But children can't help crying once in a while." Throughout his life, Selye hungered for what he never received in childhood. When he was a medical student, he dreamed of "marrying a girl with whom I could share all my concerns." I suspect that these concerns all flowed in a single direction. When he was married, he lamented that he could not carry on intellectual conversations with his wife, whom he found intellectually inferior.

Selye was powerfully moved by expressions of fawning appreciation. Once, the day before he was to undergo surgery, he was released from the hospital in time to deliver a lecture. The talk was before an important audience at one of Montreal's largest hotels. At the conclusion of his lecture, which was delivered in his usual masterful style, he explained to the crowd that he was to undergo a major operation the following day. He recounts that "the standing ovation and considerable applause was perhaps the warmest I have ever received; some of the women even had tears in their eyes as I walked through the crowd to my car." As a professor who has delivered many classroom lectures and public talks (though none ending in standing ovations), I can certainly identify with the glow resulting from being warmly received. For a gratitude addict, though, the craving can never be satisfied. There is never enough appreciation. Looking back on his life, Selye felt his work was misunderstood, his contributions unappreciated. He readily admitted wanting to hoard the gratitude, respect, and admiration of others. Because a person has little control over the reactions of others, this insecure approach to life cannot be sustained without considerable strain. It is, in effect, allowing yourself to be held emotionally hostage by the reactions of others. Incidentally, Selye's autobiography, published three years before his death in 1982, was entitled *The Stress of My Life*.

How is it possible, in the face of the monumental forces that undermine gratitude, to create and sustain a grateful outlook on life? How do we overcome forgetfulness, comparison thinking, the negativity bias, emotional conflicts, and other hindrances to gratitude? How do we live without expecting gratitude from others and not feel rebuffed when it is not forthcoming? What are the characteristics of people who are able to accomplish this? They must have developed strategies to combat these obstacles. They have created lives of pervasive thankfulness and have learned that a grateful outlook produces emotional prosperity, whereas failing to live gratefully leads to emotional poverty.

6

GRATITUDE IN
TRYING TIMES

 IN TIMES OF GREAT ABUNDANCE, gratitude can come so easily that it seems like an effortless, natural reaction. Whether we experience the joys of material success, the surprise of an unexpected job promotion, the birth of a much loved child, the euphoria of falling in love, or acclaim from our friends and peers, it is rare for us not to feel grateful on some level. In fact, those who greet such success and wealth without gratitude are sometimes viewed as flawed, arrogant, selfish, and even pathological. But such automatic gratitude deserts us in times of adversity and loss. Suffering robs us of easy gratitude; in fact, the road to recovery is one in which we must fight a hard battle to regain the ability to appreciate the good things we still enjoy, to banish anger, sullen ingratitude and depression, and to regain the ability to enjoy our lives.

The classical example of human suffering comes from the Biblical Book of Job. In this book, widely cited but rarely read in its entirety, the main character, Job, is described as a morally upright, deeply religious man with a large family and considerable wealth. He has received much good from God — family, children, possessions, esteem, and a good name. He is a man of unmatched spiritual and material prosperity, an "upright and blameless man," an extraordinary man of whom "there is none like on the earth." He's living the good life, fifth-century BC style.

Enter Satan. Satan is disgusted with Job's lifestyle of holiness, so he goads God into testing his faithful servant. He tells God that the only reason Job lives right and worships God is because he is so healthy and prosperous, and that Job is not grateful for the right reasons. Satan attributes Job's faithfulness to his dependence on God for the abundant life he has enjoyed. He accuses God of placing a "hedge" of goodness and blessing around Job so that Job could not help but praise and honor God. Satan believes that if Job were sick and broke he would quit serving God. Such easy, automatic gratitude, in other words, is not the "real thing": in essence, Satan asks God to prove that Job would still worship him even if Job's prosperity and abundance were stripped away.

In the Book of Job, God accepts Satan's challenge. God attempts to prove to Satan that Job will serve him no matter what kind of trials he goes through. From there, everything that Job has is destroyed — his children, his wealth, and his health. Children are taken, his possessions, his animals, and his servants disappear, and he becomes a person outside society — publicly regarded as a sinner, someone cursed by God. Sitting in the dust covered with painful sores, Job asks the universal question: "Why me?"

Focusing as it does on issues of suffering, the Book of Job has a timeless appeal. The question of why the righteous suffer is widely believed to be the primary theme of this book, yet it raises additional questions. Do humans get what they deserve or merit in life? How are the righteous to respond to adversity? These questions are not posed philosophically but in the context of one man's story. How would Job react when stripped of all his blessings? As a believer that all things, blessings and curses, came from the hand of God, Job was faced with that terrible question: Is God the sort of being who acts without any reason? For God said to Satan, "You have incited me against him without reason," and Job then says, "Does God give us good things without reason? And does God also give us bad things without reason?"

Three friends try to help him make sense of his predicament. Is misfortune a divine punishment for sin, they ask. Job's friends argued in the affirmative, stating that Job's misfortunes were proof that he had committed some sins for which he was being punished. His friends also advanced the converse position that good fortune is always a divine reward, and that if Job would renounce his supposed sins, he would immediately experience the return of good fortune.

In response, Job asserts that he is a righteous man, and that his misfortune is therefore not a punishment for anything. This raises the possibility that God acts in capricious ways, and Job's wife urges him to curse God and die. Instead, Job responds with equanimity: "The Lord gives, and the Lord takes away; blessed be the name of the Lord." In Job's worldview, one cannot receive the good without the bad. The climax of the book occurs when God responds to Job, not with an explanation for Job's suffering but rather with a question: Where was Job when God created the world?

Job passes the test. He does not curse God. He persists in his integrity even after he is devastated. It is evident that it was never the enjoyment of the blessed life that prompted Job's faithful gratitude. At the end of the book, we learn that Job was healed and blessed twice as much after his trial. Ultimately, he is completely redeemed. God restores Job's relationships first, granting him seven new sons and three new daughters. He is given 14,000 sheep, 6,000 camels, 1,000 oxen, and 1,000 donkeys. He is granted good health, a long life — some 140 years we are told — surrounded by four generations of his offspring.

In All Circumstances?

It is relatively easy to feel grateful when good things are happening, and life is going the way we want it to. A much greater challenge is to be grateful when things are not going so well, and are not going the way we think they should. Anger, bitterness, and resentment seem to be so much easier, so much more a natural reaction in times like these. In this way, the story of Job is instructive. Was Job grateful to God only because he was so blessed and prosperous? Passing Satan's test and maintaining his integrity, Job demonstrates that his stance of gratitude toward God was independent of his life circumstances. He did not believe that he was owed or entitled to blessings. The tools of science seem to come up short when we try to understand people living lives of gratefulness in extraordinarily difficult situations.

Beyond Job, religious literatures and inspirational writings contain stories of extraordinary figures who were able to transcend their considerable pain and cultivate a sense of gratefulness for life in spite of what was happening to them and around them. Consider Corrie ten Boom, the Apostle Paul, Dietrich Bonhoeffer, and Horatio Spafford, each a compelling example of a person who appeared to be thankful in spite of their awful circumstances.

Corrie ten Boom, whose family hid Jews in their home during the Holocaust, wrote in *The Hiding Place* that she gave thanks for the fleas in her concentration camp barracks because the fleas kept the guards at bay and allowed them some degree of privacy for their devotionals. The German theologian Dietrich Bonhoeffer was executed for plotting to kill Hitler, yet remained grateful to the end, writing in his posthumously published autobiography that "gratitude changes the pangs of memory into grateful joy." In Paul's letter to the church at Philippi, the words *joy* and *rejoice* appear sixteen times in four chapters, despite the fact that he was writing the letter from prison, where he was awaiting a trial that could have resulted in his death. From his prison cell he wrote, "I have learned to be content with whatever I have. I know what it is to have little and I know what it is to have plenty. In any and all circumstances I have learned the secret of being well-fed and of going hungry, of having plenty and of being in need . . . Rejoice always, pray without ceasing, give thanks in all circumstances."

The lawyer Horatio G. Spafford lived with his wife and four daughters in Chicago. In a trip across the Atlantic, his daughters perished when their ship was split in two after colliding with a freighter. He received from his wife a telegram that read: "Saved alone." En route to bring her home, Spafford asked the captain of his ship to let him know when they were at the location where his daughters drowned. On this spot, in their memory, he penned the words to the famous hymn, "It Is Well with My Soul."

No one signs up for a class in adversity in order to develop character. We would not choose to suffer in order to become more grateful or, for that matter, to develop any other virtue. Yet historical examples and contemporary research have shown that trials and adversities can result in positive character changes. The belief that tragedy can ultimately result in positive outcomes has been a mainstay of religious systems since the beginning of recorded time. In fact, there are those who say that the primary reason that religions exist is to help people make sense out of suffering. Buddhism and Christianity provide two strong examples. The first of the Four Noble Truths purportedly uttered by the Buddha is that "life is suffering." So central is the concept of suffering in this tradition that the Buddha is said to have made no other claim than that he came to teach about suffering, and nothing else. In Christianity, suffering is seen as resulting from mankind's estrangement from God. Yet suffering is made endurable through an identification with Christ's anguish on the cross.

Religious traditions not only identify suffering as a central aspect of the human condition, but they also articulate visions of how we should respond to the fact that life is full of suffering. People can adopt an attitude toward their suffering that allows it to be a meaningful component of life, perhaps opening the threshold to a deeper, more authentic existence. The religious traditions encourage us to do more than react with passivity and resignation to loss and crisis; they advise us to change our perspective, so that our suffering is transformed into an opportunity for growth. Not only does the experience of tragedy give us an exceptional opportunity for growth, but some sort of suffering is also necessary for a person to achieve maximal psychological growth. In his study of self-actualizers, the paragons of mental wellness, the famed humanistic psychologist Abraham Maslow noted that "the most important learning experiences . . . were tragedies, deaths, and trauma . . . which forced change in the life-outlook of the person and consequently in everything that he did."

As I write these words during the winter holidays, I think about those courageous individuals who left Plymouth and sailed to Holland and then crossed the Atlantic to New England in 1620. All but three families dug graves in the rocky soil of New England to bury a husband, wife, or child. They had brought plants and seeds with them on the *Mayflower*, along with provisions for the first winter. The barley they planted did very poorly. Other crops failed altogether. Starvation loomed large. These were, though, people of faith. They knew about ancient Israel's harvest festival: how Israel, at the end of a successful harvest, thanked God for the bounty of creation — and also for delivering them from their captivity, giving them their freedom as a people. The Pilgrims read their own story in light of Israel's story. God is thanked for the harvest but also for something more, something not actually dependent on a successful harvest: namely, God's presence and grace and love. The Pilgrims thanked God for enough corn to survive the winter, but they were also thanking God for the guiding presence they had experienced, the strong hand they had felt leading them, and the love that had sustained them. Like Job, they understood that God is to be thanked and praised in adversity as well as in prosperity.

In contemporary times, we also encounter individuals able to extract blessings from adversity. In response to an assignment asking her to identify someone in her life to whom she was grateful, a woman who participated in our research wrote the following letter describing the "gift" of her blindness:

Initially I had a difficult time identifying someone who really had a significant impact in my life that I wanted to write this letter to, and then I began to look at this homework and this state of being grateful as more of a process I needed to go through. I have many blessings in my life but have also had many hardships — I spent most of my life as a visually impaired person and ten years ago became totally blind. While I live a productive happy life with a husband, children, friends, family, etc., I have never really looked at myself or my life in a grateful way and so felt the first letter I needed to write in the process was a letter to G-D. I am a religious person, though perhaps not as spiritual as I would like to be, and my situation as well as other struggles I have had in my life have left me with ambivalence toward G-d as well as somewhat with the just taking things for granted attitude. What I realized in starting to look at gratitude more consciously was that I was grateful to G-d in many ways for the gifts of my life and my blindness. While I would be insane to ever want to be blind or choose to be blind over being sighted, there have definitely been gifts as a result of my blindness that I am grateful for. I have seen the goodness in people. I have seen and realized my own strengths. I have compassionate, responsible, independent children. I know that when I meet people I get right to their hearts and am not distracted by outward appearances. I have been given the gift of being able to help other people, which is something that is critical to me in terms of being a role model and support. While this letter is not particularly my most articulate, I wanted to thank you for helping me to see more clearly the gifts of my blindness and the thanks I feel for having had this. Now the next part of the process for me will be to thank the people who have made a difference in my life but somehow I could not get to that point before thanking either G-d or my blindness, whichever it really is. Thanks.

THE PARADOX OF HAPPINESS AND SUFFERING

The psychological literature on subjective well-being has concluded that "most people are happy." In survey research, most people, around the world, whether living in advantaged or disadvantaged circumstances, report a positive level of well-being. How can most people be happy, given the ubiquity of suffering, pain, and adversity? Is it possible for this apparent paradox to be resolved? Perhaps people are masterful self-deceivers who fool themselves into thinking they are happy when they are really miserable. On the other hand, perhaps they are masterfully adaptive creatures who are able to transform adverse circumstances into opportunities for personal growth, lasting happiness, and quality of life even in the face of pain and suffering. For some, life is often elevated to the sublime precisely under those conditions that might be expected to produce the most pain and misery.

However, this conclusion would appear to fly in the face of most assumptions of the psychological and emotional effects of trauma. For example, consider some common myths about reactions to loss. It is widely assumed, by mental health professionals, laypersons, and those themselves who encounter loss that (1) distress or depression is inevitable following loss, (2) positive emotions such as hope and happiness will be absent, (3) the failure to experience distress indicates a psychological disturbance or is somehow pathological, (4) coming to terms with or "working through the loss" is essential for ultimate recovery, and (5) attachment to the lost object must be broken. Contemporary research on coping with loss has called into question each of these widely held assumptions and the science of stress-related growth is redefining what it means to "adjust" to loss.

For example, the loss of a spouse can be emotionally devastating, and it often clearly does leave an emotional void. Yet in one study of widows who had lost their spouses within the previous month, remarkably only 35 percent were classified as definitely or "probably" depressed. In another study of parents coping with the loss of a child through Sudden Infant Death Syndrome (SIDS), by three months after their loss their positive emotions were more prevalent than their negative feelings, and this pattern held at a follow-up interview eighteen months later. Initially, researchers who toil in the field of loss and coping were understandably reluctant to ask people if they had found positives in their loss. One interviewer protested, "If you think I'm going in there and ask that quadriplegic how many times he's felt happy in the past week, you're crazy." But crazy it wasn't. Within three weeks of an injury that left them paralyzed, persons with spinal cord injuries reported happiness more frequently than anxiety, depression, or anger. In another study involving bereaved spouses, 81 percent of the respondents had found something positive eighteen months after their loss, and an astonishing 73 percent reported finding something positive just one month after the death of their spouse. Positive emotions are not "missing in action" in the aftermath of loss. Certainly no one would minimize the anguish that painful losses often bring, so even finding that losses often lead to gains should not be taken as a license to minimize the agony and suffering that trauma can produce. But these studies point to the extraordinary resilience of humans to adjust and adapt to the traumatic circumstances of their lives.

Yet it is simply the case that not everyone recovers following loss, and not everyone experiences stress-related growth. Certain factors appear to predict who will and who will not be able to find positive outcomes. Optimism is one factor. Being better copers allows optimists to adjust more quickly to their loss. Religiousness is another. Because of either their belief in an afterlife or their perception that loss is part of a larger cosmic plan, persons of faith report higher levels of posttraumatic growth than the nonreligious. Consider gratitude, though. Could gratitude be part of a person's "psychological immune system" that operates to convert adversity into prosperity? Without minimizing the severity of traumatic events, can reminding oneself to "be grateful" or to maintain a grateful attitude be an effective way of coping with particularly stressful life circumstances? An attitude of gratefulness permits a person to transform a tragedy into an opportunity for growth. Can you recall handling a crisis successfully and realizing that you grew because of the experience? In this case, you were thankful not so much for the circumstance but rather

for the skills that came from dealing with it. Alicia, a research participant whose 70-year-old father died of cancer, said:

> I tend to look at it generally as if all things that happen in my life
> are a gift, for whatever reason, or however they happen. It doesn't
> necessarily have to be only pleasant gifts, but everything that
> happens . . . there's a meaning. And through that I've learned a
> great deal. While I wouldn't want to go back and relive that, I'm
> grateful for that because it made me who I am. There's a lot of
> joys and sorrows, but they all enrich life.

The more I study gratitude, the more I have come to believe that
an authentic, deeply held sense of gratefulness toward life may require some degree of contrast or deprivation. One truly appreciates a
mild spring after a harsh winter, a gourmet meal following a fast, and
sexual intimacy after a period of abstinence. Some blessings are not
known until they are lost. Losing a valued role or goal in life may lead
the person to increase the value they see in other aspects of life. Who
is not familiar with the prototypical example of the hard-driving executive, who, after a life-threatening heart attack, now vows to spend
more time with his family? Through the process of *appreciation,* what
was once taken for granted is now seen as special. There is nothing
quite like the potential unavailability of something (or someone) to
make us value it more. Psychologists call this the "principle of scarcity" — assigning greater value to opportunities when they are less
available.

Little is known about the role of gratitude in the lives of real
people struggling with difficult life situations. In an attempt to rem-
edy this deficiency, Lisa Krause and I collected stories of gratitude
and thankfulness from the lives of persons with neuromuscular diseases (NMDs). As mentioned in chapter 2, NMDs are chronic, pro-
gressively disabling diseases of the peripheral nervous system that affect over 4 million persons in the United States. Collaborating with
colleagues in the University of California, Davis's Department of

Medicine and Physical Rehabilitation, we sent elaborate, twenty-six-page surveys assessing quality of life functioning and subjective well-being to over three hundred persons with neuromuscular diseases, including Post-Polio disease, Charcot-Marie-Tooth disease, limb-girdle muscular dystrophy, spinal muscular atrophy, and facioscapulo-humeral (FSH) disease. We received surveys from over two hundred of these individuals, and I have quoted from several in this book.

Recall Job's anguish over his physical afflictions. In the face of progressive diseases, people often find life extremely challenging, pain-ful, and frustrating. They may get angry at God, frustrated with their doctors, and bitter over life for what they perceive to be a cruel injus-tice. Thus, we initially wondered whether it would be possible for the people we interviewed to even find anything to be grateful about. As it turned out, most respondents had trouble settling on a specific in-stance — they had simply so much in their lives that they were grate-ful for. We were struck by the profound depth of feeling that is con-veyed within the essays and by the apparent life-transforming power of gratitude in many of their lives. We included one open-ended question in which we asked participants to write about a time when they felt a strong sense of gratitude or thankfulness for something or to someone. We asked them to let themselves re-create that experi-ence in their minds so that they could feel the emotions as if they had transported themselves back in time to the event itself. We then asked them to reflect on what they felt in that situation and how they ex-pressed those feelings. What is evident to us in reading these narrative accounts is that (a) gratitude can be an overwhelmingly intense feel-ing, (b) gratitude for gifts easily overlooked by most can be the most powerful and frequent form of thankfulness, (c) gratitude is indepen-dent of one's objective life circumstances, and that it can be chosen in spite of one's situation. We were also struck by the redemptive twist that occurred in nearly one-half of these narratives: out of something bad (suffering, adversity, affliction) comes something good (new life or new opportunities), for which the person feels profoundly grateful. In this narrative, a reversal in mood state proves foundational for gratefulness:

> It was difficult for me to even think of a gratitude situation until recently. My depression had recently become quite profound. I asked some friends to visualize me happy, filled with joy. The product of that request has been such an outpouring of love and words of strength and power. I had reached a point where I felt useless and worthless. Divorce, job loss, income loss, moving, loss of friends, and loss of mobility had combined to leave me feeling such despair. I thought I had moved past it in the ten months since but the feelings simply intensified as time passed. The words of my friends and family have filled me with a sense of wonder. I had no idea they all viewed me with the strength and ability to overcome that was apparent in their words. I feel a sense of peace and hope. A small beginning toward the light of joy. I feel such gratitude to these people for being mirrors to me; mirrors that reflected back not my darkness, which was all I could see, but my light which I had lost sight of.

GRATEFUL CAREGIVING

Robertson McQuilkin's wife, Muriel, who died in 2003 from Alzheimer's disease, began to show symptoms of the illness in the late 1970s. Although Alzheimer's on average claims the life of its victims in less than seven years following diagnosis, Muriel and Robertson battled the disease for nearly a quarter-century. At the age of 62, he resigned his position as a college president so that he could care for his wife full-time. Three years later, she stopped recognizing him. He wrote, "I would love her, but she couldn't love me back, and that's a painful thing." McQuilkin's story is simultaneously heart-wrenching and awe-inspiring. Here is a man who sacrificed nearly one-third of his life to caring for a woman who had no idea of who he was and would never again know. When he was asked in an interview how he continued to care for her, he replied, "Right now, I think my life must be happier than the lives of 95 percent of the people on planet Earth. Muriel's a joy to me, and life is good to both of us, in different ways. But I'm thinking of something more basic than just 'counting my blessings.' I love to care for her. She's my precious."

Assuming long-term care for a disabled spouse, an aging parent, or a chronically ill child is a unique form of stress that might even hasten the aging process. A remarkable study on this issue was carried out by researchers at the University of California, San Francisco. They compared fifty-eight women, ages 20 to 50, all of whom were biological mothers either of a chronically ill child (the caregivers) or a healthy child (the control group). Those caring for the sick children showed shorter telomeres in their immune system cells. Telomeres are DNA-protein complexes that cap the ends of chromosomes and promote genetic stability. Like the caps of a shoelace, telomeres prevent the DNA strands from unraveling. Each time a cell divides, a portion of telomeric DNA unravels, and after many rounds of cell division, so much telomeric DNA has diminished that the aged cell stops dividing. Thus, telomeres play a critical role in determining the number of times a cell divides, its health, and its life span. These factors, in turn, affect the health of the tissues that cells form, and by extension, the aging of the host organism. Experts tell us that stress is the greatest ager of all, and this revolutionary chromosomal research explains why. Stress accelerates the aging of human cells, explaining why those under chronic stress appear worn down and worn out.

It should come as no surprise that caregivers of individuals with a disease such as Alzheimer's experience an enormous amount of stress. Caregivers may become overwhelmed with their responsibilities and may eventually feel unable to provide for the needs of their relative. "Living bereavement" is a common term used to describe what it's like to see a loved one suffer from this disease. Seven years before Ronald Reagan's death, Nancy Reagan called her husband's descent into Alzheimer's "worse than the [attempted] assassination." Nancy Reynolds, a family friend, commented that at the end stages,

Mrs. Reagan had taken "responsibility for what was left" of the former president. Her privileged position meant her role as caregiver was very different from the experience of many people. However, emotionally at least, that does not mean it was any easier. Even if the caregiver decides to hand over care of their relative to a medical facility, the physical and psychological stress of watching one's relative's health decline may continue to take a toll.

It would be difficult to envision how a simple practice of gratitude journaling might provide a respite from the constant stress of providing care to a loved one with Alzheimer's. After all, the shift in outlook that gratitude provides does not change the harsh reality of this terrible disease. However, Jo-Ann Tsang of Baylor University conducted a gratitude intervention study to see if daily gratitude journals might positively impact the physical and psychological well-being of relatives of individuals with Alzheimer's disease. She recruited participants at a local group for caregivers of Alzheimer's patients. Half of the caregivers kept daily gratitude journals while the other half listed hardships they experienced each day. Both groups wrote in their journals daily for two weeks. One woman wrote, "I was very grateful that Bill called me by my name. He did not want me to go and asked me to come back." On another day, the entry in her journal read, "I was grateful today because Bill remembered it was July, not January."

The celebrations of small victories like these were frequent entries in the gratitude journals. By the end of the study, participants who kept gratitude journals experienced an increase in overall well-being and a reduction in stress and depression levels from the beginning to the end of the study. Gratefulness on a daily basis was related to higher levels of optimism and self-esteem in the caregivers and to fewer physical health complaints. Caregiving support networks advocate journaling as a mode of self-expression, and my suspicion is that keeping a daily diary of positive, uplifting experiences can be considerably therapeutic.

Paradoxically, remembering to count one's blessings and being mindful of the many ways in which life is still worth living can be life-affirming even in the midst of caring for those who are deeply forgetful. Robertson McQuilkin would gratefully hold onto memories, memories that were both sweet and bittersweet. "Muriel stocked the cupboard of my mind with the best of them," he wrote. Nancy Reagan was also buoyed by gratitude. In a speech to the Alzheimer's Association delivered a year before her husband's death, she acknowledged the power of grateful outlook:

> Just four months ago, we celebrated our 52nd wedding anniversary. And as you there understand better than anyone, this was an anniversary that I celebrated alone. Those who have Alzheimer's are on a rocky path that only goes downhill. Ronnie's long journey has taken him to a distant place where I can no longer reach him. We cannot share the wonderful memories of our years together. So many wonderful people over these last ten years have sent Ronnie and me their prayers and best wishes. To those who have been so compassionate, I will be forever grateful for your thoughtfulness. And I want you to take some comfort in knowing that Ronnie is the same gentle, humble, and kind person that he has always been. God has sent us that blessing, for which I am so thankful.

THANKFULNESS AMONG THE ASHES

On September 11, 2001, the lives of Americans were forever changed as terrorist hijackers flew commercial aircraft into New York's World Trade Center Towers and the Pentagon building outside Washington, D.C. The September 11 terrorist attacks produced more civilian casualties in a single day than has any other event in U.S. history. The horrific events of the day provided an unprecedented opportunity for mental health researchers to study the human reaction to a large-scale national trauma. Within four years, nearly one hundred studies examining various emotional and physical consequences of the attacks were published in various psychological and medical journals. The first studies to appear focused predictably on negative effects: posttraumatic stress symptoms, anxiety, depression, sleep disturbances. But soon thereafter, other studies began to appear that addressed positive emotions. Intermixed experiences of positive emotions were justifiable after the September 11 attacks. If you might wonder how, consider this. People might have felt grateful to be alive or to know that their loved ones were safe. For example, one World Trade Center survivor said, "Each day that I stay as a guest on this green Earth suddenly seems like outrageous good fortune." Related studies sought to establish whether positive psychological qualities and emotions might contribute to adjustment in the aftermath of the attacks.

In one, the then University of Michigan positive psychologist Barbara Fredrickson examined the frequency of positive and negative emotions pre- and post-9/11. Fortunately, she still had access to a group of students to whom she had administered an extensive emotions questionnaire four months prior to September 11. Participants were asked to "think back to the September 11th attacks and the days that have passed since then" and report on how often they had felt each of twenty different emotions, including those both related and seemingly unrelated to the attacks. The emotions included both positive (joy, hope, love) and negative (anxious, angry, sad). Out of the twenty emotions, gratitude was the *second* most commonly experienced. Only compassion was more frequently felt. The people who were able to feel at least moderate levels of these positive emotions had greater resilience and were less likely to suffer depression post-9/11 (72 percent of the participants evidenced clinically significant depressive symptoms). Resilient persons were those who were less likely to have experienced problems or stresses related to the terrorist attacks. Gratitude and other positive emotions seemed to exert a protective effect.

One might wonder whether all this positivity was merely a form of denial. After all, one way to cope with trauma is to seal off the negative thoughts and images from conscious awareness. Yet there was no evidence for such a suppression effect in the data. The correlation between positive and negative feelings was far from inverse, as it would be if strong defenses were operating. Most people affected by the attacks felt a mixture of pleasant and unpleasant emotions post-9/11.

Strange as it may sound, gratitude was also a reaction by some inside the World Trade Center, even as the towers were being evacuated. We've all heard many stories from that awful day. One particularly poignant account that caught my attention was told by a technology consultant for an investment company whose offices were housed in the South Tower:

> When the second plane hit the South Tower of the World Trade Center, I had just stepped out of an elevator onto the 44th floor. Dust and rubble burst out of the elevator shafts and stairways. There was a lot of panic. I clung to the need to see and feel God's love. The descent down the stairwells was orderly and efficient. So many people were actively expressing love for one another — helping them, calming their fears, embracing and comforting them. It sounds strange, but one of my abiding impressions was how much there was to be grateful for, and how many people to be grateful to . . . things got worse for a time, when the towers collapsed I was a block away . . . I was able to keep somewhat focused on the need to love and be grateful.

This was a remarkable reaction in an extraordinary circumstance. I don't know about you, but if I were in that situation, gratitude would have been one of my least likely feelings.

Soon after the terrorist attacks, media reports claimed that Americans, on the whole, had changed in many ways for the better. Despite the anger and outrage over being attacked on our own soil, we were reportedly kinder, more loving, more appreciative of life, more help-ful toward each other after 9/11. But did these changes actually occur, and if so, did they last? Christopher Peterson, a University of Michi-gan clinical psychologist and leader in the positive psychology move-ment, answered these questions using data from an online survey of character strengths. He looked for immediate changes by comparing scores before September 11 with those obtained one, two, and ten months after the attack. Seven of the strengths increased from be-fore to after: gratitude, hope, kindness, leadership, love, spirituality, and teamwork. These seven strengths remained elevated ten months later, though on average they had declined from a high point nine months earlier. On the one-year anniversary of September 11, Presi-dent George W. Bush commented that in the events that have chal-lenged us as Americans, we had also seen the character that will de-liver us. Each of us, he went on to say, was "reminded that we are here only for a time, and these counted days should be filled with things that last and matter: love for our families, love for our neighbors, and for our country; gratitude for life and to the Giver of life." Gratitude is sanctioned here by the president of the United States as a way of best handling times of uncertainty.

THE BOUNCE-BACK FACTOR

A grateful outlook on life appears to offer protection in times of cri-sis. But gratitude may also confer a more widespread and pervasive resiliency across the life span. Resiliency is an enormously popular topic in psychology today. It refers to the ability to spring back from and successfully adapt to adversity. A vast research literature has shown, for example, that optimism, hardiness, a sense of humor, so-cial support, a sense of purpose and meaning, and spirituality are po-tent resiliency factors. Recent research suggests that gratitude should be added to this list.

Kenneth Kendler and his colleagues at the Virginia Commonwealth University School of Medicine have been studying genetic risk factors for depression and other psychiatric illnesses for the last twenty years. Twin registries are compiled with the goal of understanding environmental and family-genetic risk factors for both normal and abnormal psychological traits (the strategy of examining pairs of twins allows researchers to detect unique risk factors because both twins are matched both for their genetic and their familial-environmental background). In one study, published in 2003, they looked at lifetime risk for psychiatric disorders in nearly three thousand twin pairs. High levels of thankfulness were associated with reduced risk for what researchers referred to as internalizing disorders (depression, phobias, bulimia) and externalizing disorders (antisocial personality, alcohol and drug dependence). As an epidemiological study, it does not shed light on *why* thankfulness might confer a protective effect; nevertheless this was a significant study in that most resiliency factors tend to be environmental (stress, family history, personal loss) or biological (diet, exercise) in nature, and not something as seemingly inconspicuous and unassuming as gratitude.

For people with a psychiatric disorder, gratitude might be a valuable coping tactic for responding to life's challenges. It also might be differentially effective in different gender, ethnic, and/or racial groups. An epidemiological study conducted in New York State found that "counting one's blessings" was commonly employed as a coping strategy to deal with panic disorder and agoraphobia. Counting blessings was the second most frequently endorsed coping strategy by the African American patients, who endorsed the strategy more frequently than did their European American counterparts. Other studies have found that African Americans are more resilient to chronic stress because they have been able to maintain a perspective that keeps the stress external and, in so doing, less likely to pervade their sense of self. It is also likely that religiously based attitudes of hope, faith, forgiveness, and gratitude contribute to this resilience, and the increased reliance on religion is well-documented in the African American community. Entering into a collaborative form of coping where the individual "partners" with God is more effective than is complete self-reliance, especially when stress is uncontrollable. Another study of low-income elderly women found that these women were much more likely to describe themselves as "fortunate" or "blessed" than "poor" or "old" despite two-thirds of them being below the federal poverty threshold with ages ranging from 52 to 99. Counting blessings was the most common approach for coping with poverty, mentioned by nearly one-half of all respondents.

Reminding oneself to maintain a grateful attitude might be a common way of coping with natural disasters. In one study, interviews were conducted with thirteen parents who lived in south Florida at the time of 1992's Hurricane Andrew, the deadliest and costliest hurricane in Florida's history. One of the key themes of the parents' hurricane experiences was an overwhelming sense of gratitude for what they had *not* lost during the hurricane. Although five of the families' homes had been so severely ravaged that relocation had been necessary, none of them had lost a loved one. Because they were spared the loss of what was most important to them, they experienced profound gratitude in the midst of terrible disaster. One father said, "I had this overwhelming joy to be alive . . . that's what was important . . . that elation that we were alive; that really stuck with us."

More recently etched in our memories were 2005 hurricanes Katrina and Rita. Once again, interwoven with stories of devastation from these storms were memories of recovery laced with gratitude:

Last week was a difficult week, and I saw things and met people who were living out a nightmare. Yet what struck me the hardest as I drove home was the outpouring of gratitude that those around me shared when they received something ordinary — a hot meal, a chocolate energy drink, a ride, a private place to sleep, a shower, a few words of encouragement. Deprivation was creating a new perspective for us all. We stopped taking our ordinary lives (and each other) for granted. It is the gift that I take home with me, my reward, I suppose, for hard work. Katrina can take my home but not my spirit.

Fortunately, it does not take a natural disaster to kindle a sense of gratefulness. Other life changes present their own challenges where a grateful response in the form of counting blessings can be an effective way of coping. Anyone who becomes a parent for the first time is familiar with the challenges this transition brings. In one study of new parents, researchers found that "reminding oneself of things for which to be grateful" and "telling myself I have things to be thankful for" were rated among the most helpful coping behaviors. Mothers tended to find thankfulness more useful than did the new dads (evidently those were the fathers getting up in the middle of the night).

Should children have disabilities, gratefulness might offset some of the stress associated with caretaking. Laura King, a former doctoral student of mine and now professor at the University of Missouri, asked parents of children with Down syndrome (DS) to write stories about the moment when they first learned that their children had DS. It is hard to fathom receiving more devastating news than to hear that one's child has a profound disability. Yet previous research has shown that parents of DS children actually do not significantly differ from parents of children without DS in terms of marital or family functioning. Laura coded the stories she obtained for the presence of *foreshadowing* (sensing before birth that the child might have DS), a *happy beginning*, or a *happy ending*, as well as degree of *closure* or resolution indicating the parent had come to terms with knowing that their child had DS. Most of the stories had, predictably, unhappy beginnings. But happy endings and closure in the stories were related to higher levels of well-being concurrently as well as two years later. One parent wrote, "I knew everything would be all right. He was first and foremost our baby boy, and DS was one characteristic of Jamie. He is as much or more of a blessing to our family as any child could be." The National Down Syndrome Web site even offers the tip of "adopting a grateful attitude" as a way of dealing with some of the unpleasant emotions that surface when parents learn that their child has a serious disability. Attempts on the part of the parent to stay positive will clearly be in the child's best interest. Gratitude journaling might prove helpful as it did for the caregivers of persons with Alzheimer's that I discussed earlier.

The emotional state of children with DS can itself be a source of inspiration. Richard Robison is the father of two teenage daughters with DS. He tells of the time when, at the family's Thanksgiving table, his daughter Amy came prepared with her own handwritten list of the things she is thankful for:

1. I am thankful for my family.
2. I am thankful for my friends.
3. I am thankful for my fans.
4. I am thankful for my sister.
5. I am thankful for my mom who gave me the flowers (after my play performance at school).
6. I love my mom. I love my dad. I love my sister and my brother.

There is a stereotype that persons with DS are relentlessly happy. Yet like children without DS, each child experiences a full range of emotions, struggles with the challenges of daily life, and confronts a higher than normal risk of exposure to discrimination or misunderstanding as a result of this disability. There is considerable evidence to suggest that persons with DS are also at an increased risk to be diagnosed with depression. So it's all the more inspiring when simple, enthusiastic expressions of gratitude such as Amy's brighten the lives of her parents and those around her.

THE REDEMPTIVE SELF

The Northwestern University psychologist Dan McAdams specializes in the study of lives. On campus he heads up the Foley Center, which is dedicated to advancing the rich intellectual tradition associated with Henry A. Murray, Robert White, Erik Erikson, David McClelland, Silvan Tomkins, and other scholars who established "personology" as the scientific study of the whole person in biographical and cultural context. These scholars advocated the importance of narrative (the way in which people make sense of the world through storytelling) as instrumental in meaning making. Narratives enable us to understand the past, the present, and what is humanly possible in a way that is unique. Life-narrative research assumes that the narratives people tell about their lives are imaginative reconstructions of the past and anticipations of the future, suggestive of the self-defining personal myth that a person is working on in his or her life. Few questions have a longer, deeper, and livelier intellectual history than how we "construct" our lives — and, indeed, how we create ourselves in the process. Such personal myths function psychologically to provide modern life with some semblance of order and purpose. People also use stories to make sense of lives and to help them to adapt to unexpected events.

In telling their life stories, McAdams identified "redemption sequences" as one of two distinct narrative styles that people use. In a redemptive sequence, there is a transformation from an unpleasant circumstance to a positive outcome. Something bad happens (say, the protagonist fails in some way, loses a loved one, suffers in some manner, acknowledges a personal flaw or sin), but something good comes out of it all to redeem the sequence. For instance, alcoholism and divorce might be followed by sobriety and remarriage, job failure by promotion, or a confidence-building success on the heels of a devastating failure. Notably present in the redemptive sequences generated in those interviewed by McAdams were feelings of thankfulness and appreciation. One sequence was that of an unwanted pregnancy and painful birth resulting in thankfulness and happiness for the child. Another was of a serious motorcycle injury resulting in a greater appreciation for life and a renewed commitment to life goals. Not only are these interesting real-life examples, but they also prove an impor-

tant point. Grateful, redeemed individuals are neither naively optimistic nor are they under some illusion that suffering and pain are not
real. If there is redemption, there must first be pain. The redemptive
twist does not erase the original pain. Rather, these persons have consciously taken control by choosing to extract benefits from adversity,
with one of the major benefits being the perception of life as a gift.

While people may not typically express gratitude for misfortune
in life, it is very common among highly productive adults to remark
how thankful they are about the redemptive move in their story. A
man loses his job, but as a result of this he reprioritizes his life to put
his family first and is thankful for having been given this opportunity.
A woman divorces her abusive husband, but in what follows her
friendships are strengthened and her self-esteem rises, and she is
grateful to those around her who have helped her develop in this way.
In redemptive sequences, we are reminded of the famous verse: "I
once was lost, but now am found; was blind, but now I see." Redemption can summon forth amazing grace — abundant gratitude. It may
be that gratitude promotes the construction of redemptive life sequences because individuals who approach life with an attitude that
all of life is a gift will be more likely to find the good in bad life circumstances. They are more likely to make progress and to move forward following a catastrophe. In fact, they may be more likely to label
such an event a gift.

MORE THAN A FEELING

Corrie ten Boom, the Apostle Paul, Dietrich Bonhoeffer, and Horatio
Spafford were able to maintain a grateful stance toward life in spite of
what was happening to them and around them. Gratitude can, and
often does, bloom in the soil of adversity. But how do these "pillars"
of gratefulness do it? Is gratitude one of those "unfair" gifts given to
those of sunny dispositions, those who do not instinctively feel the
anxiety, pain, and separation of living in this world? Is this an emo-

tion that comes from a chemical predisposition to positive thinking or are there choices we can make? In his book *In Search of Stones*, the psychiatrist M. Scott Peck suggests that perhaps some people carry a gene for gratitude. But can we choose gratitude? Can we choose to view everything that happens as a gift, intended for our benefit? The ability to perceive the elements in one's life and even life itself as gifts would appear essential if we are to transform tragedy into opportunity.

Conversely, the perception that one is a passive victim of unfortunate circumstances would undermine the ability to derive a sense of being gifted (compare with the African American research). Conceiving of oneself as a victim prohibits perceptions that life is a gift. Grateful people may have more psychic maneuverability than the ungrateful, enabling them to be less defensive and more open to life. As such, they are likely to express agreement with the sixteenth-century Protestant theologian, John Calvin, who wrote: "We are well-nigh overwhelmed by so great and so plenteous an outpouring of benefactions, by so many and mighty miracles discerned wherever one looks, that we never lack reason for praise and thanksgiving."

In thinking about the relations between suffering, gratitude, and growth, we need to remember the difference between *feeling* grateful and *being* grateful. As a feeling, gratitude is a natural response to a particular situation when good things happen to an individual. No one *feels* grateful when they have lost a job, received a devastating diagnosis, or seen their marriage crumble. How could they? It would be absurd and an insult to the person to suggest that they should feel grateful in spite of what was happening to them. Do you think that Job, the Apostle Paul, or Dietrich Bonhoeffer felt grateful? But gratefulness is not just a feeling. It is also an attitude, a chosen posture toward life that says, "I will be grateful in all circumstances." Brother David Steindl-Rast, the world's foremost teacher of gratitude, has written that "times that challenge us physically, emotionally, and spiritually may make it almost impossible for us to feel grateful. Yet, we can decide to live gratefully, courageously open to life in all its fullness. By living the gratefulness we don't feel, we begin to feel the gratefulness we live." Conceiving of gratefulness as a posture toward life enables us to see how it can be tested and strengthened through adversity. Grateful feelings follow when good things happen; grateful attitudes precede goodness, and they precede trials. If one is not grateful before challenges arrive, it is going to be more difficult (though not impossible) to summon up gratitude after they hit.

The philosopher Søren Kierkegaard had the following prayer:

We would receive all at Thy hand. If it should be honor and glory, we would receive them at Thy hand; if it should be ridicule and insults, we would receive them at Thy hand. O let us be able to receive either the one or the other of these things with equal joy and gratitude; there is little difference between them, and for us there would be no difference if we thought only of the one decisive thing: that it comes from Thee.

For Kierkegaard, everything that comes from the hand of God must be good, whether or not it seems so to the natural mind, *because* it comes from God who is benevolent. In gratitude, we have a way of transcending the immediate vicissitudes of circumstances. Gratitude is not only an emotion, felt when receiving a benefit gladly, but it is also a stance toward life. This was the stance that Job adopted toward life. In that sense, it can be untethered from life circumstances. A grateful stance toward life is relatively immune to both fortune and misfortune. Furthermore, trials and suffering can actually refine and deepen gratefulness. Historically, gratitude was viewed as a virtue that can contribute to living well. Virtues are habits that are the function of practice, and good habits often demand lengthy training. Classical writers focused on the good life emphasized the cultivation and expression of gratitude for the health and vitality of both citizenry and society. Across cultures and time spans, experiences and expressions of gratitude have been treated as both basic and desirable aspects of human personality and social life.

Transforming adversity into prosperity requires that no matter what happens, existence itself is seen as a gift. To see life in this fashion requires that gratefulness be a deep and abiding aspect of a person's character. The virtue of gratitude is a readiness or predisposition to respond to the actions of others by seeing the goodness and benevolence in them, and consequently desiring to return acknowledging tokens of benefit. As a virtue, gratefulness is an attitude underlying successful functioning over the life course. In his longitudinal study of male adult development, Harvard University psychiatrist George Vaillant theorizes that a key to mature adaptation to life is the ability to replace bitterness and resentment toward those that have perpetrated harm with gratitude and acceptance. According to Vaillant, "mature defenses grow out of our brain's evolving capacity to master, assimilate, and feel grateful for life, living, and experience." Gratitude is part and parcel of this creative process whereby self-destructive emotions are transformed into ones that permit healing and restoration. A dispositionally grateful person will tend to see what is good in situations and to notice less what is bad. Those with the virtue of gratefulness will become grateful for the ways in which painful circumstances allow growth. As tragedies become transformed into opportunities, grateful individuals begin to heal from past wounds and look forward to the future with a fresh affirmation toward life.

THE KINGDOM OF NIGHT

"No one is as capable of gratitude as one who has emerged from the kingdom of night," wrote Elie Wiesel, the Holocaust survivor, writer, and Nobel Peace Prize recipient. Wiesel knew firsthand the necessity of choosing to disconnect one's attitude from one's circumstances. Arrested by Nazis in his Romanian village and transported by cattle car at the age of 15 to Auschwitz in the spring of 1944, Elie suffered humiliation, loss of faith, loss of family, and finally the loss of any semblance of humanity. He experienced the great shame of caring for nothing except his own survival, and this is when daily survival brings starvation, wretchedness, and bitter cold. Somehow, Wiesel did survive the death camps and was liberated in April 1945.

A few years ago, Oprah Winfrey was interviewing Wiesel on her television program. She asked him whether, after all the tragedy that he had witnessed, he still had a place inside of him for gratefulness. His reply:

> Absolutely. Right after the war, I went around telling people, "Thank you just for living, for being human." And to this day, the words that come most frequently from my lips are *thank you.* When a person doesn't have gratitude, something is missing in his or her humanity. A person can almost be defined by his or her attitude toward gratitude . . . For me, every hour is grace. And I feel gratitude in my heart each time I can meet someone and look at his or her smile.

When I ponder the life and work of Wiesel, I am struck by his metaphor of the "kingdom of night." Fortunately, it is likely that very few of us will ever have to experience anything as horrific as the Holocaust. Yet everyone who has faced suffering of one type or another has dealt with or is dealing with his or her own kingdom of night. The "night" is those life circumstances that appear to trap us or limit our options. For one person, it might be an addiction or an abusive relationship. For another, it may be economic hardship. For yet another, it may be a limiting job or even depression. Wiesel continues to draw on his prison experiences when he explains that what others can't see is what is real to those who are trapped: people's minds build the prison walls. Their thoughts line them with barbed wire. Internal judgments become the patrolling guards. Escape requires tunneling or climbing through those barriers and walking past the guards.

How does one escape? For Wiesel, the key that opens the prison door is the key of gratefulness. Searching for and being thankful for what is positive in every situation digs the tunnel and breaks the stranglehold of despair. Wiesel writes, "This simple process has the power to transform your life. If the dust settles and you're still standing, there's a reason for it . . . now start walking! You can leave the kingdom of night. You can start walking toward the gates right now. Your freedom begins with being thankful for the small things — gaining courage and strength to reach the big things."

Our identities are closely tied to significant life memories. One could even say that we *are* because of *what* we remember. Gratitude is the way the heart remembers — remembers kindnesses, cherished interactions with others, compassionate actions of strangers, surprise gifts, and everyday blessings. By remembering we honor and acknowledge the many ways in which who and what we are has been shaped by others, both living and dead. Wiesel reminds us that, paradoxically, in gratitude we must recall the bleak times as well as the good times. Our gratitude now bears witness to the suffering that has taken place. When suffering occurs at the hands of others, such gratitude takes on a defiant character, a vigorous determination to stay grateful in spite of what one has been through. This "defiant gratitude" is a gift that Wiesel and other survivors of atrocities have given to each of us. In cheating death, he has taught us how to live. In the midst of dehumanizing conditions, he has taught us how to be human.

7
PRACTICING GRATITUDE

⁓ THERE IS AN UNDERLYING paradox about gratitude: whereas the evidence is clear that cultivating gratitude, in both our lives and in our attitude toward life, makes us sustainably happier and healthier people, it is still difficult to practice gratitude on a daily basis. Some days it comes naturally; other days, it feels as if we're taking our medicine, doing something that's good for us but that we don't really like. On difficult days, it can be like stepping onto the treadmill when you just want to sink into the couch and turn on the television. I should know. I love my work — conducting research into gratitude, thinking and writing about it, reading the insights of others on the topic, and speaking to audiences about it. But I find the sustained practice of gratitude difficult. It does not always come easily or naturally to me, and I effortfully have to redirect ingrained tendencies to take life for granted.

That may be the only thing I have in common with Einstein. He had to remind himself, a thousand times a day by his count, of how much he depended upon other people. A thousand times a day, I too have to remind myself to be grateful and to remember how much I depend upon other people. I justify myself by saying that since I am constantly thinking about gratitude, I don't need to actively practice it. But more often than not, my thinking isn't about the things in life I am grateful for, it's just about the next study, or next article, or next talk I am going to deliver. I suspect that Einstein and I are not alone. Gratitude can be hard and painful work. It requires discipline. That is why we need a chapter on how to cultivate it.

The evidence that cultivating gratefulness is good for you is overwhelming. Gratitude is a quality that we should aspire to as part and parcel of personal growth. This wisdom derives not only from ancient philosophers and theologians but also from contemporary social science research. Analyses of the Hebrew scriptures, the New Testament, and the Koran have all exposed gratitude as central among the virtues they extol. Contemporary social science research has now ratified this ancient wisdom, concluding that gratitude stimulates a host of benefits. Specifically, we have shown that gratitude is positively related to such critical outcomes as life satisfaction, vitality, happiness, self-esteem, optimism, hope, empathy, and the willingness to provide emotional and tangible support for other people, whereas being ungrateful is related to anxiety, depression, envy, materialism, and loneliness. Collectively, such studies present credible evidence that feeling grateful generates a ripple effect through every area of our lives, potentially satisfying some of our deepest yearnings — our desire for happiness, our pursuit of better relationships, and our ceaseless quest for inner peace, wholeness, and contentment. Gratitude is more, though, than a tool for self-improvement. Gratitude is a way of life.

The emotion of gratitude, like most emotions, is difficult to conjure up at short notice. As we have discussed, the feeling, like other emotions, is a reaction to external events, and without those events it is almost impossible to recapture. The cause of an emotion is something external that triggers the feeling — an elicitor, or direct cause of the feeling state. There is a particular perception or construal of the elicitor that determines the subjective feeling and its corresponding intensity. Then there is a measurable, physiological response. The emotion should cause motivational and other changes to one's thinking. Finally, there is often an expressive component that allows one to communicate the emotion to others. Those are the characteristics of an emotion, which, by definition, is transitory in nature.

As a short-term, fleeting emotion, the feeling of gratitude cannot be acquired through willpower alone. You can't *try* to be grateful and then, through sheer will, automatically achieve it, any more than you can try to be happy and succeed. There is an old saying that "happiness pursued, eludes." You cannot obtain it through conscious striving. An internal focus on whether one is happy or trying to be happy appears doomed to fail. "Ask yourself whether you are happy," wrote John Stuart Mill in 1873, "and you cease to be so." The same holds for gratitude. If you ask yourself whether or not you are grateful, you are probably not. What I'm saying here is you can't mentally change your mood into gratitude instantaneously. So relax — the feeling cannot be achieved by snapping your fingers.

The benefits of gratitude come from the long-term cultivation of the disposition of gratefulness through dedicated practice. The disposition to experience gratitude, or gratefulness, is the tendency to feel gratitude frequently, in appropriate ways in appropriate circumstances. A person with the disposition to feel grateful has established a worldview that says, in effect, that all of life is a gift, gratuitously given. Although we cannot in any direct way be grateful, we can cultivate gratefulness by structuring our lives, our minds, and our words in such a way as to facilitate awareness of gratitude-inducing experiences and labeling them as such.

Psychologists suggest that change, whether circumscribed or more far-reaching, does not occur overnight, but in stages. According to the stages of change model developed by the clinical psychologist James Prochaska at the University of Rhode Island, behavior change does not happen in one step. Rather, people tend to progress through different stages on their way to successful change. Also, each of us progresses through the stages at our own rate. This model has been successfully applied to understanding how people change unhealthy physical habits such as smoking and drinking, but it readily generalizes to unhealthy psychological habits. If you are thinking about becoming more grateful (and if you have read to this point in the book, you likely are), then you are in what Prochaska calls the "contemplation phase" of change. Here you are thinking about the negative aspects of being ungrateful and the positive consequences of a more grateful outlook. You are open to receiving information about change. But you are not yet committed to actual change. My goal in this chapter is to provide you with some very concrete tools that will enable you to get to the next stage of change, the action stage.

In the action stage, people believe they have the ability to change their behavior and are actively involved in taking steps to modify their behavior by using a variety of different techniques. Mentally, they review their commitment to themselves and develop plans to deal with both personal and external pressures that may lead to slip-ups. They may use short-term rewards to sustain their motivation and may think about their change efforts in a way that enhances their self-confidence. People in this stage also tend to be open to receiving help and are also likely to seek support from others, itself a critical factor in maintaining positive changes.

STAYING GRATEFUL ALWAYS: THE TOP TEN

I identified in chapter 5 several obstacles or barriers to gratitude. As a counterpoint, here are ten evidence-based prescriptions for becoming more grateful. Because the obstacles are considerable and their influence in our lives pervasive, the consistent, disciplined practice of the following steps is necessary to consistently feel more gratefulness. It is therefore helpful to look at different techniques of developing and experiencing gratitude. By learning and understanding these approaches, you can begin to create your own experiences and practices that help you get in touch with the capability to open the door to appreciation for the gifts you are given. I present the ten in no particular order, although they do build upon and mutually reinforce each other.

1. Keep a Gratitude Journal

One of the best ways to cultivate gratitude is to establish a daily practice in which you remind yourself of the gifts, grace, benefits, and good things you enjoy. One of the best ways to do this is keeping a daily journal in which you record the blessings you are grateful for. My research has shown, as discussed in chapter 2, that this technique makes people happier. When we are grateful, we affirm that a source of goodness exists in our lives. By writing each day, we magnify and expand upon these sources of goodness. Setting aside time on a daily basis to recall moments of gratitude associated with even mundane or ordinary events, your personal attributes, or valued people in your life gives you the potential to interweave and thread together a sustainable life theme of gratefulness, just as it nourishes a fundamental life stance whose thrust is decidedly affirming.

So you begin by cataloging, each day, gratitude-inspiring events. It does not much matter whether you begin each day journaling or make your list the last thing you do at the end of the day. There is no one right way to do it. You don't need to buy a fancy personal journal to record your entries in, or worry about spelling or grammar. The important thing is to establish the daily habit of paying attention to gratitude-inspiring events; a daily regimen is what is required. The act of writing them down translates your thoughts into words. Psychological research has shown that translating thoughts into concrete language — words, whether oral or written — has advantages over just thinking the thoughts. Writing helps to organize thoughts and facilitate integration, and also helps you accept your own experiences and put them in context. In essence, it allows you to see the meaning of events going on around you and create meaning in your own life. Writing about unpleasant, even traumatic events is widely recommended by therapists. In the context of gratitude journaling, it may help you bring a new and redemptive frame of reference to a difficult life situation.

Your gratitude list must be periodically updated. It is important not to allow your catalog to become stale. On Day 1, a participant in one of our experiments wrote down the following three gratitudes: "My cat, my dog, my apartment." On Day 2, her list consisted of "My cat, my dog, my apartment." The third day: "My cat, my dog . . ." You get the idea. Neither in content nor in ordering did she once stray from these three sources of gratitude during the three weeks of the study. This process of repeating the same blessings each day indicates "gratitude fatigue." It is true that in the first few days of journaling the content might be a bit redundant. Overlap is fine, but literal repetition should be avoided. It may even produce the opposite effect from that intended. One can only imagine, after weeks of this repetitive process, the participant suddenly writing, "My life is so empty! All I have is my cat, my dog, and my apartment!"

When reflecting upon a benefit that another has provided for us, we should break it into multiple components, meditating on each element. This will be effective for two reasons. First, it will help us avoid gratitude fatigue. Second, this will engender a greater appreciation of the effort that was expended by the benefactor and of the multiple benefits that inhere in the one big "global" one — something that a more hurried and superficial acknowledgment of gratitude might overlook. For example, to simply say that I am grateful to my wife is less gratitude-inducing than for me to consciously and deliberately try to think about the countless hours of hard work in which she took care of our home and our boys so that I could complete this book on schedule (just to name one of the kind and considerate acts she has done for me).

It may be discouraging at first; sometimes your list will seem impoverished. Corroborating ancient wisdom, though, through research I have found that becoming aware of one's blessings actually leads to having more to be grateful about. As our perceptual focus becomes sharpened, we are more likely to notice blessings where before we saw curses. We start to no longer take things for granted. We begin to be grateful for the ability to feel gratitude. The spiral grows. The important thing is to get started wherever you are, even if the only item on your list is "nothing bad happened today." If you are currently at a −5 on a −10 to +10 ungrateful-to-grateful scale, it may be necessary to first move to a zero-point before you can begin to clearly see positive blessings and move to the plus side of the ledger.

When you identify in your daily journal those elements in your life for which you are grateful, the psychologist Charles Shelton recommends that you see these as "gifts." As you reflect on or contemplate an aspect of your life for which you are grateful, make the conscious effort to associate it with the word *gift*. Be aware of your feelings and how you relish and savor this gift in your imagination. Take the time to be especially aware of the depth of your gratitude. In other words, don't hurry through this exercise as if it were just another item on your to-do list.

2. Remember the Bad

For most people, life is generally perceived to be pleasant. Research has shown that memories of past events tend to be biased toward the positive. A recent study showed that over 90 percent of research participants listed more pleasant than unpleasant autobiographical memories. Despite this preference for the positive, there is no reason why the blessings that are listed in our daily gratitude inventories should be only pleasant. We need to remember the bad things as well. During one Thanksgiving sermon, the Reverend Peter Gomes encouraged his congregation at Harvard to "think of your worst moments, your sorrows, your losses, your sadness and then remember that here you are, able to remember them . . . you got through the worst day of your life . . . you got through the trauma, you got through the trial, you endured the temptation, you survived the bad relationship, you're making your way out of the dark . . . remember the bad things . . . then look to see where you are." When we remember how difficult life used to be and how far we have come, we set up an explicit contrast in our mind, and this contrast is fertile ground for gratefulness.

Why would remembering the worst that life offered be an effective strategy for cultivating gratitude? Because it capitalizes upon natural mental tools and normal human thought processes. For one, psychological research has established the empirical truth that "bad is stronger than good." Negative stimuli often evince powerful reactions that can be difficult to ignore or surmount. The adversities of life, seasoned with strong emotions, are deeply etched in our memories and for this reason are easy to recall. Yet a competing tendency is that the feelings associated with unpleasant events tend to fade faster than the feelings associated with pleasant events. We yearn to reconcile with our ex-spouse because the memories of stormy encounters and icy contempt have faded. Therefore, to be grateful in our current union, it is helpful to remember just how awful a previous marriage was. Second, our minds think in terms of counterfactuals — mental comparisons we make between the way things are and how things might have been different. At times these counterfactuals may be counterproductive to our mental well-being, as we lament opportunities lost or regrets over what might have been. But we can harness the power of counterfactual thinking by reminding ourselves of how much worse life might be than it is.

3. Ask Yourself Three Questions

In working on a daily moral inventory, you might find it effective to incorporate aspects of a Buddhist meditation technique known as *Naikan*. Naikan was developed by Yoshimoto Ishina, a self-made millionaire and devout Buddhist from Japan. He developed the method as a way of helping others look inside (the word *Naikan* means "looking inside"), become introspective, and "see oneself with the mind's eye." The practice involves reflecting on three questions:

What have I received from _____?
What have I given to _____?
What troubles and difficulty have I caused _____?

These questions can help us address issues or relationships. It helps us to see the reciprocal quality of relationships and provides a structure for self-reflection. This can be directed toward work situations, social interactions, or toward developing higher aspects of oneself.

The first step or question involves recognizing all the gifts we receive. Remembering a person's smile, kind words, or helpful actions can elicit feelings of gratitude. When we focus on the good that comes to us every day, we can be filled with deep appreciation rather than drowning under the burden of our problems. Once when I traveled, I reflected on how many people were responsible for helping me get from Point A to Point B. Having arrived at my hotel room, I was shocked by the sheer number who were involved (the shuttle bus driver, ticket agent, baggage handler, security screener, pilots and flight attendants, rental car agent, and hotel desk clerk, among others; I'm sure I left some out). Focusing on what these people are giving has reduced the stress of travel for me far more than any other factor.

Next we focus on what we give to others. This helps us realize how connected we are to others and helps remove a sense of entitlement that might come from feeling that we are due things from others without a need to give back. Ask yourself the question: In what ways might I "give back" to others as an appropriate response for the gratitude I feel? Be creative in finding ways to give back for the many blessings you have received. At the very least, I owe and I express a heartfelt thank-you for all those people in the previous example.

The last step is a difficult one of acknowledging not the things that bother us, but how we cause pain in the lives of others by our thoughts, words, and deeds. The author Greg Krech, who wrote on the practice of Naikan, says of this step, "If we are not willing to see and accept those events in which we have been the source of others' suffering, then we cannot truly know ourselves or the grace by which we live."

This practice of asking the three questions can be practiced daily for twenty minutes or so in the evening. It can be used to reflect on the day's activities in a general way. Another method is to reflect on a specific relationship over a period of fifty to sixty minutes. One can view a relationship chronologically or focus on a particular situation that might need attention. Regardless of the relationships under meditation, the process of Naikan emphasizes two themes: (1) the discovery of personal guilt for having been ungrateful toward people in the past and (2) the discovery of feelings of positive gratitude toward those persons who have extended themselves on behalf of the person in the past or present.

A more intensive practice of Naikan can take place at one of several retreat centers in the United States. This usually takes place over the course of a week or so and does not include making lists or writings one's reflections, but sitting in meditation and looking at a blank screen on which to replay the story of one's life. Participants spend most of the day reflecting on their relationship with significant persons in their lives, especially parents. These retreats produce profound experiences for the serious and sincere meditator.

4. Learn Prayers of Gratitude

Surveys have revealed that people spend more time praying than doing just about anything else. Survey research has revealed that 72 percent of people asked say that they pray at least once a day; 75 percent of people say they would like to spend more time in prayer, and over half (51 percent) say they pray before a meal. Most of the prayers are casually conversational rather than liturgically formal.

Prayer is at the front and center of the spiritual life. It has been referred to as "the soul and essence of religion" and "the most spontaneous and personal expression of intimacy with the divine." Prayers of gratitude are among the most common form of prayer, and religious scriptures of various traditions are replete with prayers of this type. Even college students, who are not generally regarded as a particularly prayerful group, pray prayers of thanksgiving more frequently than any other type of prayer (except for petitionary requests).

Praying for gratitude is strongly sanctioned in religious scriptures. The Hebrew Bible is replete with the motif that man owes God gratitude for life, health, and sustenance. There are numerous "thanksgiving" psalms and other prayers in which the person or the community that is praying pours forth expressions of gratitude. The message is clear: Be thankful. Accept the gifts you have been given. Don't forget God. Liturgies and rituals are built to help believers remember. For example, in the liturgy of the Lutheran Church, once the offering and the Communion bread and wine are brought forward to the altar, the minister enunciates what the *Lutheran Book of Worship* calls the *Great Thanksgiving*:

> Minister: The Lord be with you.
> Congregation: And also with you.
> Minister: Lift up your hearts.
> Congregation: We lift them to the Lord.
> Minister: Let us give thanks to the Lord our God.
> Congregation: It is right to give him thanks and praise.

Or you may prefer a significantly different, less ritualized version, this one by the famed *Prairie Home Companion* Lutheran, Garrison Keillor:

> Thank you, Lord, for giving me the wherewithal not to fix a half-pound cheeseburger right now and to eat a stalk of celery instead. Thank you for the wonderful son and the amazing daughter and the smart sexy wife and the grandkids . . . Thank you for the odd delight of being sixty, part of which is the sheer relief of not being fifty. I could go on and on. . . . List your blessings and you will walk through those gates of thanksgiving and into the fields of joy.

Although gratitude is most at home in monotheistic traditions, there is not a religion on earth that believes that thanksgiving is unimportant. It is universally endorsed. In many spiritual traditions, prayers of gratitude are considered to be the most powerful form of prayer, because through these prayers people recognize the ultimate source of all they are and all they will ever be. One of my favorites is the following Native American prayer:

> We thank Great Spirit for the resources that made this food
>   possible;
> we thank the Earth Mother for producing it,
> and we thank all those who labored to bring it to us.
> May the Wholesomeness of the food before us,
> bring out the Wholeness of the Spirit within us.

The noted Buddhist teacher Thich Nhat Hanh is a prolific author and developer of a movement known as "engaged Buddhism," which intertwines traditional meditative practices with active nonviolent civil disobedience. Once nominated by Martin Luther King Jr. for the Nobel Peace Prize, Thich Nhat Hanh is considered to be one of the most revered teachers of Buddhism in the West, second only to the Dalai Lama. He has the following morning prayer that is undemanding and can be practiced by those of any faith or the faithless:

> Waking up this morning, I see the blue sky.
> I join my hands in thanks
> for the many wonders of life;
> for having twenty-four brand-new hours before me.

If you find that because of circumstances you cannot pray from gratitude, then I would suggest praying for the ability to be grateful. We can pray to experience the feeling of gratitude, to find gratitude hidden within our circumstances, and to be reminded of our gifts.

In addition to praying prayers of thanksgiving, gratitude and prayer connect in other ways. A serendipitous finding from one of our experimental studies on gratitude was that progress in achieving a goal was facilitated when participants prayed about their desired outcome. At the beginning of the gratitude journaling study, we asked participants to provide a short list of goals they wished to accomplish over the next two months. As these were students, most goals fell into the interpersonal or academic domains. The interesting finding was that prayer was correlated with perceived goal success, but only for students who were keeping gratitude journals. For students in the hassles and control groups, prayer was unrelated to goal outcomes. This suggests a synergistic effect, where prayer seems to matter more in the context of heightened gratitude. Students who prayed about their goals also actually took more active steps toward reaching them (breaking them down into subgoals, recruiting social support, shielding them from competing activities), perhaps because of an energy boost they received from the gratitude exercise. The upshot of this is that petitionary prayers "work" better if people also practice gratitude.

5. Come to Your Senses

Good health; being alive; no more skin allergies; I'm not fat; white teeth; exercise; eyes; ears; touch; physical strength; afternoon nap; ability to breathe; modern medicine, energy to get through the day; no broken bones. Each of these bodily-related blessings appeared in journals that my research participants have kept. The physicality of gratitude is noticeable as gratefulness for the functioning of one's body, recovery from illness, or for just being alive are some of the most commonly mentioned themes. Nearly 80 percent of our research participants say they are grateful for their health, or the health of family members, making it *the* most cited trigger of gratitude. Another frequently mentioned source of gratitude is the senses — the ability to touch, see, smell, taste, and hear. In her remarkable book *The Natural History of the Senses,* the author Diane Ackerman wrote that "nothing is more memorable than a smell." Smells transport us back to earlier times, perhaps to childhood vacations, or adolescent romances, or family holiday traditions that we now look back on with nostalgic gratitude. I can still remember the intoxicating smell of Christmas trees in our living room when I was a child. In fact, I'd begun ordering balsam pine trees from the East Coast for our California home in an attempt to recover that smell. When the shipping costs began to exceed the price of the tree, our family rediscovered the joys of the annual pilgrimage to the local tree lots.

Through our senses, we gain an appreciation of what it means to be human, of what an incredible miracle it is to be alive. Could there be a more fitting response than that of joyous gratitude? For millennia, poets, philosophers, and physicians have praised the miraculous and beautiful nature of the body. Seen through the lens of gratitude, however, the body is more than a miraculous construction. It is a gift, freely and gratuitously given, whether one perceives the giver to be God, evolution, or good family genes. Even though some bodily parts may not function as reliably as they once did, if you can breathe, there is cause for gratitude.

Speaking of breathing, Dr. Frederic Luskin suggests in his popular book, *Forgive For Good,* the following exercise, which he calls the "Breath of Thanks":

1. Two or three times every day when you are not fully occupied, slow down and bring your attention to your breathing.
2. Notice how your breath flows in and out without your having to do anything . . . continue breathing this way.
3. For each of the next five to eight exhalations, say the words "thank you" silently to remind yourself of the gift of your breath and how lucky you are to be alive. He suggests practicing this at least three times per week.

It is a good reminder that gratitude begins with the basics. Breathing gratitude is a practice that is available to all of us, regardless of our current life circumstances.

6. Use Visual Reminders

Enter our home and one of the first things you will see is a ceramic plaque above the hallway mirror with the words GIVE THANKS carved in the center. Help yourself to a drink from the refrigerator and you might see a magnet on the door quoting Eleanor Roosevelt: "Yesterday is history, tomorrow is mystery . . . today is a gift." Now go over to the family room and look at the bookcase to the right of the windows. On one shelf is a pewter paperweight given to me by a close friend containing a passage from the author Melody Beattie: "Gratitude can turn a meal into a feast, a house into a home, a stranger into a friend." Around Thanksgiving season, our home becomes one big gratitude shrine.

Recall that two of the primary obstacles to being grateful are (1) forgetfulness and (2) a lack of mindful awareness. Forgetfulness. That human tendency. We forget our benefactors, we forget to take time to count our blessings, and we forget the many ways in which our lives are made easier because of the efforts of others. Awareness is a precondition for gratitude: we must have *noticed* whatever we are to be thankful for — we cannot be thankful for something of which we are unaware. Therefore, we need to remind ourselves and to become aware. There is no shortage of suggestions available for how to incorporate daily rituals and practices with the goal of reminding ourselves to be grateful. Articles with titles such as "27 Ways to Live a Spiritual Life Every Day," "30 Ways in 30 Days," and "100 Blessings a Day" regularly appear in popular magazines. I like visual reminders that serve as cues to trigger thoughts of gratitude. Some people, such as my wife and I, attach Post-it notes listing blessings to their refrigerators, mirrors, steering wheels, or other noticeable locations. Others set their pagers, beepers, or Personal Digital Assistants (PDAs) to signal them at random times throughout the day. When they are signaled, they pause and count their blessings on the spot. They might even record them on their PDAs as a high-tech form of journaling. A trial lawyer whom I read about found that his shower each morning evokes thankfulness, for he had spent considerable time in remote areas where hot water was an unthinkable gift.

The best visual reminders might be other people. You may have engaged in some self-improvement program only to have abandoned it after a short time. Exercise programs have notoriously high drop-out rates. Most Americans fail to engage in regular physical activity. One of the primary reasons why people don't exercise is that they lack someone to exercise with. Social support encourages healthy behaviors. One study found that participants recruited alone for a weight-loss program had a 76 percent completion rate and 24 percent maintained their weight loss, whereas those recruited with friends boasted a 95 percent completion rate and 66 percent maintained their weight loss in full for six months.

I know of people who have accountability partners to remind them to be grateful. Accountability partners and accountability groups were brought to the public's attention when former President Clinton organized a group of pastors to aid in his redemption following his Oval Office indiscretions. Accountability partners make us, well, accountable. We become answerable to a trusted inner circle or partner who will challenge us when we begin to stray off the moral path. Just as it is easier to maintain the discipline of physical exercise when you have a partner, maintaining the discipline of gratefulness also benefits from a partner with whom you can swap gratitude lists and who will challenge your ungrateful thoughts. You can talk with others about what you are learning about gratitude and the difference that it makes in your life. Your partner may be able to help you find hidden blessings in your life, identify barriers to your gratitude, or help you give thanks for aspects of your life that may be particularly challenging. Perhaps even more important, a partner can challenge our ungrateful attitudes toward life when we need that prompting. Those of you already in accountability groups (whether you call them that or not) might use part of the group time for gratitude.

It stands to reason that an accountability partner would be effective in kindling our sense of gratitude. Gratitude is, after all, a social emotion that is activated in relational contexts. You might find yourself developing a deep sense of gratefulness toward your accountability partner that then generalizes to others in your social sphere.

Internal strategies are good but are not enough. We live in social contexts, and other people can facilitate or hinder our desire to become more grateful. You might consider hanging out with grateful people and commit to spending less time with people who themselves lack this virtue. You may already do this, since ungrateful people, like chronic depressives, tend to be shunned. A well-established social psychological law is the law of emotional contagion: an emotion expressed within a group has a ripple effect and becomes shared by the group's members. People are susceptible to "catching" other people's emotions. Examples readily abound. When my son was 4 he became easily distressed when one of his nursery school classmates was upset; similarly, he laughed at movies he didn't even understand if his older brother was amused. Therapists find treating depressed persons a drain because it makes them feel depressed. We find a movie funnier when the people around us in the theater are laughing, and find it sadder if they are crying. There is evidence that children catch their parents' emotions as well as evidence that parents catch their children's emotions.

If we hang out with ungrateful people, we will "catch" one set of emotions; if we choose to associate with more grateful individuals, the influence will be in another direction. Find a grateful person and spend more time with him or her. When you yourself express buoyant gratitude, you will find that people will want to "catch" your emotions.

7. Make a Vow to Practice Gratitude

In *Harry Potter and the Half-Blood Prince,* Severus Snape makes an unbreakable vow with the dark witch Narcissa Malfoy to kill Professor Dumbledore. Does he succeed? In case some of you have not yet reached Book 6 in the Harry Potter series (unfathomable as that might be), I'll not spoil your reading. There is some research, though, which shows that swearing a vow to perform a behavior actually does increase the likelihood that the action will be executed. In one such study, members of a local YMCA who decided to participate in the Twelve-Week Personal Fitness Program agreed to "exercise three days per week for twelve weeks and beyond at the Y." Once making the decision to participate, the experimental group was sworn to perform the promised behavior. A second group signed a written commitment to perform the promised behavior, and a third, control group, did not make any form of commitment. The impact of the manipulation was examined for its effect on adherence to the program. Subjects in the vow condition did demonstrate greater adherence than the other conditions as measured by consecutive weeks of three exercise sessions without relapse. The effect of breaking the vow in this case was assuredly less dire than it would have been for Severus Snape; nevertheless, it appeared to increase motivation above and beyond even a written contract to engage in the same behavior.

Why is swearing an oath an effective motivator of behavior? For one, a vow, when made before others, constitutes a public pronouncement of an intention to perform an action. Breaking a vow thereby becomes a profound moral failure (as dissolution of a marriage is for those who taking wedding vows seriously). Fear of sanctions, either internal (in the form of guilt) or external (in the form of social disapproval) is a powerful motivator. For those spiritually inclined, making a vow to God is serious business. If we made a vow to others and they forgot about it, we'd be off the hook. But God's hook is deeper. God does not forget. A vow to God carries greater moral weight and authority than a vow to a mere human. The Hebrew Bible states, "If you make a vow to the LORD your God, do not be slow to pay it, for the LORD your God will certainly demand it of you and you will be guilty of sin . . . whatever your lips utter you must be sure to do." When a teenager, for example, makes a "Vow of Purity" pledge before God and witnesses to remain pure and chaste until marriage, the vow has a tighter hold on behavior than one without a divine promise. In the mind of the pledge maker, breaking a divine vow would bring severe punishment, whereas performing the behavior would bring ultimate rewards. But God's role goes beyond that of moral enforcer. When we make a vow to God, we, in effect, bring God along as a powerful ally to help us summon the energy to keep our promises.

What might a vow to practice gratitude look like? It need not be elaborate. It could be something as simple as "I vow to not take so many things in my life for granted. I vow to pause and count my blessings at least once each day. I vow to express gratitude to someone who has been influential in my life and whom I've never properly thanked." If your vow is formalized, post it somewhere conspicuous where you will be frequently reminded of it. Better yet, share it with your accountability partner.

8. Watch Your Language

In the late 1930s, the amateur linguist Benjamin Lee Whorf posed the theory that language determines the nature and content of thought. This "Whorfian" hypothesis inspired decades of research in a variety of disciplines, including linguistics, psychology, philosophy, anthropology, and education. To this day, it has not been completely disputed or defended but has continued to intrigue researchers around the world. Many have adopted a weaker form of the hypothesis, namely that language *influences* how we think rather than *determining*, in a rigid fashion, the very content of the thoughts.

I introduce the Whorfian theory here because of its relevance for thinking about how to stimulate more grateful living. The way we describe events in our lives, and ultimately, life itself, is a direct window on how we perceive and interpret life. This theory says that the language we use influences how we think about the world. Carried further, the Whorfian view is that the words we use create reality. Compare grateful discourse with ungrateful discourse. Grateful people have a particular linguistic style. They tend to use the language of gifts, givers, blessings, blessed, fortune, fortunate, abundance. They traffic in the discourse of thankfulness. Ungrateful people, on the other hand, tend to focus on deprivation, deservingness, regrets, lack, need, scarcity, loss. In one study, sixty-two females, aged 40 to 100, were interviewed in a semistructured conversational format to elicit open self-descriptions. Overall, the terms that most women used to describe themselves were "fortunate" and "blessed." One of the poorest women in the study, scraping by with an income far below the poverty level, said, "I know I'm poor. But I thank the Lord in a way. He ain't gonna let his children starve. Even if it ain't nothing but milk and bread, I'll eat . . . I don't consider myself poor, but I consider myself . . . blessed." The ability to see oneself as fortunate may be a significant component of successful aging, and, as we learned from the famous nun study I described in chapter 3, may be even be associated with longevity.

Cognitive therapists observe that depressed persons walk around chronically engaged in negative self-talk ("Nobody likes me," "I'll never find a partner," "I'm such a loser," and so on). "We are what we think about all day long," said Ralph Waldo Emerson. The talk becomes so automatic that we don't even realize that we are doing it or realize the pervasive effect it is having. We can change our mood by changing what we say to ourselves. The goal of cognitive therapy is to shake up these internal monologues and to replace the negative, dysfunctional thoughts with more positive, functional ones.

What would be grateful counterparts to the self-defeating talk of depressives? I don't have in mind here a new-age "I love myself" mantra spoken in front of the mirror to oneself (in a *New Yorker* cartoon a mother answers her little boy's query, "Why are you special? Because I'm your Mommy, and I'm special"). In gratitude, we are not focusing on how inherently good or special *we* are, but rather on the inherently good or special things that *others* have done on our behalf. We might say to ourselves, "I have so much in life to be thankful for," "I am truly blessed," "Everyday is a surprise," or "My life is a gift." Seemingly flying in the face of much pop psychology advice, gratitude self-talk that draws our attention to the positive contributions that others have made to our lives will simultaneously favorably impact our emotional well-being while strengthening our social bonds.

9. Go Through the Motions

An ingenious series of experiments conducted a number of years ago showed that when people mimicked the facial expressions associated with happiness, they felt happier — even when they did not know they were moving the "happy muscles" in their face. Researchers have found that smiling itself produces feelings of happiness. How were they kept in the dark? Simple. They were asked to hold a pencil with their teeth. Doing so tends to activate the muscle we use when we smile (the zygomatic major). This muscle lifts the corner of the mouth obliquely upwards and laterally and produces a characteristic smiling expression. Try it now. You will smile. Now, take that pencil and hold it in your lips, pointing it straight out. A different set of muscles are now activated, those that are involved in frowning (these are the ones targeted by Botox treatments). Why this clever ruse? You can't let subjects in the study know that they are supposed to be feeling happy, because that would have unintended consequences on the behavioral rating of interest.

It turned out that the people with the pencils in their teeth, who were, unbeknownst to them, activating their zygomatic muscles, rated cartoons funnier than those who held the pencils with their lips. It appears that going through the motions can trigger the emotion. Technically stated, involuntary facial movements provide sufficient peripheral information to drive emotional experience.

The relevance for practicing gratitude is direct. If we go through grateful motions, the emotion of gratitude should be triggered. What is a grateful motion? Saying thank you. Writing letters of gratitude. Isn't this the way we socialize our children to become grateful members of a civic society? Expressing gratitude toward someone whom you've never properly taken the time to thank can have profoundly positive consequences, for both the person expressing and the recipient. Research I described in chapter 2 indicated that the positive glow resulting from sharing a gratitude letter can last for several months.

So what if the motion has to be forced? The important thing is to do it. Do it now, and the feeling will come. There is a great deal of psychological evidence showing that attitude change often follows behavior change. Good intentions are often crushed by old habits. If we stand around waiting for a feeling to move us, we may never get going. Get a person to perform a behavior, and, with some exceptions, their feelings will fall in line. Get people to attend church, and pretty soon they will start believing in what they are hearing. Get people to volunteer in soup kitchens, and they will become more generous. Effective churches plug people in right away. Effective managers know that successful training focuses on changing behavior first. Marriage therapists tell spouses who have lost the love to pretend that they like each other. In each case, going through the motions can trigger the desired emotions, setting the stage for emotions to reinforce the behavior.

10. Think Outside the Box

If we want to make the most out of opportunities to flex our gratitude muscles, then we must creatively look for new situations and circumstances in which to feel grateful. Just when I thought I had fully grasped the conceptual basis of gratitude, an article came across my desk describing two "anomalous cases" of gratitude not fitting the usual dynamic of the giving and receiving of goodness between benefactor and beneficiary.

The first case is being grateful to those who do you harm. In other words, being grateful to our enemies. What a preposterous notion this seems to be. Because of our natural inclination to either defend or retaliate (the "flight or fight" response), this is a very difficult notion for most of us to comprehend. Yet this is a common ideal within Buddhism. The Dalai Lama often repeats this Buddhist teaching by telling his audiences that he is grateful to the Chinese for giving him the opportunity to practice love for his enemies. If love is too much to swallow, then be grateful that our enemies give us opportunities to practice patience. Similar examples can be found in other spiritual traditions. The Sufi poet Rumi writes about a priest who prays for his muggers "because they have done me generous favors. Every time I turn back toward the things they want I run into them. They beat me and leave me in the road, and I understand again that what they want is not what I want. Those that make you return to the spirit . . . be grateful to them." Gratitude to those who harm us is a highly advanced form of gratitude that most of us are not easily capable of.

You may be able to more readily identify with the second anomalous case of gratitude. It is being grateful to someone whom *you* benefit. Individuals who perform volunteer work sometimes speak of the benefits they receive from their service and express gratitude for those who gave them the opportunity to serve. Mother Teresa often spoke of being grateful for the sick and dying she ministered to in the Calcutta slums, because they enabled her to deepen her compassion. The psychologists Ann Colby and William Damon studied "moral exemplars" — people who made extraordinary moral commitments to the social organizations where they volunteered or worked.

One quality that these moral exemplars had in common was a strong positive attitude — they took joy in their lives and were determined to make the best of whatever happened. Notably, they expressed this positivity as a deep gratitude for the satisfaction they got from their work, and especially, from helping others. Since service to others helped them to find their own inner spirituality, they were grateful for the opportunity to serve. These exemplars have a profound sense of themselves being gifted. Purposeful actions then flow from this sense of giftedness so that they can share and increase the very good they have received. We are reminded that gratitude is incomplete until it is manifested in outward action. We have to, as the psychologist Charles Shelton so fittingly describes, "give back the goodness."

SOME FINAL THOUGHTS

A few years ago, I cowrote a small, inspirational book on gratitude. Shortly after it was published, I received an e-mail from my coauthor that was originally sent to her by a 78-year-old man who had read the book. He testified that it had completely changed his life — his relationship with his wife, his children, and his grandchildren, the way he thought about himself, the world, everything. That is a pretty radical statement to make, especially for a man nearing the ninth decade of his life. I recall thinking at the time, "This is why I do what I do." For people like him — people who avail themselves of the transformational power of gratitude. Gratitude is a new way of seeing. For him, it was a novel way of seeing. It is a stance, a posture, a way of positioning oneself so that one is attuned to the gifts that come one's way. For some, such as this man, it can be a profound change in how we observe and experience the world. He proved that it is never too late to start reaping the benefits of grateful living. And by the way, he ordered twelve more copies of the book for his children and grandchildren.

For better or for worse, we research psychologists are what we study. When I was an undergraduate psychology major, I was fascinated by the relationship between the researcher and the researched. Why did people choose to study the topics they did? By the time I got to graduate school, I thought I had it all figured out. People generally studied what they were lacking or deficient in. Introverts studied extroversion, shy people researched assertiveness, vengeful people yearned to learn about forgiveness, absent-minded professors explored the particulars of human memory.

Nowadays, I prefer to think of this "deprivation theory" more as a "concordant self-perfection" model. We yearn to become more of what we already are. We are works in progress. Gratitude, from this angle, is not a day, or an event, or a moment. It is a process, a journey. When I contemplate why I have chosen to study gratitude, I am reminded that a famous writer once said that authors don't choose their topic, their topic chooses them. I feel compelled to study gratitude, to learn as much about it as I can, and to share what I have learned with as many people as possible. I've confessed that the practice of gratitude is hard and does not come naturally to me. The dividends, though, are well worth the struggle. I'd always been someone who struggled with attitudes of deservingness and entitlement. I did not want to give credit to others for whatever I had been able to accomplish. It was difficult for me to experience peace and contentment. Gradually, I've come to experience the freedom of gratitude. By appreciating the gifts of the moment, gratitude frees us from past regrets and future anxieties. By cultivating gratefulness, we are freed from envy over what we don't have or who we are not. It doesn't make life perfect, but with gratitude comes the realization that right now, in this moment, we have enough, we are enough.

It's highly unlikely that I will ever find again a topic as satisfying and inspiring to devote my research energy to. For the opportunity to learn about gratitude and inform others of my findings in the hope that this knowledge will produce for them the best life they are capable of, I am deeply grateful.

NOTES

1. The New Science of Gratitude

PAGE

1 "*I cannot tell you anything*": Stein, Ben (2005). "American Gratitude," *The American Enterprise*, 18–21.

2 "*gratitude is the most pleasant*": Comte-Sponville, Andre (1996). "Politeness," in *A Small Treatise on the Great Virtues*. New York: Metropolitan Books/Henry Holt and Company.

4 "*The quality or condition*": "Gratitude," in *The Oxford English Dictionary* (2nd ed.). New York: Oxford University Press.

5 "*Denken ist Danken*": Heidegger, Martin (1968). *What Is Called Thinking?* New York, Evanston, and London: Harper & Row.
The French expression": Steindl-Rast, David (2004). "Gratitude as Thankfulness and as Gratefulness," in *The Psychology of Gratitude*, ed. Emmons, R., & McCullough, M. New York: Oxford University Press, pp. 282–89.

6 "*gratitude is the heart's*": Edel, Abraham (1961). "Science and the Structure of Ethics," in *International Encyclopedia of Unified Science. Foundations of the Unity of Science* 2(3). Chicago: University of Chicago Press.
"*the delightful emotion*": Brown, Thomas (1820). *Lectures on the Philosophy of the Human Mind*. Edinburgh: Tait.

7 "*Yet I have found*": Bartlett, Elizabeth Ann (1997). *Journey of the Heart: Spiritual Insights on the Road to a Transplant*. Duluth, MN: Pfeifer-Hamilton.
"*the willingness to recognize*": Bertocci, Peter Anthony (1963).*Personal-*

ity and the Good: Psychological and Ethical Perspectives. New York: David McKay Co.

Perceive grace and you will: Peck, M. Scott (1995). *In Search of Stones: A Pilgrimage of Faith, Reason, and Discovery.* New York: Hyperion.

8 *"Dear God, we paid":* Lobdell, William (2001). "D'oh God! 'The Simpsons' and Spirituality," in *The Simpsons Archive.* Retrieved on January 25, 2006, from http://www.snpp.com/other/articles/dohgod .html.

9 *"if every grateful action . . .":* Simmel, Georg (1950). *The Sociology of Georg Simmel.* Glencoe, IL: Free Press.

11 *Our experimental research:* Emmons, R. A., & McCullough, M. E. (2003). "Counting Blessings versus Burdens: An Experimental Investigation of Gratitude and Subjective Well-Being in Daily Life," *Journal of Personality and Social Psychology* 84: 377–89.

12 *happiness yields numerous rewards:* King, Laura, & Lyubomirsky, Sonja (2005). "The Benefits of Frequent Positive Affect: Does Happiness Lead to Success?" *Psychological Bulletin* 131: 803–55.

14 *Gratitude is a "hypocognized":* Solomon, Robert C. (2004). Foreword, in *The Psychology of Gratitude,* ed. Emmons, R., & McCullough, M. New York: Oxford University Press: pp. v–xi.

15 *American men were less likely:* Kosmitzki, Corinne, & Sommers, Shula (1988). "Emotion and Social Context: An American-German Comparison," *British Journal of Social Psychology* 27: 35–49.

"In ordinary life we hardly": Bonhoeffer, Dietrich (1966). *The Way to Freedom.* New York: Harper & Row.

16 *"Of all the crimes":* Harpham, Edward J. (2004). "Gratitude in the History of Ideas," in *The Psychology of Gratitude,* ed. Emmons, R., & McCullough, M. New York: Oxford University Press, pp. 19–36.

gratitude "is the meanest": Dorothy Parker, quoted in Gomes, Peter J. (2003). *Strength for the Journey: Biblical Wisdom for Daily Living.* New York: HarperSanFrancisco.

"When I saw the Christmas": Gomes, Peter J. (2003). *Strength for the Journey: Biblical Wisdom for Daily Living.* New York: HarperSanFrancisco.

17 *"Once we have been liberated":* Ibid.

18 *"Gratitude as a discipline":* Nouwen, Henri J. M. (1992). *The Return of the Prodigal Son.* New York: Doubleday Publishing Group.

"I must exert myself": Einstein, Albert (1931). "The World As I See

It." Retrieved February 1, 2006, from http://aip.org/history/einstein/essay.htm.

2. GRATITUDE AND THE PSYCHE

19 *Commentators on the life of Chesterton*: Alhquist, D. (2003). *G. K. Chesterton: The Apostle of Common Sense*. San Francisco: Ignatius Press. Schall, J. V. (2000). *Schall on Chesterton: Timely Essays on Timeless Paradoxes*. Washington, DC: Catholic University of America Press.

20 *I like the Cyclostyle ink*: Fagerberg, D. W. (2000). "The Essential Chesterton," *First Things* 10: 23–26.

21 "*The test of all happiness*": Ibid., p. 25.
    "*[Gratitude] is the doctrine*": Harp, R. L. (1991). "Orthodox Wonder," *The Chesterton Review* 17: 33–45.

22 *majority of U.S. respondents*: Freedman, Jonathan (1978). *Happy People: What Happiness Is, Who Has It, and Why*. New York: Harcourt Brace Jovanovich.
    each person has a chronic: Fugita, Frank, & Diener, Ed (2005). "Life Satisfaction Set Point: Stability and Change," *Journal of Personality and Social Psychology* 88: 158–64.

23 *lottery winners were less happy*: Brickman, P., Coates, D., & Janoff-Bulman, R. (1978). "Lottery Winners and Accident Victims: Is Happiness Relative?" *Journal of Personality and Social Psychology* 36: 917–27.

24 *faithfully engaging in a new*: Babyak, M., Baldewicz, T. T., Blumenthal, J. A., Herman, S., Craighead, W. E., Doraiswamy, M., Khatri, P., Krishnan, K. R., & Moore, K., (2000). "Exercise Treatment for Major Depression: Maintenance of Therapeutic Benefit at 10 Months," *Psychosomatic Medicine* 62: 633–38.

26 "*the greatest thing is to give thanks*": Schweitzer, A. (1969). *Reverence for Life*, trans. R. H. Fuller. New York: Harper & Row.
    "*Whatever we are waiting for*": Breathnach, Sarah Ban (1996). *The Simple Abundance: Journal of Gratitude*. New York: Time Warner Company.
    Enlarge your vision: Osteen, Joel (2004). *Your Best Life Now: 7 Steps to Living at Your Full Potential*. New York: Warner Faith.
    "*Reflect upon your present blessings*": Dickens, Charles (1835). "A Christmas Dinner." Retrieved February 1, 2006, from http://www.fidnet.com/~dap1955/dickens/a_christmas_dinner.html.

27   *the impact of a gratitude intervention*: Emmons, R. A., & McCullough, M. E. (2003). "Counting Blessings versus Burdens: An Experimental Investigation of Gratitude and Subjective Well-Being in Daily Life," *Journal of Personality and Social Psychology* 84: 377–89.

35   *viewing good things as gifts*: Watkins, P. C. (2004). "Gratitude and Subjective Well-Being,", in *The Psychology of Gratitude*, ed. Emmons, R., and McCullough, M. New York: Oxford University Press, pp. 167–92.
      "Life is the first gift": Piercy, Marge (2006). "Listening with Understanding and Empathy." Retrieved February 1, 2006, from http://www.habits-of-mind.net/listening.htm.

36   *"All goods look better"*: Chesterton, Gilbert Keith (1954). *St. Francis of Assisi*. Garden City, NY: Doubleday & Co.

38   *if the receiver thinks the giver*: Bartlett, M., & DeSteno, D. (2006). "Gratitude and Prosocial Behavior: Helping When It Costs You," *Psychological Science* 17: 319–25.
      clinically depressed individuals: Grimm, D. L., Kolts, R., & Watkins, P. C. (2004). "Counting Your Blessings: Positive Memories Among Grateful Persons," *Current Psychology: Developmental, Learning, Personality, Social* 23: 52–67.

41   *depressed individuals engage in self-focus*: Ingram, Rick (1990). "Self-Focused Attention in Clinical Disorders: Review and a Conceptual Model," *Psychological Bulletin* 107(2): 156–76.
      participants who had something good: Atchley, Leslie (2005). "Don't worry; be . . . grateful?" Retrieved June 13, 2005, from http://aands.virginia.edu/x5325.xml.

42   *upward social comparisons* : Smith, Richard (2000). "Assimilative and Contrastive Emotional Reactions to Upward and Downward Social Comparisons," in *Handbook of Social Comparison: Theory and Research*. Amsterdam, Netherlands: Kluwer Academic Publishers, p. 28.

43   *men who viewed photographs*: Goldberg, L. L., Gutierres, S. E., & Kenrick, D. T. (1989). "Influence of Popular Erotica on Judgments of Strangers and Mates," *Journal of Experimental Social Psychology* 25(2): 159–67.
      "From my childhood": Dickens, Charles (1977). *Bleak House*. New York: Norton.

44   *"age of loneliness"*: Bernston, G. G., Cacioppo, J. T., & Hawkley, L. C. (2003). "The Anatomy of Loneliness," *Current Directions in Psychological Science* 12(3): 71–74.

45   *positive emotions . . . build enduring*: Fredrickson, Barbara (2001). "The

Role of Positive Emotions in Positive Psychology: The Broaden-and-Build Theory of Positive Emotions," *American Psychologist* 56: 218–26.

optimal mental health is associated: Fredrickson, Barbara (2005). "Positive Affect and the Complex Dynamics of Human Flourishing," *American Psychologist* 60(7): 678–86.

46 *[Gottman] can predict with 90 percent*: Gottman, John M. (1999). *The Seven Principles for Making Marriage Work*. New York: Crown Publishers.

"*When couples struggle*": Hochschild, Arlie Russell (1989). *The Second Shift: Working Parents and the Revolution at Home*. New York: Viking.

48 "*the things for which they are grateful*": Lyubomirsky, S., Sheldon, K. M., & Schkade, D. (2005). "Pursuing Happiness: The Architecture of Sustainable Change," *Review of General Psychology. Special Issue: Positive Psychology* 9(2): 111–31.

49 *the importance of expressing gratitude*: Maslow, Abraham (1979). *The Journals of A. H. Maslow. The A. H. Maslow series*. Monterey, CA: Brooks/Cole Pub. Co.

Seligman and his colleagues: Park, N., Peterson, C., Seligman, M. E. P., & Steen, T. A. (2005). "Positive Psychology Progress: Empirical Validation of Interventions," *American Psychologist* 60: 410–21.

50 "*Ingratitude! thou marble-hearted fiend*": Shakespeare, William (1608). Quoted from *King Lear*. Retrieved February 1, 2006, from http://www.shakespeare-online.com/quotes/kinglearquotes.html.

51 *what school-age children said*: Gordon, A. K., Mushner-Eizenman, D. R., Holub, S. C., & Dalrymple, J. (2004). "What Are Children Thankful For? An Archival Analysis of Gratitude Before and After the Attacks of September 11," *Applied Developmental Psychology* 25: 541–53.

52 *By fostering the positive emotion*: Froh, J. J., Sefick, W. J., & Emmons, R. A. (2006). "Counting Blessings in Early Adolescents: An Experimental Study of Gratitude and Subjective Well-Being." Manuscript submitted for publication.

53 *parents emphasize the sense of community*: Baumgarten-Tramer, Franziska (1938). "'Gratefulness' in Children and Young People," *The Journal of Genetic Psychology* 53: 53–66.

54 *humans as "dependent rational animals"*: Macintyre, Alasdair (1999). *Dependent Rational Animals: Why Human Beings Need the Virtues*. Chicago: Open Court Publishing.

3. How Gratitude Is Embodied

57 *the emotion of elevation*: Haidt, Jonathan (2003). "Elevation and the Positive Psychology of Morality," in *Flourishing: Positive Psychology and the Life Well-Lived,* ed. Haidt, Jonathan, & Keyes, Corey L. M. Washington, D.C.: American Psychological Association, pp. 275–89.
"*the most substantial*": Kottler, Jeffrey (1996). *The Language of Tears.* San Francisco: Jossey-Bass Publishers.
"*There are times when*": Ibid.

58 "*because of the violent pain*": Meissner W. W. (1992). *The Psychology of Saint Ignatius of Loyola.* New Haven and London: Yale University Press.

59 *The expressive component*: Camras, L. A., Holland, E. A., & Patterson, M. J. (1993). "Facial Expression," in *Handbook of Emotions, ed. Lewis, M., & Haviland, J. M.* New York and London: The Guilford Press, pp. 199–208.

60 *In every culture they studied*: Ekman, Paul (1989). "The Argument and Evidence About Universals in Facial Expressions of Emotion," in *Handbook of Social Psychophysiology,* ed. Wagner, H., & Manstead, A. Oxford, John Wiley & Sons, pp. 143–64.

61 *voice as a carrier of emotional information*: Darwin, Charles (1890). *The Expression of the Emotions in Man and Animals.* London: John Murray, Albermarle Street.
correctly infer true emotional state: Pittam, J., & Scherer, K. R. (1993). "Vocal Expression and Communication of Emotion," in Lewis & Haviland, pp. 185–98.

62 *observers were shown videotapes*: Ekman, Paul (1975). "Unmasking the Face; A Guide to Recognizing Emotions from Facial Clues," in *Spectrum Book.* Englewood Cliffs, N.J.: Prentice-Hall.

63 *explanation a person fashions*: Affleck, G., Croog, S., & Tennen, H. (1987). "Causal Attribution, Perceived Benefits, and Morbidity After a Heart Attack: An 8-Year Study," *Journal of Consulting and Clinical Psychology* 55: 29–35.

64 *People who are anger-prone*: Goodman, Troy (2005). "Anger-Prone People More Likely to Have Heart Attacks." Retrieved October 6, 2005, from http://www.beliefnet.com/story/23.story_2345_1.html.

65 *A study conducted at the Duke*: Bosworth, H. B., Feaganes, J. R., Mark, D. B., Siegler, I. C., & Vitaliano, P. P. (2000). "Personality and Coping

with a Common Stressor: Cardiac Catheterization," *Journal of Behavioral Medicine* 24: 17–31.

66 *Thankfulness was also predictive*: Dew, M. A., & Harris, R. C. (1996). Department of Psychiatry: University of Pittsburgh School of Medicine.

   A number of recent studies: Gallo, L. C., & Matthews, K. A. (2003). "Understanding the Association Between Socioeconomic Status and Physical Health: Do Negative Emotions Play a Role?" *Psychological Bulletin* 129: 10–51.

67 *A thirty-five-year longitudinal study*: Peterson, Christopher (1988). "Pessimistic Explanatory Style Is a Risk Factor for Physical Illness: A Thirty-Five-Year Longitudinal Study," *Journal of Personality and Social Psychology* 55: 23–27.

   researchers found evidence suggesting: Geleijnse, J. M., Giltay, E. J., Hoakstra, T., Schouten, E. G., & Zitman, F. G. (2004). "Dispositional Optimism and All-Cause and Cardiovascular Mortality in a Prospective Cohort of Elderly Dutch Men and Women," *Archives of General Psychology* 61: 1126–35.

   people who scored high on optimism: Colligan, M. R., & Offord, M. M. (2002). "Optimism-pessimism Assess in the 1960s and Self-Reported Health Status 30 Years Later," *Mayo Clinic Proceedings* 77: 748–53.

68 *the research team was able to predict*: Danner, D. D., Friesen, W. V., & Snowdon, D. A. (2001). "Positive Emotions in Early Life and Longevity: Findings from the Nun Study," *Journal of Personality and Social Psychology* 80: 804–13.

69 *"How thankful I am"*: Snowdon, D. D. (2001). *Aging with Grace: What the Nun Study Teaches Us About Leading Longer, Healthier, and More Meaningful Lives*. New York: Bantam.

   "The life-extending effects": Pressman, S.D., & Cohen, S. (2006). "Positive Emotion and Social Word Use in Autobiography Predicts Increased Longevity in Psychologists." Presented at the Annual Meeting of the American Psychosomatic Society Conference, Denver, CO.

70 *"Close your eyes and relax"*: Atkinson, M., McCraty, R., Rein, G., Tiller, W. A., & Watkins, A. D. (1995). "The Effects of Emotions on Short-Term Power Spectrum Analysis of Heart Rate Variability," *American Journal of Cardiology* 76: 1089–93.

73 *"I'm a changed man"*: (2005). "You Can Meet Him at McGuire's." Retrieved October 6, 2005, from http://www.mayoclinic.org/patient stories/robertmcguire.html.

73 *[Feinberg] attributed his 180-degree turnaround*: Tyler, Aubin (2004). "Feinberg: Town Council Should Be 'Pro-People.'" Retrieved on January 12, 2006, from http://www.explorernews.com/articles/2004/03/10/oro_valley/oro_valley06.prt.

Increases in DHEA were significantly: Atkinson, M., Carrios-Choplin, B., McCraty, R., Rozman, D., & Watkins, A. D. (1998). "The Impact of a New Emotional Self-Management Program on Stress, Emotions, Heart Rate Variability, DHEA, and Cortisol," *Integrative Physiological and Behavioral Science* 33(2): 151–70.

74 *positive emotions are physiologically beneficial*: Branigan, C., Fredrickson, B. L., Mancuso, R. A., & Tugade, M. M. (2000). "The Undoing Effect of Positive Emotions," *Motivation and Emotion* 24: 237–58.

"Hatred cannot coexist": Saizberg, Sharon (2002). *Lovingkindness: The Revolutionary Art of Happiness*. Boston: Shambhala Publications.

each type of emotion is controlled: Davidson, R., Maxwell, J. S., & Shackman, A. J. (2004). "Asymmetries in Face and Brain Related to Emotion," *Trends in Cognitive Sciences* 8: 389–91.

76 *Experiments have shown*: Hener, T., Raz, T., & Weisenberg, M. (1998). "The Influence of Film-induced Mood on Pain Perception," *Pain* 76(3): 365–75.

77 *loving-kindness program*: Carson, J. W., Carson, K. M., Fraz, A. M., Goli, V., Keefe, F. J., Lynch, T. R., & Thorp, S. R. (2005). "Loving-Kindness Meditation for Chronic Low Back Pain," *Journal of Holistic Nursing* 23(3): 287–304.

79 *close relationship between gratitude*: Teigen, Karl (1997). "Luck, Envy, and Gratitude: It Could Have Been Different," *Scandinavian Journal of Psychology* 38(4): 313–23.

counterfactual deficit in patients: Brown, A., Durso, R., Lynch, A., & McNamara, P. (2003). "Counterfactual Cognitive Deficit in Persons with Parkinson's Disease," *Journal of Neurology, Neurosurgery, and Psychiatry* 74: 1065–70.

82 *There is a ritual exchange*: Kornai, Janos (2000). "Hidden in an Envelope: Gratitude Payments to Medical Doctors in Hungary," in *The Paradoxes of Unintended Consequences*, ed. Dahrendorf, L., & Elkana, Y. Budapest: CEU Press.

83 *providing our surgeon with $27,000*: Balabanova, D., & McKee, M. (2002). "Understanding Informal Payments for Health Care: The Example of Bulgaria," *Health Policy* 62: 243–73.

84 *the full range of day-to-day emotions*: Braddock, C. H., Fryer-Edwards,

K., & Kasman, D. L. (2003). "Educating for Professionalism: Trainees' Emotional Experiences on IM and Pediatrics Inpatient Wards," *Academic Medicine* 78: 730.

Resident "Sam" explained: Ibid.

"I was clearly struggling": Ibid.

grateful emotions lead: Estrada, C., Isen, A. M., & Young, M. J. (1997). "Positive Affect Facilitates Integration of Information and Decreases Anchoring in Reasoning Among Physicians," *Organizational Behavior and Human Decision Processes* 72(1): 117–35.

85 *"Physicians may also be more likely to develop"*: Schwenzfeier, E. M. et al. (2002). "Psychological Well-Being as a Predictor of Physician Medication Prescribing Practices in Primary Care," *Professional Psychology: Research and Practice* 33: 478–82.

86 *Bicycle helmet use nearly doubled*: Buchholz, C., Clarke, S. W., & Ludwig, T. D. (2005). "Using Social Marketing to Increase the Use of Helmets Among Bicyclists," *Journal of American College Health* 54(1): 51–58.

a longing for something: Gabbard, Glen (2000). "On Gratitude and Gratification," *Journal of the American Psychoanalytic Association* 48(3): 697–716.

87 *"You know, it's an amazing feeling"*: "Special Coverage of the Aftermath of Hurricane Katrina: NBC Special." (2005, September 3). Retrieved on January 12, 2006, from http://web.lexis-nexis.com/universe/document?_m=1dc5f96469cb23d6d6f916e38de8b197&_docnum=3.

88 *the electromagnetic field generated*: Bradley, R. T., McCraty, R., & Tomasino, D. (2004–2005). "The Resonant Heart," *Shift: At the Frontiers of Consciousness, December 2004–February 2005: 15–19.*

4. THANKS BE TO GOD: GRATITUDE AND THE HUMAN SPIRIT

90 *"Grace and gratitude go together" "If the only prayer you say" "To speak gratitude is courteous and pleasant"*: All quotes cited in Emmons, Robert A., & Hill, Joanna (2001). *Words of Gratitude for Mind, Body, and Soul.* West Conshohocken, PA: Templeton Foundation Press.

91 *A "thank-you note" committee*: Lewis, G., McCaughey, B., McCaughey, K., & Shaw Lewis, D. (1998). *Seven from Heaven: The Miracle of the McCaughey Septuplets.* Nashville: Thomas Nelson Publishers.

92   *the proper response to divine gifts*: Miller, Patrick D. (1994). *They Cried to the Lord: The Form and Theology of Biblical Prayer.* Minneapolis: Fortress Press.
"*Religious leaders could not have asked*": Lewis, et al., *Seven from Heaven.*

93   "*The Pilgrims came here seeking freedom*": Anonymous author. Retrieved January 26, 2006, from http://www.sermons.org/thanksgiving.html.
"*What else can we say*": Buchanan, John M. (2002). "Stammering Praise," *Christian Century,* Nov. 20–Dec. 3: 3.
"*the best general-purpose hymn*": Ibid.
Two-thirds of those surveyed: Moore, David W. (1996). "This Thanksgiving Day Americans Most Thankful for Family and Health," *The Gallup Poll Monthly.*

94   *gratitude was one of the main motivations*: Allport, Gordon W., Gillespie, James M., & Young, Jacqueline (1948). "The Religion of the Post-War College Student," *Journal of Psychology: Interdisciplinary and Applied* 25: 3–33.
those who regularly attend religious services: Emmons, Robert A., & Kneezel, Teresa T. (2005). "Giving Thanks: Spiritual and Religious Correlates of Gratitude," *Journal of Psychology and Christianity* 24(2): 140–48.
"*In this attitude*": Streng, Frederick J. (1983). "Introduction: Thanksgiving as a Worldwide Response to Life," in *Spoken and Unspoken Thanks: Some Comparative Soundings,* ed. Carman, John B., & Streng, Frederick J. Dallas: Center for World Thanksgiving, pp. 1–9.

95   "*grace and gratitude go together*": Boulton, Matthew (2001). "'We Pray by His Mouth': Karl Barth, Erving Goffman, and a Theology of Invocation," *Modern Theology* 17: 67–83.

96   *Many of the sacrifices offered*: Schimmel, Solomon (2004). "Gratitude in Judaism," in *The Psychology of Gratitude,* ed. Emmons, R., & McCullough, M. New York: Oxford University Press, pp. 37–57.
"*It is forbidden to a man*": Ibid.

97   "*Sam . . . when I regained consciousness*": All quotes cited in Buchanan, "Stammering Praise."
"*A true Christian is one who never*": Baillie, John (1963). *A Reasoned Faith.* New York: Scribner.
"*True religion is right tempers*": Quote cited in Emmons and Hill, *Words of Gratitude for Mind, Body, and Soul.*

98   "*The Holy Scriptures do everywhere*": Edwards, Jonathan (1959). *Religious Affections*. New Haven, Conn.: Yale University Press.

100 "*Gratitude for the abundance*": Sanneh, Lamin O. (1983). "Thanksgiving in the Qur'an: The Outlines of a Theme," in *Spoken and Unspoken Thanks*, pp. 135–44.

101 *There is gratitude for the capacity*: Fadiman, James, & Frager, Robert (1999). *Essential Sufism*. New York: HarperSanFrancisco.
     "*Let us rise up*": Quote cited in Emmons and Hill, *Words of Gratitude for Mind, Body, and Soul.*

102 "*The mother is pregnant for 270 days*": Shoshu, Nichiren (2003). "The Four Debts of Gratitude." *The Doctrines and Practice of Nichiren Shoshu.* Retrieved January 26, 2006, from http://www.nsglobalnet.jp/page/d_and_p/chapter_43.htm.

104 "*happiest people on earth*": Shakarian, D. (1975). *The Happiest People on Earth: The Long-Awaited Personal Story of Demos Shakarian.* Old Tappan, NJ: Chosen Books.
     Today, Pentecostalism is the most: Jenkins, Philip (2002). *The Next Christendom.* New York: Oxford University Press.
     Historical narratives of Pentecostal women: Griffin, R. Marie (1998). "'Joy Unspeakable and Full of Glory': The Vocabulary of Pious Emotion in the Narratives of American Pentecostal Women, 1910–1945," in *An Emotional History of the United States*, ed. Stearns, Peter N., & Lewis, Jan. New York: New York University Press.

105 "*was of a spiritual nature*": Judd, Carrie F. (1936). *The Life and Teachings of Carrie Judd Montgomery.* Oakland, CA: Office of Triumphs of Faith.

107 "*Over its career*": Geertz, Clifford (1968). Cited in *Anthropological Approaches to the Study of Religion*, ed. Banton, Michael. London: Tavistock Publications.
     This belief in God(s): Barrett, Justin L. (2004). *Why Would Anyone Believe in God?* Walnut Creek, CA: AltaMira Press.
     the design of our minds: Ibid.

108 *A related contemporary theory*: Bulbulia, Joseph (2004). "Religious Costs as Adaptations that Signal Altruistic Intention," *Evolution and Cognition* 10: 19–42.

110 *the communal character of praise*: Miller, Patrick D. (1994). *They Cried to the Lord: The Form and Theology of Biblical Prayer.* Minneapolis: Fortress Press.

111 *"When the sacred is seen working"*: Pargament, Kenneth I. (1997). *The Psychology of Religion and Coping: Theory, Research, Practice.* New York: The Guilford Press.

112 *some caregivers appraised their situation*: Park, Crystal L. (2005). "Religion as a Meaning-Making Framework in Coping with Life Stress," *Journal of Social Issues: Religion as a Meaning System,* 61: 707–30.
a sample of Spiritualists: Ibid.
"It makes things bearable": Claypool, John (1995). *Tracks of a Fellow Struggler: Living and Growing Through Grief.* Harrisburg, PA: Morehouse Publishing.

114 *We who lived in concentration camps"*: Frankl, Viktor Emil (1984). *Man's Search for Meaning: An Introduction to Logotherapy.* New York: Simon & Schuster.

115 *Litanies of remembrance*: Peck, Morgan Scott (1995). *In Search of Stones: A Pilgrimage of Faith, Reason, and Discovery.* New York: Hyperion.

116 *one out of every eight people*: Hargrove, Thomas, & Stempel, Guido H. III (2004). "13 Percent Don't Plan to Celebrate Thanksgiving," *Scripps Howard News Service.* Retrieved November 19, 2004, from http://web.lexis-nexis.com/universe/document?_m=13963096ea94456 98ea07a0b2e39b9.
"recognition of tragedy": Cox, Harvey Gallagher (1969). *The Feast of Fools: A Theological Essay on Festivity and Fantasy.* Cambridge, MA: Harvard University Press.

117 *"Blessed be Your name"*: Redman, Beth, & Redman, Matt (2005). *Blessed Be Your Name: Worshipping God on the Road Marked with Suffering.* Ventura, CA: Regal Books.

5. An Unnatural Crime: Ingratitude and Other Obstacles to Grateful Living

123 *record donations poured in*: (November 2005). "Hurricane Katrina Draws Record Donations." Retrieved on January 25, 2006 from http://web.lexis-nexis.com/universe/document?_m=4f5c243e3011ed28d7cea2 2e63c78d49&_docnum=2&wchp=dGLzVlzzSkVA&_md5=777d37d5a5 4fcba16e8e401b55361cf7.

125 *"I won't help anyone"*: Gray, Steven (2005, November 11). "Good Inten-

tions: A Katrina Family Tries to Start Over in Minnesota Town," *Wall Street Journal*, pp. A1.

Sometimes gifts bring joy: Scheibe, Karl E. (2000). *The Drama of Everyday Life*. Cambridge, MA: Harvard University Press.

127 *natural tendency of the mind*: Cacioppo, J. T., Ito, T. A., Larson, J. T., & Smith, N. K. (1998). "Negative Information Weighs More Heavily on the Brain: The Negativity Bias in Evaluative Categorizations," *Journal of Personality and Social Psychology* 75(4): 887–900.

128 *"positivity offset" is a slight*: Berntson, G. G., & Cacioppo, J. T. (1999). "The Affect System: Architecture and Operating Characteristics," *American Psychological Society* 8(5): 133–37.

129 *areas of the brain responsible*: Mather, M., Canli, T., English, T., Whitfield, S., Wais, P., et al. (2004). "Amygdala Responses to Emotionally Valenced Stimuli in Older and Younger Adults," *American Psychology Society* 15(4): 259.

The inability to acknowledge dependency: Dickens, Charles (1997). *Great Expectations*. New York: Doubleday.

"*I could not have spoken one word*": Ibid.

130 "*The law of benefits*": Emerson, Ralph W. (1844). Retrieved on January 31, 2006, from http://www.rwe.org/comm/index.php?option= com_content&task=view&id=139&Itemid=42.

132 *the prevalence of internal conflicts*: Emmons, Robert A., & King, Laura A. (1990). "Conflict Over Emotional Expression: Psychological and Physical Correlates," *Journal of Personality and Social Psychology* 58(5): 864–67.

134 "*love, anxiety, and anger*": Vitz, Paul C. (1999). Retrieved on January 31, 2006, from http://www.catholiceducation.org/articles/marriage/mf0002.html.

135 *A gift that is lavishly disproportionate*: Scheibe, *The Drama of Everyday Life*.

The secretary of a physician: Weijer, Charles (2001). "No: Gifts Debase the True Value of Care," *Western Journal of Medicine* 175: 77.

136 *Because of the ethical complexities*: Ibid.

hazardous ritual of classroom holiday gift giving: Flanagan, Caitlin (2004, December 6). "What Teachers Want," *The New Yorker*, p. 64.

One group was to finish: Myers, David G. (1992). *The Pursuit of Happiness: Who Is Happy and Why*. New York: William Morrow and Company.

137 "*Do not spoil what you have*": Epicurus (341 BCE — 271 BCE).

Retrieved on January 31, 2006, from http://www.brainyquote.com/quotes/quotes/e/epicurus133089.html.

a segment of the psychological industry: Dineen, Tana (1998). *Manufacturing Victims: What the Psychology Industry Is Doing to People.* Montreal: Robert Davies Multimedia Publishing.

139 *individuals who suffered disabling spinal cord injuries*: Brickman, P., Coates, D., & Janoff-Bulman, R. (1978). "Lottery Winners and Accident Victims: Is Happiness Relative?" *Journal of Personality and Social Psychology* 36: 917–27.

Over 5 million iPods: Fernandez, Sandy M. (2005, August 21). "Hear What I'm Saying?" *Washington Post.* Retrieved on February 6, 2006, from http://pqasb.pqarchiver.com/washingtonpost/access/884798331.html?dids=884798331:884798331&FMT=ABS&FMTS=ABS:FT&fmac = &date=Aug+21percent2C+2005&author=Sandy+M.+Fernandez& desc=Hear+What+I percent27m+Saying percent3F.

"People were just walking by": Ibid.

140 *"Nothing more detestable" "I hate ingratitude" "Ingratitude is treason to mankind"*: All quotes cited in Harpham, Edward J. (2004). "Gratitude in the History of Ideas," in *The Psychology of Gratitude,* ed. Emmons, R., & McCullough, M. New York: Oxford University Press, pp. 19–36.

Shakespeare uses the terms: Leithart, Peter J. (2004). "The Politics of Gratitude," *First Things* 148: 15–17.

141 *"healthy independence and strength"*: Mencken, H. L. (1924). *Prejudices: Second Series.* New York: Alfred A. Knopf.

"We have been the recipients": Lincoln, Abraham (1863). "Presidential Thanksgiving Proclamations." Retrieved on January 31, 2006, from http://www.pilgrimhall.org/thanxproc1862.htm.

143 *"How will he meet his God"*: Knott, Tom (2004). "Finishing First in Gratitude," *Washington Times.* Retrieved on September 15, 2004, from http://web.lexis-nexis.com/universe.document?_m=36de7ad286e42ce 06d4be5150bf80ca7.

144 *"If Noor stayed in Iraq"*: Weinstein, Joshua L. (2005). "A Father's Thanks, A Daughter's Smile," *Portland Press Herald: Maine Sunday Telegram.* Retrieved on March 1, 2005, from http://pressherald.maine today.com/news/local/050301heart.shtml.

Violations of this type: Algoe, Sara, & Haidt, Jonathan (2003). "Moral Amplification and the Emotions that Attach Us to Saints and Demons," in *Handbook of Experimental Existential Psychology.* New York: Guilford Press.

145 *"In the light of the Divine Goodness"*: Shelton, Charles M. (2003). "Graced Gratitude," *The Way* 42(3): 137–49.

147 *A psychodynamic perspective*: Bergler, Edmund (1945). "Psychopathology of Ingratitude," *Diseases of the Nervous System* 6:226–29.

148 *"no other vice is so hostile"*: Seneca (1935). "On Benefits," in *Moral Essays, with an English translation by John W. Basore: Vol. III*. Cambridge, MA: Harvard University Press.

   "All the women on The Apprentice": Trump, Donald (2005). "Profile: Donald Trump," *Money Week*. Retrieved on January 31, 2006, from http://www.moneyweek.com/file/4794/trump-1111.html.

   "There has never been anyone": Quoted in Robins, Richard W., & Paulhus, Delroy L. (2001). "The Character of Self-Enhancers: Implications for Organizations," in *Personality and Psychology in the Workplace: Decade of Behavior, ed.* Roberts, Brent W., & Hogan, Robert. Washington, DC: American Psychological Association, pp. 193–219.

149 *These items come from the Narcissistic Personality Inventory*: Raskin, Robert, & Hall, Calvin S. (1981). "The Narcissistic Personality Inventory: Alternate Form Reliability and Further Evidence of Construct Validity," *Journal of Personality Assessment* 45(2): 159–62.

150 *[narcissists] might be reluctant to express gratitude*: McWilliams, Nancy, & Lependorf, Stanley (1990). "The Denial of Remorse and Gratitude," *Narcissistic Pathology of Everyday Life*. New York: W.A.W. Institute.

152 *psychiatrists estimate that only one percent*: Diagnostic and Statistical Manual of Mental Disorders (4th ed.). (1994). Washington, DC: American Psychiatric Association.

   "Act with kindness": Confucius (nd.) Retrieved on January 31, 2006, from http://en.thinkexist.com/quotes/with/keyword/gratitude/.

153 *"Among all emotions"*: Selye, Hans (1956). *The Stress of Life*. New York: McGraw-Hill.

   "was the awakening in another person": Ibid.

154 "I don't remember my mother": Ibid.

   "marrying a girl": Ibid.

   "the standing ovation": Ibid.

6. Gratitude in Trying Times

157   *the Book of Job has a timeless appeal*: Wharton, James A. (1999). *Job*. Louisville, KY: Westminster John Knox Press.

158   *[Job] is granted good health*: Good, Edwin M. (1990). *In Turns of Tempest: A Reading of Job*. Stanford, CA: Stanford University Press.

159   *Corrie ten Boom. . .wrote*: ten Boom, Corrie, & Scherrill, John (1984). *The Hiding Place*. New York: Bantam.
      "gratitude changes the pangs": Bonhoeffer, Detrich (1971). *Letters and Papers from Prison*, trans. Eberhard Bethge. London: SCM Press.
      "I have learned to be content": Beck, James R. (2002). *The Psychology of Paul: A Fresh Look at His Life and Teaching*. Grand Rapids, MI: Kregel Publications.

160   *His wife received a telegram that read*: Spafford, Horatio G. (1873). "It Is Well With My Soul." Retrieved on February 6, 2006, from http://www.gracelivingstonhill.com/spafford.htm.

161   *"the most important learning experiences"*: Maslow, Abraham H. (1987). *Motivation and Personality*. New York: Harper & Row.
      Like Job, they understood: Gomes, Peter J. (2002). *The Good Life: Truths That Last in Times of Need*. San Francisco: HarperSanFrancisco.

162   *The psychological literature on subjective well-being*: Diener, Carol, & Diener, Ed (1996). "Most People Are Happy," *Psychological Science* 7(3): 181–86.

163   *the science of stress-related growth* : Wortman, Camille B., & Silver, Roxane C. (1987). "Coping with Irrevocable Loss," in *Cataclysms, Crises, and Catastrophes: Psychology in Action*. Washington, DC: American Psychological Association, pp. 185–235.
      Yet in one study of widows: Ibid.
      In another study of parents: McIntosh, D. N., Silver, R. C., & Wortman, C. B. (1993). "Religion's Role in Adjustment to a Negative Life Event: Coping With the Loss of a Child," *Journal of Personality and Social Psychology* 65: 812–21.

164   *persons of faith report higher levels*: Park, C. L., Cohen, L. H., & Murch, R. L. (1996). "Assessment and Prediction of Stress-Related Growth," *Journal of Personality* 64(1): 71–105.

165   *Psychologists call this the "principle of scarcity"*: Cialdini, Robert B. (1985). *Influence: Science and Practice*. Upper Saddle River, NJ: Scott Foresman and Company.

168 *They compared fifty-eight women*: Adler, N. E., Blackburn, E. H.,
     Cawthon, R. M., Dhabhar, F. S., Epel, E. S., Lin, J., & Morrow, J. D.
     (2004). "Accelerated Telomere Shortening in Response to Life Stress,"
     *Proceedings of the National Academy of Sciences of the United States of
     America* 101(49 & 50): 17312–25.

169 *Jo-Ann Tsang of Baylor University conducted*: Ciras, Heather J. (2005).
     "First Give Thanks, Then Do No Harm." Retrieved on January 12,
     2006, from http://www.stnews.org/atruism-1632.htm.

170 *"Muriel stocked the cupboard"*: McQuilkin, Robertson (2005). "CT
     Classic: Muriel's Blessing." Retrieved on October 11, 2005, from http://
     www.ctlibrary.com/print.html?id+11608.

     "Just four months ago": Retrieved on March 14, 2006, from http://
     www.alz.org/Media/newsreleases/ronaldreagan/reagannancyletter
     .asp.

171 *"Each day that I stay as a guest"*: Mason, Kelly Murphy (2001). "The
     Sacrament of Gratitude." Retrieved on February 7, 2006, from http://
     www.beliefnet.com/story/89/story_8926.html.

     Fredrickson examined the frequency: Fredrickson, B. L., Tugade, M. M.,
     Waugh, C. E., & Larkin, G. R. (2003). "What Good Are Positive Emo-
     tions in Crisis: A Prospective Study of Resilience and Emotions Fol-
     lowing the Terrorist Attacks on the United States on September 11th,
     2001," *Journal of Personality and Social Psychology* 84: 365–76.

172 *"When the second plane hit"*: "Survivors' Stories" (n.d.). Retrieved on
     February 7, 2006, from http://www.11-sept.org/survivors.html.

173 *These seven strengths remained*: Peterson, Christopher, & Seligman,
     Martin (2003). "Character Strengths Before and After September 11,"
     Psychological Science 14: 381–84.

     "reminded that we are here": Bush, George W. (2002). "President's Re-
     marks to the Nation." Retrieved on February 7, 2006, from http://
     www.whitehouse.gov/news/releases/2002/09/20020911-3.html.

174 *lifetime risk for psychiatric disorders*: Kendler, K. S., Liu, X. Q., Gardner,
     C. O., et al. (2003). "Dimensions of Religiosity and Their Relationship
     to Lifetime Psychiatric and Substance Use Disorders," *American Jour-
     nal of Psychiatry* 160: 496–503.

     "counting one's blessings": Smith, L. C., Friedman, S., & Nevid, J. (1999).
     "Clinical and Sociocultural Differences in African American and Eu-
     ropean American Patients with Panic Disorder and Agoraphobia,"
     Journal of Nervous and Mental Disease 187: 549–60.

175 *Entering into a collaborative form*: Naim, Raymond C., & Merluzzi, Thomas V. (2003). "The Role of Religious Coping in Adjustment to Cancer," *Psycho-Oncology* 12: 428–41.

Counting blessings was the most common: Barusch, Amanda Smith (1999). "Religion, Adversity, and Age: Religious Experiences of Low-Income Elderly Women," *Journal of Sociology and Social Welfare* 26: 125–42.

"*I had this overwhelming joy*": Coffman, Sherrilyn (1996). "Parents' Struggles to Rebuild Family Life After Hurricane Andrew," *Issues in Mental Health Nursing* 17: 353–67.

"*Last week was a difficult week*": Afton, Jo (2005). "Letter from Jo Afton." Retrieved on February 7, 2006, from http://sistercitysupport .net/index.php?s=but+not+my+spirit.

176 "reminding oneself of things" "Telling myself": Ventura, Jacqueline N., & Boss, Pauline G. (1983). "The Family Coping Inventory Applied to Parents with New Babies," *Journal of Marriage and the Family* (Nov. 1983): 867–75.

"*He is as much or more of a blessing*: Kind, L. A., Scollon, C. K., Ramsey, C., & Williams, T. (2000). "Stories of Life Transition: Subjective Well-Being and Ego Development in Parents of Children with Down Syndrome," *Journal of Research in Personality* 35: 509–36.

177 "adopting a grateful attitude": The National Down Syndrome Society Web site (n.d.). Retrieved on February 6, 2006, from http://www .ndss.org.

The emotional state of children with DS: Robison, Richard (2003). "Dad of the Month." Retrieved on February 6, 2006, from http://iparenting .com/dad/0903.htm.

178 *McAdams identified "redemption sequences"*: McAdams, Dan P. (2006). *The Redemptive Self: Stories Americans Live By*. New York: Oxford University Press.

179 "*I once was lost, but now am found*": McAdams, Dan P., & Bauer, Jack J. (2004). "Gratitude in Modern Life: Its Manifestations and Development," in *The Psychology of Gratitude*, ed. Emmons, R., & McCullough, M. New York: Oxford University Press, pp. 81–99.

180 *Peck suggests that some people*: Peck, Morgan Scott (1995). *In Search of Stones: A Pilgrimage of Faith, Reason, and Discovery*. New York: Hyperion.

"*We are well-nigh overwhelmed*": Calvin, Jean (2001). *Institutes of the Christian Religion*. Grand Rapids, MI: Wm. B. Eerdmans.

"*times that challenge us physically, emotionally, and spiritually*": Rast, Brother David Steindl (n.d.). "Practicing the Art of Gratefulness." Retrieved on February 8, 2006, from http://www.gratefulness.org.

181 "*We would receive all at Thy hand*": Kierkegaard, S., & LeFevre, P. D. (1996). *The Prayers of Kierkegaard.* Chicago: University of Chicago Press.

182 "*mature defenses grow out*": Vaillant, George (2002). *Aging Well: Surprising Guideposts to a Happier Life from the Landmark Harvard Study of Adult Development.* Boston: Little, Brown and Company.
"No one is as capable of gratitude": Wiesel, Elie, & Heffner, Richard D. (2001). *Conversations with Elie Wiesel.* New York: Schocken Books.

183 "*Absolutely. Right after the war*": Wiesel, Elie (2000). "Oprah's Cut with Elie Wiesel," *O, The Oprah Magazine, Nov. 2000.* Retrieved on February 6, 2006, from http://www2.oprah.com/omagazine.200011/ omag_200011_elie_b.jhtml.

184 "This simple process": Retrieved on January 10, 2006, from http:// www.pubs.org/eliewiesel/life/henry.html.

7. Practicing Gratitude

187 "*Ask yourself whether you are happy*": Mill, John Stuart (1873). *The Cambridge History of English and American Literature in 18 Volumes (1907–21), volume XIV. The Victorian Age, Part Two.* Retrieved on February 8, 2006, from http://www.bartleby.com/224/0107.html.
Psychologists suggest that change: Prochaska, James O. (2000). "Change at Differing Stages," in *Handbook of Psychological Change: Psychotherapy Processes & Practices for the 21st Century,* ed. Snyder, C. R., & Ingram, R. E. . New York: John Wiley & Sons, pp. 109–127.

189 *Psychological research has shown*: Niederhoffer, Kate G., & Pennebaker, James W. (2002). "Sharing One's Story: On the Benefits of Writing or Talking About Emotional Experience," in *Handbook of Positive Psychology,* ed. Lopez, S. J., & Snyder, C. R. New York: Oxford University Press, pp. 573–83.

191 "*think of your worst moments*": Gomes, Peter J. (2003). *Strength for the Journey: Biblical Wisdom For Daily Living, A New Collection of Sermons.* San Francisco: HarperSanFrancisco.

192 "*bad is stronger than good*": Baumeister, R. F., Bratslavsky, E., & Finke-

nauer, C. (2001). "Bad Is Stronger Than Good," *Review of General Psychology* 5(4): 323–70.

Naikan was developed by Yoshimoto Ishina: Hedstrom, L. James (1994). "Morita and Naikan Therapies: American Applications," *Psychotherapy* 31: 154–60.

193   *"If we are not willing to see"*: Krech, Greg (2002). *Naikan: Gratitude, Grace, and the Japanese Art of Self-Reflection.* Berkeley, CA: Stone Bridge Press.

194   *people spend more time praying*: Gallup, George, & Bezilla, Robert (1992). *The Religious Life of Young Americans: A Compendium of Surveys on the Spiritual Beliefs and Practices of Teen-Agers and Young Adults.* Princeton, NJ: G. H. Gallup International Institute.

"the soul and essence of religion" "the most spontaneous and personal": Clark, Walter Houston (1961). *The Psychology of Religion: An Introduction to Religious Experience and Behavior.* New York: Macmillan.

Even college students: McKinney, John Paul, & McKinney, Kathleen G. (1999). "Prayer in the Lives of Late Adolescents," *Journal of Adolescents* 22: 279–90.

195   *the minister enunciates*: *Lutheran Book of Worship.* (1978). Minneapolis, MN: Augsburg Publishing House.

"Thank you, Lord, for giving me ": Keillor, Garrison (2006). "With All the Trimmings: A Thanksgiving Essay." Retreived on March 1, 2006, from http://www.javaforjesus.com/allthetrimmings.html.

196   *"We thank Great Spirit for the resources"*: "Prayers of the Day: Native American" (2006). Retrieved on March 1, 2006, from http://www.beliefnet.com/prayeroftheday/more_prayers.asp?paid=49&faid=10.

"Waking up this morning": Hanh, Thich Nhat (1993). *Call Me by My True Names.* Berkeley, CA: Parallax Press.

197   *"nothing is more memorable than a smell"*: Ackerman, Diane (1991). *A Natural History of the Senses.* New York: Vintage Books.

198   *"Breath of Thanks"*: Luskin, Fred (2002). *Forgive for Good: A Proven Prescription for Health and Happiness.* New York: HarperCollins Publishers.

199   *Articles with titles such as*: Compiled by Frederic A. Brussat (1994). "27 Ways to Live a Spiritual Life Every Day: Who Says Gossiping and Brushing Your Teeth Can't Be Sacred?" *Utne Reader* (July/August 1994): 91–95.

200   *One of the primary reasons*: Coscarelli, L., Ford, Maire, & Plante, T. G.

(2001). "Does Exercising With Another Enhance the Stress-Reducing Benefits of Exercise?" *International Journal of Stress Management* 8(3): 201–13.

201 *the law of emotional contagion*: Doherty, William (1997). "The Emotional Contagion Scale," *Journal of Nonverbal Behavior* 21: 131–54.

Severus Snape makes an unbreakable vow: Rowling, J. K. (2005). *Harry Potter and the Half-Blood Prince*. New York: Scholastic.

202 *Subjects in the vow condition*: Dean, Mark Lawrence (2002). "Effects of Vow-making on Adherence to a 12-week Personal Fitness Program, Self-Efficacy, and Theory of Planned Behavior Constructs," *Dissertation Abstracts International: Section B: The Sciences and Engineering* 62(12-B): p. 5959.

"If you make a vow to the LORD": The Holy Bible: New International Version, Containing the Old Testament and the New Testament. (1984). Grand Rapids, MI: Zondervan Bible Publishers.

203 *Whorf posed the theory*: Whorf, Benjamin Lee (1966). *Language, Thought, and Reality; Selected Writings. Edited and With an Introduction by John B. Carroll. Foreword by Stuart Chase.* Cambridge, MA: MIT Press.

204 *"I know I'm poor"*: Barusch, Amanda Smith (1997). "Self-Concepts of Low-Income Older Women: Not Old or Poor, But Fortunate and Blessed," *International Journal of Aging and Human Development* 44(4): 269–82.

"We are what we think about": Emerson, Ralph Waldo (2006). Ralph Waldo Emerson Quotes. Retrieved on March 1, 2006, from http://www.brainyquote.com/quotes/quotes/r/ralphwaldo108797.html.

205 *They were asked to hold a pencil*: Strack, F., & Martin, L. (1988). "Inhibiting and Facilitating Conditions of the Human Smile: A Nonobtrusive Test of the Facial Feedback Hypothesis," *Journal of Personality and Social Psychology* 54: 768–77.

206 *two "anomalous cases" of gratitude*: Fitzgerald, Patrick (1998). "Gratitude and Justice," *Ethics* 109: 119–53.

207 "because they have done me generous favors": Ibid.

people who made extraordinary moral commitments: Colby, Anne, & Damon, William (1992). *Some Do Care: Contemporary Lives of Moral Commitment*. New York: The Free Press.

208 *"give back the goodness"*: Shelton, Charles (2002). "Gratitude, Moral Emotions, and the Moral Life." Monograph adapted from a lecture

presented April 15, 2002, at Indiana University, Bloomington, Indiana. *The Poynter Center for the Study of Ethics and American Institutions.* Bloomington, IN: Indiana University Foundation.

208 *a small, inspirational book on gratitude*: Emmons, Robert A., & Hill, Joanna (2001). *Words of Gratitude: For Mind, Body, and Soul.* Philadelphia: Templeton Foundation Press.

INDEX